Acts of Consciousness

Drawing on compelling material from ~~~~~~ interviews with former hostages and political prisoners, Guy Saunders reworks three classic thought experiment stories: Parfit's 'Teleporter', Nagel's 'What is it like to be a bat?' and Jackson's 'Mary the colour scientist' to form a fresh look at the study of consciousness. By examining consciousness from a social psychology perspective, Saunders develops a 'Cubist Psychology of consciousness' through which he challenges the accepted wisdom of mainstream approaches by arguing that people can act freely. What makes 'Cubist Psychology' is both the many examples taken from different viewpoints and the multiple ways of looking at the key issues of person, mind and world. This is a unique and engaging book that will appeal to students and academics in the field of consciousness studies and other readers with an interest in consciousness.

GUY SAUNDERS is a senior lecturer in the Department of Psychology at the University of the West of England, Bristol, where he teaches courses on 'Psychology of Consciousness' and 'Psychology and the Arts'.

Acts of Consciousness

A Social Psychology Standpoint

GUY SAUNDERS

CAMBRIDGE
UNIVERSITY PRESS

University Printing House, Cambridge CB2 8BS, United Kingdom

Cambridge University Press is part of the University of Cambridge.

It furthers the University's mission by disseminating knowledge in the pursuit of education, learning and research at the highest international levels of excellence.

www.cambridge.org
Information on this title: www.cambridge.org/9780521128544

© Guy Saunders 2014

First published 2014

A catalogue record for this publication is available from the British Library

Library of Congress Cataloguing in Publication data
Saunders, Guy, 1954–
Acts of consciousness : a social psychology standpoint / Guy Saunders.
    pages   cm
ISBN 978-0-521-11124-9 (Hardback) – ISBN 978-0-521-12854-4 (Paperback)
1. Consciousness. 2. Social psychology. I. Title.
BF311.S375 2014
302–dc23   2013040562

ISBN 978-0-521-11124-9 Hardback
ISBN 978-0-521-12854-4 Paperback

Contents

Contents

Contents

Contents

Preface

This book is about how we come to be a person, how we develop a mind of our own and how we come to have an impact on the lives of others through the acts of consciousness we make in the world about us. I want to engage you and I hope you might suspend belief and test your worldview against mine. I will write as plainly as I can about life and living and discuss the familiar, commonsensical and commonplace.

I will discuss three stories as a way of examining our basic beliefs about life and living. The three stories are written as 'thought experiments'. A *thought experiment* is an exercise in thinking about something we wish to investigate for which an actual experiment would be unethical and / or impossible to carry out with current technology. I'll take a fresh look at the stories from a different standpoint.

My focus will be on the familiar features of persons and places, such as minds, points of view and experiences, but with the emphasis on action. I'll take the root verbs – 'to be', 'to have' and 'to know' – and use these as a starting point for an investigation of consciousness and as headings for the three parts of this book.

I will draw on the accounts of former hostages and political prisoners and the research I carried out with their help. I think that the extreme situation of solitary confinement amplifies what it is to be human. Our everyday lives may be drowned out by the noise of normal life such that we are caught up in all manner of matters that take our attention. I'll systematically examine what happens to people in solitary confinement and apply understanding from this to the burning question: what's this life and living all about?

Preface

I offer this book as my contribution towards the field of consciousness studies. I will put a case *for* the standpoint I am taking rather than argue against other standpoints in the field. I'll refer you to other works I've read so that you can hear other voices on these matters. I'll add some notes on recommended further reading all of which I've further read myself.

I recommend reading this book from the beginning through to the end as an unfolding story, but it is structured to allow those who like to dip in to do so. The Introduction is essential but can be read in conjunction with any of the three parts of the book. There is a name and subject index so that you can find explanations of key terms.

I will be raising questions about how we conventionally think about consciousness both in common practice and in more specialist enquiries. I believe that the artist René Magritte was on the right track when he said he wanted to 'sabotage the familiar' and 'to put the real world on trial'.[1] I would put it less confrontationally: I want to suspend belief, to try out and to test out the familiar world of person and place, to explore the world about us, to ask what life and living is all about.

Care to join me?

Acknowledgements

Very many people have a voice in this book and some may go unacknowledged here. Much of what follows may have been picked up in one way or another from others: casual conversations, unattributed reading and the general social affairs of living that contribute to all of us. Where this book is good it is because of the help people gave me; where it is not, then it is down to me. In particular, I should like to thank John Hodgson, whose skilful editorial help – showing me how I could make my writing clearer – has made this book much more readable. I should like to thank Harriet Powney who also gave editorial help, particularly in the early stages of writing. My wife Frances read drafts and offered ideas that helped improve the clarity of this book. To all those who read drafts and offered encouragement: thank you.

Where I know sources, I have cited them. The sources cited may be the ones that set my thinking in train and need not be the original source of any particular argument. All errors are mine and I hope to address these and other matters as an ongoing process. I have included a list at the back of the book of those works that are the main influences and that I would recommend readers to follow up; this list includes some comments suggesting why I think it's worth taking the time to read, view or listen to some or all of the recommended works. There is a list of references to films, paintings and other artworks where I think these may help you understand the main themes. There are no illustrations, but you should easily find all the images you need online. There is also a simple bibliography of works that, even if not directly cited, form the main backdrop of scholarship.

Acknowledgements

Many have helped me and the following have done more than their fair share. So, a big thank you to Vladimir Bukovsky, Brian Keenan, Terry Waite and Anthony Grey for their previous participation in interviews from which I derived much of my doctoral thesis (Saunders 1998) and for permission to quote material in this book. Thanks are also due to the Economic and Social Research Council (ESRC) who funded the doctoral research work that led to my thesis on consciousness and captivity.

Thanks are due to Ciarán Benson, who has always been open-handed in his academic support. A special thanks to Dave Chalmers, John Pickering, Martin Skinner, Ray Tallis, Les Lancaster, Robert Pepperell and Charles Whitehead for the rich conversations and material derived from them that I have used here; and for reading or reviewing draft manuscripts. I owe a debt to those who have encouraged me: to Ray Land, who encouraged me to go to university, and a special thanks to William Wood-Davies, my uncle Bill, who started me off on this academic adventure exploring consciousness when he suggested that I read Julian Jaynes's book *The Origin of Consciousness in the Breakdown of the Bicameral Mind*.

Many who have helped I have met through the Consciousness and Experiential Psychology section of the British Psychological Society, and I would like particularly to thank Jane Henry, Debbie Biggerstaff, Max Velmans, John Pickering, Steve Torrance, Richard Stevens, Susan Stuart, Mike Beaton, Gethin Hughes, Bryony Pierce and Lesley Graham. If you go to events organised by this group, you will be further engaged on the subjects treated in this book. See http://cep.bps.org.uk/ for further information.

I am indebted to my colleagues in Psychology at the University of the West of England in Bristol, and particularly Mick Emerson with whom I've shared an office for over ten years. Thank you to those in the Centre for the Understanding of Social Practices for academic support and a research home. A very particular thank you goes to Sue Blackmore, who taught a 'Consciousness' course at UWE – which I continued when she left – for many conversations

xiv

and for writing the best introduction to consciousness book on the market. I would like to thank all the students who have taken my 'Consciousness' course, and particularly Duncan Gillard.

The lyrics from the song 'I wish I knew how it would feel to be free' are used by permission of Duane Music and © 1964 Duane Music Inc., USA assigned to Westminster Music Ltd, Suite 2.07, Plaza 535 King's Road, London sw10 0sz. International copyright secured. All rights reserved.

I would like to thank my publishers Cambridge University Press for daring to sanction such a book as this, and the Syndicate for reading and accepting my proposal. Thank you to my anonymous reviewers who offered much encouragement and many helpful suggestions. Thank you to Andy Peart who was the original commissioning editor and helped me through the proposal process, to Hetty Marx who was always there for me throughout the review process, to Carrie Parkinson for her help taking the manuscript through to final publication and to Kay McKechnie for her help in copy-editing the final typescript. This book is the fulfilment of the proposal.

Finally, I would like to thank my wife Frances for her continuous support; my friends, family and loved ones, and particularly John, Gerry and Rosie; Zowie, Lorena, Ruby-May, Luca and especially my son Paul to whom this book is dedicated.

Introduction

I don't know about you, but I suppose you are a person like me; that you have thoughts and feelings and experiences as I do; that these are *your* experiences that *you* know about. And I would call these features *consciousness*. Consciousness is how it is for us to live this life of ours, so it is a person's subjective experience; it is *psychological*. Consciousness is about how we share our world and what we have in common one with another, so although it is *my* conscious experience or *your* conscious experience, it is also *our* conscious experience; it is a *social psychological* feature of people's lives. We do things in this shared world about us and these acts have an impact on our lives and the lives of others, so we live in a world of people and relationships. We may come to take responsibility for this because we not only know consciously what we do, we can also reflect beforehand on what we will do and its impact. Over time, we may commit to people and perhaps to ideas. We can know consciously and act freely.

I want to think through the implications of this interpretation of consciousness and ask what this means for us not as a final explanation, but as a way station that may help us make a start on some big issues: issues of how we treat one another and ourselves, and issues to do with those things we most take for granted. In a sense the very character of consciousness that I am setting out calls for reflection on our life and living.

I accept this is a very partial work: I am making a selection and dealing with this selectively. The idea is to take the space to go slowly over the research work I have carried out.

The research background: the genre of captivity

I wanted to research imagination but I couldn't think how to do it. While I was doing my degree in psychology in the 1990s I came across an account of solitary confinement written by Joseph Kovach, I believe.[1] The title was 'Freedom through mental activity' and in it the author described how he had survived his time as a political prisoner, in what was the Soviet Union, by his use of imagination. At once I could see how the research I wanted to do could be done. I would research the experiences of those who had been held in solitary confinement as a way of researching the use of imagination. And that is what I did.

At first it was imagination that was the focus, but as I worked I found that the wider field of consciousness added to my interest, and still does. Also, in the early stages the stories of captivity were the backdrop to help me understand imagination; but as I got interested in this extraordinary body of work, I found myself bringing captivity to the foreground of the research project.

Accounts of captivity are legion: the prison writings of former political prisoners and hostages that make up a body of work deserve to be called a 'genre'.[2] I read extensively from the genre of captivity and I wrote to former captives asking to meet them. I met and interviewed four former captives.

Two of the conclusions I drew from the research are relevant to this book. The first is that *we are made from the lives of others. Consciousness is made from the social interactions made by others with us in early life and by the exchanges we make with others as we get older*. In captivity, we make a virtual social world in order to sustain ourselves. I will say how I think this is done and how I think this has a bearing on the life we lead. The second is that *consciousness is polyphonic.* Consciousness consists in features running next to each other (as well as the more usual configuration of a continuous, sequential, one-after-another conscious mental life). By polyphonic, what is meant is that consciousness has many things going on at the same time. The many things going on side by side simultaneously compose our acts of consciousness and conscience. Far from being a different kind of existence, captivity turns down the volume of ordinary life and living and serves to amplify our humanity. It is unsurprising that books written by former hostages and political prisoners are so successful. They speak to us about who and what we are.

Under conditions of solitary confinement where little or nothing is happening, everything rests on the psychological life of the captive, how they deal with their situation. And I came to see this situation as something that could stand in for conscious life and living because it pared down a person to all that there is when there is nothing else. When a person is separated from those they love and know, from everything they would normally do, and from the world of events, what is left *is* what a person is.

It may seem as if this is a topsy-turvy standpoint where I've turned things on their heads, but studying what something *is not* in order to study what something *is* has had other successes. In fact, studying things directly rarely works. I came to see how studying captivity was studying how we are free and that by studying a person in isolation I was studying what it was to be a person in relation to our world.

This book is a series of investigations about consciousness that takes apart the world about us and how it seems to us to be, and puts it back together again differently. I will be using three stories that have been much discussed in the field of consciousness studies as a means of investigation. The stories will allow me to discuss various features of consciousness such as subjective experience, point of view and knowing what we know.

I am a realist social psychologist who believes that the world about us really exists. I believe we contribute to the world about us that makes us who and what we are. I believe we are minded and capable of consciously knowing and acting with conscience. I believe we are persons in our own right. Persons are minded to act. Persons make the world about us as it is by leading lives the way they do. I believe that we are neither alone nor can we accomplish anything in isolation from others; life and living is about doing things together even if others are in the form of remembered conversations, or books, or films or other times and places in which we do things with others. We are fundamentally social in character and this is indivisible. If we break this, we really do disintegrate and there's no person left. I believe we are made from other people and speak others' voices in our own; it is our own voice, but it is always resonant with the voices of others. This isn't a contradiction in terms, but any other explanation would be.

How the book is set out

This book is in three parts that selectively focus on something that has come to characterise consciousness. These three parts are anchored on three stories; these are sometimes called 'thought experiments'. A thought experiment is a way of testing an idea where it would be unethical or impossible to carry out an actual experiment. To test the ideas, it is important to try to imagine what is said in the set-up of the basic story. We should try to imagine what the philosopher supposes in the way that they set it up even though parts of the set-up may seem ludicrous. The idea is to think through what follows from the set-up as if it could be really carried out. This might lead us to form certain conclusions and think that these are obvious. So, the idea is then to think of how the set-up might be systematically varied to see where our ordinary beliefs get in the way of a fair test. I want to focus selectively on features of life and living that seem common to all of us even if our appreciation of them varies. Necessarily, I'll be taking a particular viewpoint, but this should allow you something to lean against so that you may test the worldview you hold.

The three stories

The three thought experiments or stories have been much discussed in debates about consciousness and in the field of consciousness studies. I have put references in the further reading so that you can follow the ideas back to the original papers if you wish, although it isn't necessary to do so in order to follow discussions in this book. I will give sufficient background in the text. I don't claim to be able to unpick all that these papers allude to. I'm not a philosopher and these are difficult papers, containing much that probably goes right past me. But I think difficulty should not be a bar to us, particularly when they offer such an engaging way into examining consciousness. You might be able to access the original papers online and I give some suggestions for websites, but of course these may have changed since this book was published. As the originals were written by philosophers, you might find them a little hard to follow, but if you do wish to get the general idea of the originals, I would encourage you to reread rather than give up. There is often a lot of insight in a philosophical paper, but it may take some careful reading and rereading to get the idea. It does for me. I will try to put the stories and discussions in plain English, but this will change the stories in ways that follow interpretations I am interested in. By changing the stories at all, it is likely to mean that some of the complexity of the original papers will be lost. I found these stories rewarding because they forever throw up questions that test our familiar world. And it is in this spirit that I invite you to join my discussions of the three stories. As far as possible when reading this book, try to keep these stories in mind. I will be referring to them, but even when I do not do this directly, the stories and your familiarity with them will help you get the idea of what I am saying.

Part I takes the story of an imagined teleporter – in science fiction, a teleporter is a futuristic machine that can instantly transport you from one place to another – and examines questions about being a person and how it is for us *to be conscious*. The story is taken from a thought experiment devised by Derek Parfit.[3]

Chapter 1 sets out the basic story and also some variations. The main feature of consciousness discussed in this chapter is what it means to be a *person*. Chapter 2 addresses questions raised by the thought experiment asking not only who am I but also what, when and where am I? I will introduce the idea of *negative shapes, spaces and contours* as an alternative way we can conceive of ourselves as persons. We will examine variations on 'to be' such as the sense of self, memory and identity as, for example, in a discussion of the film *The Return of Martin Guerre*. Chapter 3 takes a first look at the genre of captivity and asks what is it *to be captive*? How does a person sustain themselves in solitary confinement? What do they do to stop themselves from psychologically disintegrating? I will quote from interviews I carried out with former captives, so that you can hear their voices in this discussion, and to make a case for the importance of the lives of others even when we are separated from other people. The idea of *polyphony* will be introduced here.

Part II takes the story told by Thomas Nagel that asks the extraordinary question, 'What is it like to be a bat?'[4] In this part we examine what it is *to have conscious experience*. This includes our sense of 'point of view'; the sense that we are located in our time and place (and *this* body). I will introduce some ideas associated with a movement in painting called *Cubism* and from which I have coined the term *Cubist Psychology*.[5] The mind–body problem is outlined in the introduction to Part II. Chapter 4 directly deals with the thought experiment about bats and examines what it is to have a worldview. Chapter 5 examines treatments in the arts concerning experience, point of view and mind; we discuss films such as *Being John Malkovich*, *Blade Runner* and *The Diving Bell and the Butterfly*. This chapter also has a brief discussion of the novel and how novelists have dealt with the idea of conscious subjective experience. Chapter 6 returns to my research work on captivity and examines the captive's mind.

Part III tackles what it means to know consciously and deals with issues such as Theory of Mind and reflexivity; these are discussed in the introduction and throughout. Chapter 7 examines the idea of 'landscape and the world about us'. Chapter 8 takes the story of 'Mary the colour scientist'. The story is taken from a thought experiment devised by the philosopher Frank Jackson. We examine a variation devised by me as a way to explore how it is to be free. Chapter 9 takes the song 'I wish I knew how it would feel to be free' as a medium for discussing all that's been discussed so far in the book: how it is to be conscious, to have conscious experience and to know consciously. This chapter includes further commentary on the genre of captivity.

The Conclusions chapter pulls the book together around the main themes of captivity/freedom, acts of consciousness and conscience, person/mind/world and Cubist Psychology.

The Notes pages that follow the final chapter contain the endnotes from each raised figure shown in the book. After these, there is a section with comments on recommended further reading, viewing and listening. This is followed by a list of references to films, paintings and other artworks, and a bibliography, which gives a full reference for all of the sources I have used. Finally, there is an index of subject matter and author names with the page numbers where these occur, so that you can easily look up a particular idea or particular people.

How the book is written

This book is written in the form of returning loops so that we're never far from readdressing matters that came up earlier or turning our attention forwards to matters still to come. These loops are not simply repetitions; they are opportunities to return to an issue from another direction. You may need to read some parts twice because material placed later may help with material placed earlier. Earlier chapters tend to be longer because they include extra material explaining key terms, which are referred to later in the book.

I will try to write plainly and explain any jargon as we go along. Writing plainly will also mean using everyday language and expressions that mean some readers may start reading into this book interpretations that are unintended. For example, the word 'thing' or 'something' is one such useful word that could be misinterpreted as meaning an object, particularly a separate object distinct from other objects.[6] Sometimes plain English can make it seem as if I am talking about consciousness as a thing when I am just using convenient everyday language.

It might look as if the distinctions I make between, for example, inside and outside are intended to convey a division between two things. I don't mean to imply a division as I take the distinctions only to be helpful ways of characterising how things seem for us. The twofold way of talking that most of us use ordinarily is not a problem in itself; it helps us to say what we mean because we can make distinctions between this and that. Dividing the world into how it seems to be only becomes a problem if we believe that the world really is divided up and that the twofold way we talk about this and that really depicts how the world is. Sometimes, the way languages are structured seems to imply that there really are sets of opposites that represent real and distinct separate categories of existence. In order for me to speak plainly about consciousness, sometimes it may seem as if I'm saying the world is really divided into two on any subject, when I do not believe this to be the case.[7] In most examples that I will discuss I will say that there are many ways of characterising rather than simply two.

The idea in this book is to discuss issues slowly and at length so that the sense of what I am saying is eventually conveyed. Where I am unable to do this it is largely because I do not understand the issue well enough myself. And these paragraphs will contain the most important three and a half words I know: 'I don't know.' Where possible, I will say why I am unable to explain further or where I think others may have a better grasp on an issue, but also where I don't think anyone knows.

Much of what follows has been written about elsewhere and some of the sources are listed at the back. I find that much of the discussion seems to stop at the point where it most needs to go on to say more. For example, the development of us as persons is discussed and sometimes explained, but not what a person can do as a person. I'll point towards contributions that have fed my thinking. You can read this book without looking up the notes; they are mostly there to refer to further reading and sometimes give more background details about the point just made. For example, many of the notes acknowledge a source for what has just been discussed. Although this book is aimed at the interested layperson, some readers may want to see my sources and so place my work in relation to the academic field to which it contributes. Some readers may wish to follow up my main sources, so I have also included a short section of recommended further reading together with some remarks about each one.

There are some terms that I have found it difficult to do without and these will be illustrated with an example either when they are first mentioned or where I think an explanation best fits.

Some of us have got used to using the plural 'them' when 'he' or 'she' would seem to be grammatically correct. The idea is not to use pronouns for male and female because use of either is clearly exclusive and use of both as in 'he/she' is off-putting. I know some readers will be offended by the use of 'them' and 'their' as singular pronouns, but I think it is more important that my book is inclusive and that most readers get plain English.

I am at a point in my life and work where it seems the more I learn the more I find myself saying I don't know, but I have some ideas. This book focuses on what can be said about the living of this life of ours, and, as such, it touches on the *meaning* of life in its discussion of the *manner* of life and living and what it is to have conscious experience. I would like to think some ideas in my book might be important for all of us, but I am well aware of the problems caused by many in what writers have already written on these matters: I have no wish to add to the pile of supposedly expert texts. I will argue *for* this contribution rather than against others. By putting one clear voice and set of ideas, the reader can try out and test out their views against mine. And this is only possible by taking a clear position. More than one view can have merit in a complex field of study like consciousness. My aim is to add to the field. Much of what follows may be a kind of madness dressed up as an interesting discussion, but I will let others be the judge of that and just get on with it.

Part I

To be conscious

INTRODUCTION

What does it mean to be conscious and to live a conscious life? In Part I we will take the verb 'to be' as the act of consciousness and 'to live' as how it is for us when we sustain 'to be' *over time*. We endure and I will take duration as more important than any one snapshot even when duration is much like a series of snapshots, as any analysis of life and living often is. In this part I want to suspend belief about how it is to live this life of ours, to test what is commonplace and familiar about life and living and to begin to think about what it is for us to be temporal beings, or beings that have a sense of their time and place.

I will take Derek Parfit's story of the 'teleporter' and examine beliefs about what it is to be a person; but first, what do I mean by the term 'person'?

I believe persons are made of other people. This may sound outlandish at first pass, but we will go around this idea many times in this book. The idea of person can be related to how we think of parts and wholes. Parts and wholes can be quite a useful way of conceptualising our world. We are, as an example, individual members of the human family.[1] As such, we are each one part of a larger whole that consists solely of all those many parts put together.

Persons are what we know and do not know about someone. After my father died, I realised that I didn't know why he had come to live in Ramsgate, Kent. My grandfather moved there, but

11

I have no idea why that was; they had come from Taunton in Somerset. It could have been to find work, but I am just guessing. When we read a well-drawn character in a book, it is because the writer has only drawn it sufficiently for us to produce the virtual person that moves through the pages. We do this as the reader. Much that we imagine about the person is ours and is not drawn from the book at all. If someone turns the book into a film, we may see it and respond, 'That's not how *I* saw them!'

From this standpoint persons are psychological and exist psychologically for others and for the person themselves. This is the kind of consciousness that I am trying to discuss. This is consciousness placed in the world, having a standpoint and minded towards a person's situation. It is because others think of me that I continue to live. This shifts Descartes' famous 'I think therefore I am' to the social world of persons.[2]

For example, one of the former captives I interviewed was Terry Waite. In his book *Taken on Trust* he reports receiving a postcard that starts 'Dear Terry, You are not forgotten.'[3] He has said how important this message was when it was given to him in his cell. Later, it was removed by one of Waite's more unpleasant guards, but the consolation of it remained with him.

To know that others are thinking about them is extraordinarily personally sustaining for a hostage. It helps to maintain a person's integrity against the psychologically disintegrating effects of solitary confinement.

Chapter 1 sets out Parfit's basic story or thought experiment and includes a discussion of some of the variations on his original theme. We will examine two forms of integrity – the feelings of unity and continuity.

Chapter 2 moves from the basic story to tackle our beliefs about persons, senses of self, identities and the like. We have many words and ways of talking about who and what we are and this in itself is evidence of the changing historical nature of persons. This is quite a long chapter, so I have broken it down into a series of smaller sections that can be taken one at a time. The first section, with the heading 'Negative spaces, shapes and contours', introduces one of the book's main conceptual themes through illustrative examples and exercises. In the second section, on 'The making of persons', there is a discussion of how our development is as much about how we are brought up as it is about how we grow up. The third section, on 'Senses of self', includes a discussion of the feeling that we are a single unified presence deserving of explanation. The fourth section, on 'Social identities', deals with how we are composed by our place in social groups. In the fifth section, headed 'What collects us together?', examples are used to discuss the alternative social theory of persons.

Chapter 3 examines what it is like to be captive and what happens to prisoners held in solitary confinement. I believe that the stories of captivity can help us make sense of what it is to be us because conditions of solitary confinement pare down the person, the action and the situation in ways that bring to our notice what is often drowned out by the deluge of distractions in our modern world. Captivity is not a distinct state of affairs different from ordinary living; rather, it amplifies ordinary living. The accounts of captivity turn up what is usually taken as background and turn down the volume of the busy everyday world that is normally to the fore.

The Conclusions for Part I pull together the key themes: persons and our relationships with other people. From a social psychology standpoint a person is never alone. Persons can be physically separated – we can be a long distance apart or cut off from a person and this may create the illusion of separation. But as a person you are as much a part of me as I am of you. We are interrelated, or to put it plainly, we are related. To understand what a person is doing in any situation, we need to start from a social standpoint and to ask what a person brings to a situation. In solitary confinement, where there are no people present, a captive simply makes people up and creates a virtual social world in which they continue to live the life they lead.

1   To teleport or not to teleport? (Parfit)

The story of the teleporter

Imagine a future situation where, on a regular basis, you can teleport from one place to another. Imagine a place you want to travel to. Imagine that you enter a chamber that has all the equipment and a button you press to start the teleporting process. The equipment scans you: all of you. Nothing is left out. The equipment transmits the scan to a receiver at the new location. The receiver equipment then remakes you in the new location using the perfectly copied information to make a perfect organic copy from local materials. As part of the process, the equipment deletes the original you as well as the scan used to remake you at your destination. Imagine that the equipment is completely reliable. From your point of view, there is a moment or two of unconsciousness, but then, there you are again, the next moment, in the teleporter chamber at your new location. It is like momentarily dropping off to sleep and waking up again.[1]

The teleporter is one hundred per cent safe and completely copies everything about you.

Would you use the teleporter? At this point, write down what you think and some of the feelings and thoughts that have arisen in response to the story. Think about the following questions and write down your response to these:

- If you would use the teleporter, can you imagine why someone would not use it?
- If you would not use it, why would you not use it? Can you imagine someone who would, why they might use it, and how this standpoint differs from yours?

You may know exactly what you would do without thinking about it, but please entertain the alternative answer and reflect on what your decision says about what it is *to be* you.

If you're not quite sure what teleporting is, it was used extensively in the *Star Trek* television series and films as well as in more recent science fiction. Teleporting means being transported from one place to another by some process of matter transport whereby you are dematerialised, transported by some kind of information transfer to new coordinates, and then rematerialised. In reality, scientists soon realised that not only would the energy required for matter transfers be beyond any capacity currently imaginable, but also that it would only be necessary to send the information. So instead of a matter transport, the idea was revised to information transport. If we could make this work, it would be ultra-fast travelling. It might one day be possible to achieve transport through a kind of quantum entanglement and I gather – but can't say I understand – that this is how it has already been done with photons.[2] But let's get back to consciousness. It's not the actuality that we are concerned with here: all we need to believe for the thought experiment is to entertain the possibility that the teleporter works and then we can discuss what follows from this and think about the assumptions we are making about ourselves, our life and living.

As the idea in the teleporting story is that your replica brain is exactly like yours, it will seem to remember living your life up to the point where you entered the teleport chamber. The replica you will be psychologically continuous with you and its unified character will be just like yours. The original you and the replica you would be indistinguishable, even to you.

So is your replica you, you? I don't know. But I have a notion that *you* – original or replica – need not *be* some kind of unique continuous existence running through the core of your life like the writing in a stick of rock. If a person for you is this kind of core, then you died in the teleporter when your molecules were deleted by the scanner. If what we are is scannable or can be transformed into something scannable, there could be continuity, that is, there would not be a period during which you had ceased to exist *in some form*; however, what would be your status were you to remain as a scan stored in some kind of retrieval system? Would you be in some kind of suspended animation? Would you be conscious of this? This way of thinking supposes that we could be transformed into 'information' and that as information we would still retain our first-person perspective – the way it seems to us that we are located somehow in time and place, and that we have a subjective viewpoint on the world.

As 'information', however complex, would you still have a first-person perspective on anything? We don't know, but this is one of the most argued-about questions in consciousness studies.[3] Of course, the transformation of information needs to work both ways. It is necessary to both scan you at your departure point and use the information transferred in the scan to put you back together again at your destination.

Each introduction of new technology also opens the way to new and more horrific forms of torture. If you were conscious and stored in some kind of teleport computer and you knew this was your condition, wouldn't this be even worse than being locked in a cell as a political prisoner or hostage? If you didn't know this was your condition, in what sense has all that you are been scanned? If we go from something that gives a first-person perspective to information that doesn't, something just got lost. If we get this back on arrival, in what sense has point of view been continuous with who we were at our departure point? At least the captive has some freedom through mental activity: to imagine, to reflect and to remember. If you were held in some kind of computer limbo would this mean being aware of being in limbo, as if you were locked in or had locked-in syndrome?

Locked-in syndrome is one of the most extraordinary conditions. A person is 'locked in' because, although conscious, they are unable to communicate as they are completely paralysed. Hence they are 'locked in', as if trapped inside a house, with no means of contact with other people. Some can move their eyes and have used this as a means of contact. Recent work has allowed communication to take place via brain scanning technology.

We would normally take consciousness to be given in the ability of a person to deliberately respond to conversation. In normal circumstances if I say something to you and you say something back that relates to it, I assume you are conscious in the same way as I take myself to be. In circumstances where a person has locked-in syndrome, normal checks through conversation may be unavailable. If the person can make voluntary movements, these can stand in for conversation and work as a way to signal their conscious presence. By scanning a person's brain activity and looking for certain tell-tale patterns of activation, it is possible to set up a simple signalling system for responses such as *yes* and *no*.[4] We do not know that the locked-in person is responding much as we would were we to be put in a scanner and asked to employ the same system ourselves, but then we do not know how it is we are conscious deliberators either.[5]

Jean-Dominique Bauby dictated a book about his experience of being locked in and a film of the same name based on the book tries to show what it is like to be locked in and is faithful to the account Bauby gave in his book.[6]

If what we are is pared down to our conscious life and living – given that any engagement with our world was impossible for us – would we want this to be teleported? Would we accept a replica that, like an avatar, gave us a renewed embodied basis complete with movement and conversation? Would this be us?

Are we a person if we are refabricated? I believe that what makes us persons is our social treatment of one another and not simply the physical form that we take. We accept an exchange with others over diverse technologies many of which offer nothing more than a disembodied voice. I believe that it is because we treat each other as persons the way we do that we are the people we treat each other to be.

If the person with locked-in syndrome is completely paralysed and has no contact and never achieves contact, they are no longer a person for us; however, they are still a person for themselves. But this makes the point: the only way that they continue to be a person is because they can use an imagined virtual world, which also includes themselves in interactions with others. This is tragically and comically portrayed in the film of Bauby's story, where a voiceover gives us a flavour of Bauby's virtual world.[7] It might, on this basis, be possible to survive the death of the physical body *if* it were to become possible to occupy a virtual world. The only requirement for being able to act could be that you can still think and feel. We can see this from the cases of being locked up as a hostage or political prisoner, particularly where this involves solitary confinement.

There are problems, however. If you were never to have an interaction with others, but were conscious, it would be as if you were dead. It's not too pleasant to think about, but we need to think this through. Without the prospect of ever being able to interact with others, we would be likely to descend to utter despair. We might be able to accept the situation rather as in meditation, where the idea is to accept thinking and thoughts and not grasp at them or seek to banish them from our minds. We could let go of life. If our bodies were kept alive under circumstances where the medical profession envisaged that there might be a cure in the future, we might have to endure this state for a long time.

A locked-in person could communicate via a yes/no system that, as with Bauby, could even allow them to dictate how they are feeling. Of course, this then means we're talking about real inter-actions with the world that allow original actions that have conse-quences in the world. This is likely to be sufficient to sustain the person as a person. Bauby wrote a book and this has subsequently been adapted into a film; this meant Bauby had an impact from his locked-in condition: on this basis he was a person *for us* as well as for himself.

The following series of discussions pick up on some of the main conceptual issues where what it is to be a person is concerned. Some issues will be introduced here and then developed more fully in Chapter 2.

Persons and integrity: unity and continuity

Conventionally, we have two defining characteristics for being a person. First, we require continuity; for someone to be one and the same person over time. We require that a life is continuously led for it to be the same life of the same person; their lifetime. Second, we require unity; to be one and the same person requires that whatever is associated with a life is integral to the life continuously led. We are the sum of all our parts unbroken at any one time. To be a person is to be a unity, to be fully or wholly myself, to be all of me and to be continuous, to be all of me over all of my life. In keeping with earlier discussions, we could liken what it is to be us to the idea that parts are integrated into some kind of symphonic whole like a piece of music.[8]

One way we tend to think of ourselves is as some kind of continuous existence, but beyond the idea of something like memory or the way we trace events over human time, the way it appears to us to be could be wrong. It may seem that we have a core feature that leads our lives, but in fact this could be simply a variety of ways of relating 'you' to time and place, events and experiences and the you that seems to have a core could be a collection or bundle of related elements joined artificially one to another by one social practice or other much as the brush strokes on a painted surface are given the collective name of *painting*.

I used to think that my life was continuous from birth to death and possibly each side of each. I thought that I started from birth, or before, and had been a single continuous life ever since, and that I might have continued to live after my death. I had a unique soul or I was a unique soul: probably both. I was that unity. In keeping with the principles of this book, I am not about to criticise this position. Souls could sit inside the cavern of the diaphragm, in the spine, in the head, move from spine to head, or simply not be located.

Parfit describes this and similar views as types of 'ego theories' about the nature of persons. An ego is simply an 'I'. When you say 'I', to what does 'I' refer? It is conventionally thought that the ego or 'I' somehow sits inside your head and looks out on the world from a vantage point somewhere behind the eyes as if in a movie theatre.[9] But does 'I' refer to anything or does it just indicate that you are the speaker?

To be a person in the ego theory sense of the word is to have this commonplace commonsensical view that the person that is me was there at the beginning and is continuous through to the end; that if the teleporter does what it says, it copies and sends *everything* to my destination where the high-fidelity replicator restores me to my former glory. If this is what it does, there is no reason to suppose that I am not also there. If you teleport everything that makes me *me* to a location that can use this to replicate me, what if anything would be left out or left over?

To be a person, does our life have to be continuous? Consciousness of events is normally broken by sleep or possibly by other forms of unconsciousness, such as coma or anaesthetisation, so just because teleporting is a different kind of break in continuity it need not make us think that it is different from the ordinary commonplace breaks in the living of our lives. What do we think happens when someone is in a coma or comes out of a coma? Are they a person when anaesthetised? Are they the same person when the anaesthetic wears off and they 'wake up'? What happens if someone has locked-in syndrome but as yet is not in contact with others? Is an uninterrupted life necessary for being a person? What constitutes continuity? If I, in the form of information that the scanner has turned me into, am stored in a retrieval system and then I'm replicated later, is this a continuous life running through the time when I was information or is this period time out and thus a new life and new person is started up afterwards? But, if I can accurately recall my life prior to being stored, am I not the same person? Am I not at least as much the same as I'm the same person when I wake up after an anaesthetic or simply wake up in the morning even if I've spent much of the night in slow-wave sleep?[10]

If a person is a separate entity then lack of continuity equals death. When you scan me and destroy the original, you kill me. If only the original can *be* you, then when you were scanned the original you was destroyed, so you were destroyed too. The entity that was me at the point of scanning no longer exists. On this basis teleporting is dying. But, if I'm not a separate entity, then ordinary life is the same as teleporting, as Parfit suggested. My moment-to-moment existence is a series of teleports in which the collection of elements that I call 'me' are assembled and reassembled, collected up and bundled, but the manner of my collective status lends itself to teleporting because the reality of my discontinuous life is about the same. If consciousness of my situation is continuous – or at least it picks up where I left off and I have recollections of my life before sleeping/teleporting – I would probably believe this to be sufficient for the person also to be continuous against the standard I adopt in ordinary living.

When my body (including the brain) dies, the physical features of me as a person are no longer alive; but I may be remembered by those that knew me and this is a kind of continuance. I may be discussed. In the social sense I have some continuance that survives at least until those that knew me die. Were I to produce something longer lasting, I could persist in some social or cultural form beyond this point too.

I can see reasons – other than religious and spiritual reasons – why we would assume persons are continuous and united wholes. I want to be treated as such by the law because to do so would treat me as having rights to act, to move around, to mix with others, to speak freely but also to have responsibility for the consequences of my actions such that I can be treated as the knowing cause of something that happened. We do treat others this way. If you are old enough and developed enough and you do something, you will be treated as a knowing subject and the cause by your intentions and actions of some event. We could assume from these that a person just is the elements and features already discussed, that they are recognised and treated as a person as part of our conventions of how we treat each other. Treating each other this way may mean we treat each other better.

Persons as positive shapes: the boundary of the skin

The greatest assumption on this view is just the idea that persons are like things and can be separated out and treated as distinct units in isolation.

We conventionally draw the person as if in isolation. We get schooled in images of isolated brains with outlines around them. We do the same when we draw the body and we assume that we have outlined the person.

Conventionally, a person is drawn as a positive space. We learn various conventions as we learn to look at images. Conventions are the uses of representations that have become established; they are the customary ways in which we are used to representing the world and our place in it. Drawing a line or an outline around an object is a conventional way of depicting an object. We draw it or

23

picture it *as if* it really had a line drawn around it that we were simply copying; no such lines exist in nature of course. We draw an outline around a body or a brain and the person or brain is enclosed by that outline as if separated from everything else and hanging in empty space unsupported and unrelated to anything else. Too often this view prevails. Magritte's series of paintings of everyday objects such as pipes, hats and bicycles highlighted this familiar view of objects as separable from the world about them by painting them as if hanging in space. Magritte 'sabotaged' this taken-for-granted standpoint by painting the wrong labels on the images.[11]

The usual assumption is that we are separate entities detached from each other; that whatever is enclosed by our skin *is* us. As long as we scan all of this, we have copied everything. But how does copying what's enclosed by our skin copy our relationships with other people? We can draw a line round the skin as a boundary and call this positive shape us, but our relationships with other people could be likened to all the negative shapes that exist in between. George Herbert Mead said:

> If mind is socially constituted, then the field ... of any given individual must extend as far as the social activity ... extends; and hence that field cannot be bounded by the skin of the individual organism to which it belongs.[12]

We will examine the alternative standpoint of negative spaces, shapes and contours in Chapter 2. For now, negative spaces are those found between people and objects or between objects and other objects; thus, they are often simply thought of as background.

Persons characterised as social kinds

As I think persons are human or social 'kinds' (rather than natural 'kinds'), I would say that there are no persons at birth and then one person if and only if brought about by others. In answer to

24

the great question 'What exists and what is its character?' some would say that there are natural and human kinds of things. Most would understand natural kinds of things as being in some sense universally true: 'organisms' are universally agreed to be a natural kind. Whereas many terms in psychology – some would say most – are human kinds of things, they vary across both period and place. I will use the term 'social kind' because as a social psychologist I would say all that exists for us as persons is social in character. As Kurt Danziger says:

> The sorts of things that psychology takes as its objects, people's actions, experiences and dispositions, are not independent of their categorization.[13]

When we categorise human life the way that we do – for example when we categorise our relationships with other people – these categories are of human making; there is nothing in the world that exists of these relationships independently of our human standpoint.

Natural kinds are such things as bodies, brains and planets. Natural refers to the idea of natural categories, the patterns and regularities that we can make out across the natural world and perhaps across the universe as we know it. Human kinds are those things that are entirely human in manufacture and classification. So the term human refers to those things that are part of the world of our own making. Person, Mind and World (among many others) are human classifications and need not refer to a natural order, although they may seem to. As Charles Taylor wrote:

> What has been argued in the different theories of social nature of [human beings] is not just that [they] cannot physically survive alone, but much more that they can only develop their characteristically human capacities in society. The claim is that living in society is a necessary condition of the development of rationality, in some sense

25

of this property, or of becoming a moral agent in the full sense of the term, or becoming a fully responsible, autonomous being.[14]

There are natural kinds such as bodies, brains and planets, and characteristically human or social kinds such as persons, minds and worlds.

Persons transformed: growing up and upbringing

There is a time endured during which we are coming about, when we develop into what we become. There is evidence that suggests that whatever we are develops. We cannot say for sure whether there was a person at the beginning, so we cannot say whether or not this self-awareness grows upon some kind of core body like a copper sulphate crystal grows in copper sulphate solution on a seed crystal. Of course, a seed crystal has to be produced first before you can grow it into something bigger. In much the same way, I think we are seeded by others and whatever it is that we are grows from that beginning.

We are primed. Our development is like the priming of a water pump. You have to put water into the pump first before you can get water out of the pump.

A clearer analogy might be the way many of us may have learned that pearls grow in an oyster shell. What really happens fits what I want to suggest, while the urban myth is what I would like to debunk. The myth is that pearls grow upon some kind of grit such as a grain of sand, when what really happens is that an alien organism gets into the oyster shell and the oyster secretes nacre, which is the same substance that makes the oyster's shell, and it is this nacreous growth that becomes the pearl. The oyster is isolating the irritant much as our immune response might wrap up a bacterium that got into our system. In effect the process neutralises and naturalises such that the pearl is very much part of the oyster.

By analogy, I think that is how we get started. Others get into us by engaging us in play and conversation and it is this that we naturalise to become persons such that we could say that we are made from other people. Over time we become the person others have made us into and a person that endures in their own right.

Whatever name we use for ourselves, I think we get started socially by the way others engage us and make us like them. The raw materials are there in most cases, but unless others who are already persons engage us in play, conversation and other social practices, we will not become persons by ourselves. We both develop and are transformed. Some developmental processes are a matter of maturation. As long as we are well nourished we will mature and grow. Others are facilitated or even caused by others and the situation into which we are born. 'How we grow up is mostly a matter of how we are brought up.'[15] Persons are made of social practices such as the 'rites of passage' that are peculiar to different cultures. It is only because we come to use our bodies and brains in the ways others show us that we are made persons the way we are. We fit our social and cultural worlds because they made us. We are made of the same patterns so it is entirely natural that we feel at home in our particular social and cultural setting. But none is exactly the same as us. We are persons in our own right. If we go to another setting, however, we may experience the kind of alienation that would be predicted by being the product of our former home culture. If we stay away long enough, we act according to local convention in the cultural setting that we have come to call home. If we then return home supposing that we will regain our familiar place, we will get a second shock: that of being an alien in our original home country. All these point to the idea that person is a social or human kind.

Persons and place: copying background

Much of the debate about teleporting assumes a level of copying that we may never achieve. The kind of high fidelity that can copy memories, dreams and reflections is a long way from copying molecules and cells, even whilst acknowledging that cells and molecules are necessary for memories, dreams and reflections. We have a problem and it relates to the difference between single notes played separately in a sequence of equal intervals and a melody brought about by playing the same notes as a series with emphases, timing and pauses. Negative spaces in music help to give music its idiosyncratic feel and it is the musicality of the musician, or the phrasing of the singer, that gives the piece or song a particular character. A piece of music is more than the sum of its various quantities. Simply copying the quantities will not guarantee music played at the other end of the teleport. If copying us as persons is like copying music, copying us may involve copying the whole orchestrated score. It may be that copying at any point in the music is enough to get us started at our destination, but if who and what we are is extended socially in what Ciarán Benson calls 'place-time', we might need to copy all our orchestration and all that orchestrates us.[16]

Ciarán Benson's term 'place-time' is the human kind equivalent of the natural kind 'space-time'. Place-time is a 'humanised, personalised space' and relates to 'experiential time', that is, 'time as a person experiences it'. He says that 'Our sense of the familiarity of places is intimately connected to the idea of place-time.'[17] It is the sense of self that makes the world about us navigable and gives us an orientation. The world about us is treated as the lives of others.[18] That I am made by the world about me is certain; that the world about me is changed by my actions is equally certain. The world as it is was not inevitable; it has been made the way it is by how we are. We can make a distinction between me and my world, but this does not make the world exist separately from me as a discrete object I can observe. Nor am I separable from the world. If I ceased to make exchanges with my world, I would cease to exist. Neither is the world fixed; rather, it changes and in some small part this is due to me. Nor am I fixed for I can do things that will have consequences in the world.

It is not clear today what would constitute copying you and your place-time so that a copy could be teleported. 'You' also includes others, aspects of others that are only evident when they are absent, so the 'you' is not a distinct entity existing separately from anything around it as if completely enclosed. Any single piece of music only makes sense as music because of other musical pieces. 'Here' includes other places that help us set this one and also our standpoints on these settings. 'Now' includes knowing of our likely tomorrows and of how things might be as well as recollected past times and how things might have been. As in music, a single note is set within other notes yet to be played or those already played. If you are an important part of another's life and living, would it be expected that you be scanned to enable their teleport? Without the settings of our life – the social ground on which we stand – we literally do not figure.

To be one and the same person: making more than one replica

But what happens if I make two or more replicas? What happens if the original scanning process fails to destroy the original when copied? Which one is me? Are they all me? In one version of the teleporter thought experiment devised by Derek Parfit, there is a fault. The teleport is successful in that the original 'you' has been scanned and copied. Your scan has arrived safely and you have been faithfully replicated. A replica you now exists on Mars, let's say, and has arrived at your destination; however, instead of the original you at your departure point being destroyed by the process, the original you still exists on Earth. Parfit calls this the 'branch line case' and he suggests that we should think of it as time limited.[19] Imagine the original is going to die very soon so that even though it should have been destroyed in the scanning process, it will not live much longer, perhaps a matter of hours or days. The replica you will continue to do what the original you was going to do so that even though the original and replica overlap, once the original dies, only one of you continues to exist. You might even be able to use a video link to speak to the replica you at the destination. If we thought that teleporting would successfully transport us to our destination, we must still believe that we have arrived there, even if via a video link we are faced with the very real presence of what appears to be our identical twin still living at the departure point. But who is it that speaks to us from Earth? Where matters of identity are usually concerned, I am identified as being *one and the same* person and recognised as unique. There could not be more than one of me, could there? So who is it?

Where two persons exist there will always be questions over which is the real and which the imitation or impostor. The questions asked highlight some of our assumptions about what it is for us to be a person. In the film *The Return of Martin Guerre* (*Le Retour de Martin Guerre*) – better than the transposed remake *Sommersby* – we the audience always know that the hero, played by Gérard Depardieu, is an impostor.[20] Warning: plot spoiler. If you would prefer to see the film without knowing important plot points, do it before reading on.

In the film, we are taken right up to the point at which a court is about to decide in the impostor's favour, that is, that he really is the real Martin Guerre when the really real Martin Guerre enters the courtroom and proclaims himself. We had learned early in the film that the real Guerre has lost a leg and so visually we have a symbol of the real Martin Guerre when we see just a close up of the peg leg as a man walks into the courtroom. We know this stands for the real Martin Guerre.

Had the impostor got away with the trick, for all intents and purposes he would *be* Martin Guerre. If he could suspend disbelief about himself, he could indeed *be* Martin Guerre for himself. What is Martin Guerre but the person recognised to be such by others, treated as such by others and sanctioned as such by his home culture and its authorities and institutions? Others think of him as Martin Guerre, so he exists as such a person. What then does this mean that a person is?[21]

Further discussion of the *Martin Guerre* film can be found in Chapters 2 and 5.

Persons and identity: partial duplication

There is another part to the thought experiment and it involves partial duplication of you.[22]

Imagine what happens if instead of scanning all of you in a teleporter, we simply substitute some of your original cells with exact duplicates. Once again it is necessary to imagine that the process of duplication and substitution is completely reliable and safe. It could become normal practice for making exact duplicates of neurons (brain cells) or neural circuits (assemblies of brain cells that are physically interconnected), or all the way up to complete brain substitution. At the 100 per cent level this would be the same amount of copying of the brain as in the above story of teleporting. But what happens to you when, let's say, 2 per cent of your brain is replaced with cells that exactly duplicate your original neurons? What happens when 49 per cent or 51 per cent is replaced? What about 98 per cent? The question is, 'will you as a person survive the substitution process?'

What does this mean you think you are? Who or what do you think you are? What we're asked to consider is what happens at each stage. If you think that a small amount of substitute cells would still mean that you are the original you, but that 51 per cent rather than 49 per cent would make the substitute a replica you, why would the substituting of 2 per cent more cells tip the balance then but not when 2 per cent was *all* that was replaced? In the way we normally frame the idea of a person, we would have to be that person or not be that person. If I am to be operated on, particularly if I am to have brain surgery, it seems natural that I would ask, will what results from the surgery be me? Am I about to die? Is this the end of my life? There must be an answer even if we do not know today what that answer is. Where persons are concerned I must either survive the operation or not. Questions about persons are all-or-nothing-type questions. I cannot half survive a life-threatening experience: I do or I don't survive.

If we were to scan you and not destroy the original, it seems obvious that the replica would be just that: a replica and therefore not the original you; more like a clone than a continuance of the original. You, after all, still exist. At the other end, where we only replace 2 per cent of your cells with duplicates, the result is still you. Therefore at cases in between the result must be you or a replica. There must therefore be a critical point or percentage at which it would be a replica, let's say 51 per cent. But we have already said that changing a few cells, up to say 2 per cent, would result in it still being you. We could of course try to have it both ways and, in a sense, this is what the social view does. But we need to think through the contradictions where cell replacement is concerned.

We tend to assume that copying and replacing (and transplanting) means that you, the original you, sets about taking over any new material. It is as if we liken ourselves to owners of our body and whatever is in its positive space. But is this a misconception of our situation based on a set of beliefs that are not themselves under examination? We may want to keep a notion of identity that is somehow separate from the physical basis of our being. We may want to be some kind of owner-occupier of the bodily house we live in. We may not be wrong to do so, but we may be assuming one kind of extra ingredient when other kinds will work. We need not assume we are an entity or something that inhabits a body; we could equally well be the psychological product of a social developmental process. But I'll need to say more about this.

Of course, the view here uses the principle of replacement parts only a little at any one time, but if we accept that we could replace all of our body parts over a period of time, we need to ask what happens should we decide instead to do all the replacement work as part of the same operation. What differs between doing operations over, say, a few years and doing the replacement work all in one operation?

We could say we are both the elements bundled together to carry out any action *and* something that exists as a unity with the power to effect an impact. But both of these ideas have about them the recognition of ourselves as bundles: the bundle is a unity and the bundled are elements. The problem concerns how we deal with continuity. We seem to accept some level of repair and cell substitution, but many doubt continuity if repair or substitution is on either a large scale or all at once. We need to think this through.

It could be said that the reproduced you at your destination is only you after the original is destroyed. As long as the original survives, any replica can only ever be a copy of the original you. But this is where the paradox lies: if the teleporter has successfully rebuilt you at the receiver location, this you has continuity too. If both experience a moment of unconsciousness as if awakening out of sleep, neither would know *by itself* which was the original. Therefore both teleported *you* on Mars and undestroyed original *you* on Earth are both 'you'. Of course, if neither knew of the existence of the other, the question would not arise.

There are limitations to this kind of debate: this is a thought experiment the reality of which may never be do-able and the consequences of which may vary from the above if it ever becomes do-able. Nonetheless, it may help us to think through our basic beliefs where questions of who and what we are as persons are concerned.

Bundle or collection theories of persons

Let's re-examine the nature of persons from an alternative point of view. If no such extra thing as a continuous entity we call person exists, questions about what happens to *it* are meaningless. Parfit says that there is not an entity *as well as* the collection of

33

elements, so he concludes that the number of persons is none. A separate entity, however named – self, soul, person, among other names, does not exist. The named entity *only and entirely* consists in the name we give to the collection of elements. Parfit thought that the Buddha, Siddhartha Gautama, held this belief and I am introducing it here because Parfit refers to it. Parfit thinks that the Buddha may have been the first bundle theorist and he quotes part of a piece attributed to him:

> A sentient being does exist, you think, O Mara? You are misled by a false conception. This bundle of elements is void of Self, in it there is no sentient being. Just as a set of wooden parts receives the name of carriage, so do we give to elements the name of fancied being.[23]

This suggests that the Buddha thinks we may have a misconception of what a person is because we are using how a person seems to us. The same misconception may be evident in the way we name things. So, an assembly of car parts gets the name 'car', but there is no such *extra* thing as 'the car itself'. And we can go further and apply this to elements too. There is no such thing as a car door. And so on.[24]

We may not be so easily fooled here, but some things seem to carry a life of their own independent of the parts that make them up. A university may consist of lecture theatres, laboratories, the students' union, staff offices, among other things; but do you think there is something over and above this that we might call 'the university itself'? This is a contentious area because it makes us set out the kinds of things that we think exist. Those that take a materialist worldview may happily rest on the idea that once you have a complete list of the physical elements of a university – the buildings and equipment, let's say – you have described all there is. A social psychologist may want to include the network of relationships between people working, studying and running the university, and argue that universities also consist in these, though they would be harder to map.

Charles Horton Cooley wrote that the words society and individual 'do not denote separable phenomena, but are simply collective and distributive aspects of the same thing'.[25] He gave examples such as the terms 'class' and 'students' and I want to take this idea and use it for 'people' and 'person'. We shift our viewpoint; we do not change what it is we view. Individual and social cannot be opposites as one always implies the other; they are complementary terms. They are useful only because they are two different standpoints on human life and living. If we ask which came first, person or persons, we can see the absurdity. We could examine how some people have a higher status and we could compare high- with low-status groups, but it would necessarily be a discussion of status, power and supposed superiority. When we shift standpoint, we do not shift to a different subject, rather we shift to a different standpoint on the *same* subject. I think that sometimes we only get into this confusion because we take it as read that there are only two positions and that, therefore, these are opposite views. I think it would be helpful to take it that there are many standpoints on any subject. I will come back to this when we discuss social identities in Chapter 2.

What kind of bundle are we? If we are collections, collections of what? What makes a collection, a collection? What collects us together or bundles us up? Could we be bundled up by other people who have played a part in our life or by the parts we play?

We have many beginnings and most of these we share with everyone else born during the same time as us. I am always held fascinated by any film clips from around the time I was born. The period often looks so different from the periods I have known as an adult such that it is almost like looking at another life. Yet what shapes these clips was shaping me. If I am to know what I am like it is at least as important to know about the historical influences that have shaped me.[26] What kind of family was I born into? What were they like? How did they bring up their children? What were the conventional standpoints people held?

Could we be collected in memories of the events and experiences that a person has been through? Are we bundled together by how others treat us? Let's suppose that you are a bundle of elements that are held together by some kind of unifying process or idea that relates them, much like a number of different items, such as small presents, could be tied up with string to keep them all together. A bundle could also be thought of as a collection. David Hume wrote about this and used the term 'collection' as well as 'bundle'.[27] I think the term 'collection' is very useful. We might think of ourselves as collections of memories, of the tales we tell of ourselves – literally the stories of our lives – and we might consider this to still have about it the conventional sense of the individual we are used to. But I want to put a spanner in the works of that way of thinking.

If we are the kind of bundle of elements that we think of as our memories, these clearly involve the shared experiences of past events too. Many past events will have been shared experiences. The collection or bundle of elements is not ours because we fundamentally share a common humanity. And this means any experience would have more than one *owner*. What bundles you is not just you but other persons. Is there a difference between you recalling a shared past experience and you and the persons you shared the experience with recalling the past experience together? I think there is a difference. The way that we pattern experiences in memories is a kind of fiction: we fashion experiences into a narrative that usually puts us at the centre of the story (whatever role we played in the event). When someone else remembers the event from their point of view, they will tend to be the centre of events.

Collections of memories: John Dean's testimony

When it was not known that there were tapes of discussions between the then president of the United States, Richard Nixon, and others about the Watergate break-in, John Dean's testimony to the senate committee was given greater credibility.[28]

Dean was an advisor on legal issues to the president. He seemed to be able to report on lengthy and complex meetings had by the principal players in Nixon's government. When the tapes were revealed and played, the differences between the recordings of discussions and Dean's testimony could be analysed. In particular, Dean's testimony distorted what was actually said and placed Dean as more central to the discussion than he in fact was. What this highlighted was how we tend to remember our role in events and how we remember events from our point of view. Remembering involves what was retained of an actual event as well as our role in the episode. Because memories are stories rather than strict archival recordings, there are likely to be changes made. Remembering may put us at the centre of the action when we were one of many or even on the fringe. Remembering may conjure up the general idea of an event rather than a mirror on what really happened. Remembering may change the roles played by the principals at the event such that we may simplify the number of characters and merge two or more roles into one. Dean's testimony allowed researchers to see the scale of the problem: how much remembering is partial, selective and revised to place the person remembering at the centre of events. We tend to emphasise our role in events.

There are different kinds of accuracy. We would not expect memory to be word-for-word recall of discussions. We would look for the kind of accuracy that fairly captured the general idea of what took place. We are much more likely to remember discussions where what we said had been previously prepared or repeated material we had previously discussed, as does Dean. Nonetheless, Dean's testimony was substantially consistent with what was going on at the White House and when Nixon released the actual transcripts, these did not undermine John Dean's testimony.

Dean's testimony has the hallmarks of the kind of partial, selective and revised versions of an event found in stories, scripts and roles. These are evident in the way a film reconstructs actual events. An event may have taken place over a number of separate periods that a film compresses into one that has all the significant action. Similarly, many people may be involved in an actual event and a film may encapsulate a number of different people in one role that plays out the significant characteristics. A film may not be faithful to any particular event or person, but fidelity is to the general idea of what happens, to the pattern of events, and thus may fairly represent it.

In my work as a university lecturer, I may be able to present a detailed account of a particular academic viewpoint without notes. It is so much easier for the lecturer to recall material than it is for a student; the lecturer has prepared and also may have previously discussed it. For the student the lecture may be the first and only occasion where they go through the material. Nonetheless, recall is always going to be to some extent constructive, or 'imaginative reconstruction' to use Bartlett's phrase, simply because events cannot be recalled in their entirety.[29] Events may not be solely based on retained information, but they are partly so. Others present at an event are likely to agree that some of the details are faithful to what happened.[30]

If we had all the archive recordings of all possible kinds, we could never put an event together exactly as some actual event because there is no such thing as an actual event. All events are constructed by us including present events. We decide where an event starts and ends. Our recordings betray our acceptable distortions. By placing a single camera at a meeting, we are likely to bias the weight given towards those at the centre or on a raised platform and away from those at the fringe. Even the idea of a centre and fringe is one we get from *framing* events.

Taking memory to be any memory of an event cuts the event into my point of view of my part in it. We can do this but we should acknowledge when memory is not broken up except artificially. There are no joints at which to cleave our memory of an event or indeed someone else's memory from ours. Patterns do not necessarily have convenient places to divide parts from other parts;

decisions about how to do this may be arbitrary. It may seem as if the points at which we cleave things apart are convenient or even obvious points for a cut, but to cut it there is arbitrary because we could have chosen differently, or even not to have cleaved what we cleaved at all. Experiences of events, and the memories of them: neither of these is easily framed in a positive space. Experience is not so easily divided up as yours or mine. My experience may also be your experience, particularly if we were together. All experiences have shared contours such that to call something *my* experience is only ever partially true.

Our memories highlight particular parts of events and our role in them seen from our point of view, but it's only when someone else was also present that our version of events can be seen for what it is: a partial telling of what happened from a particular point of view. Memories often take particular forms because there are conventional ways in which certain kinds of human events are told. As film directors do, we may parcel up several incidents into one, several people into one character giving us a convenient package. When others remember events, they may pick out things we have forgotten or relegated to the fringes.

Chapter conclusions

So, what is the nature of persons? The response we give to this will highlight the beliefs we hold. If there are no such things as separately existing distinct egos, questions about what happens to 'you' in the teleporter become non-questions: no such *thing* called person exists, therefore there is nothing to copy and nothing to leave behind in the copying process, nothing to be left free-floating when the original 'you' is destroyed in the scanning. If the number of persons was none to begin with, it makes no difference how many replicas are made, they will not be more of or less of a person by this process, nor will they seem to be some kind of automaton or undead or zombie lacking in vital spirit. Each replica, like the original, is simply a bundle of elements onto which a variety of characteristics can be applied: this is a person; this is Guy; this is Guy's identical twin. But we will know that these are names and descriptions for the bundle of elements and not the naming of any distinct entity that somehow exists separately from them.

Of course, if you think you are not a distinct person, ordinary survival is the same as this: your replica on Mars is just like a future you. After all, the only continuity is that fashioned by your memories and the other ways in which you relate yourself as a bundle or collection.

We should not forget the ways that others collect us together by their responses to us and our absence. How are we collected or bundled together? What does the bundling or collecting? One way in which we collect ourselves together is through memory. In English, we are even said to re-collect our past experiences. My standpoint throughout this book is the view that persons are relational and that therefore the properties of who and what we are vary according to how a person is related to others. We get collected in the remembrances others have of us and with their expectations of us. So other people collect us together too: whether, for example, our relationship with others is to do with the place in which we live or work. Workplace colleagues do this for us, so work collects us. Our movement around our local area collects us, so places do it. We are part of our home town and all that goes on in it. We are related to place-time. Work, rest and play do it. When we die others may continue to do it.

To suspend belief is not easy. Belief glues us to the familiar and commonplace in ways that are transparent for us most of the time. Reflecting on Parfit's teleporter story confronts us with our basic beliefs and assumptions about the nature of persons. There are a variety of depictions of what a person, their sense of identity or their sense of self looks like. We have Parfit's useful distinction between ego and bundle theories that cover much of how a person appears to us to be. But I want to contribute a social theory standpoint to the explanatory mix. From this point of view we are part of the fabric of our shared humanity, of the social practices such as those connected with birth and rites of passage to adulthood, and of the institutions that make and break us as people. We are also part of the lives of others as they are part of ours: there isn't an easy separation between you and me. If we were to teleport, we would need to scan the world about us too or else fail to turn up at our destination as we were at our departure point.

If we are assuming a boundary around the object we call persons and that boundary is the skin, we are also definitely not including anything else: no setting, no one else, no background, context, anything. Are we assuming that these features are automatically available to us at our destination? This was not stated in the teleporter design. Our assumptions belie our beliefs and show that the nature of persons goes beyond the skin.

We need to think about who and what we are and that is what the next chapter is about. In it we will examine some key psychological ideas, such as sense of self, memory and identity. I will develop the concept of negative shapes, spaces and contours as a way for us to see ourselves differently.

2   To be a person: ego, bundle and social theories

The question 'who am I?' also asks what am I, which am I, when am I and where am I? Rather than place a division between who and what questions, I will ask a greater variety of questions that all address 'who am I?' There are of course two other questions, 'how and why am I as I am?' We should see the 'who am I?' questions as incorporating all the other questions that we want to ask about persons and what it is to live this life of ours. Before getting into the details, the following sets out the big picture ideas from Chapter 1 where ego, bundle and social theories of persons are concerned.[1] So, what exactly is a person – whether or not it's at home – and are we all one of these?

In ego theories, we are mostly concerned with what unifies someone's experience, what gives it its continuous feel, what makes it someone's singular experience. Ego theories often present the traditional view of the person as an individual sense of self that is a persistent continuous mental thing that is consistent throughout life, the subject of our experiences, our very subjectivity or sense of the personal, our thoughts and feelings as had by one person as the experiencer. The quintessential ego theory is the idea of a soul. It is the soul that orchestrates us, conducts our lives and, according to some versions, is like our bodily form but non-physical. It is sometimes called a 'vital spirit'. As it is a non-physical body, it can travel the universe. It may enter a human body and animate it at some point of time during pregnancy. The soul leaves the physical body at the point of death. Scientists have tried to weigh the soul by measuring the change in weight after the soul's departure; at one time it was thought to weigh 21 grams.[2] So the person is the single continuous, unified form taken by the soul throughout life. The soul is likened to a charioteer holding the reins of life and steering our life course. It is unclear how a non-physical form acts on the physical. Where ego theory is concerned, *the number of persons is one.*

In bundle-type theories, we think about persons as collections: what is unified is in reality a series of experiences as, for example, in someone's memories. From this standpoint, we are a collection of experiences that make up our lifetime. We can ask, 'What bundles or collects them up?' The collection of elements may have been causally related in memory as the collection of experiences that make up someone's life at any given time. The quintessential bundle theory is the idea that the concept of person rests on a misconception. We think that there is both a person and all the characteristics a person has such that the word 'person' refers to something unified and unifying: the person is something that *has* these characteristics. From the bundle standpoint, thoughts and feelings exist as a series that we may call a person's life. These thoughts and feelings may be collected up, as, for example, in memories that we may call that person's life experiences. We may call the bundle, *person*; but no such *thing* as person exists over and above the bundle of thoughts and feelings. Just as a car is a collection of car parts this doesn't mean that the word 'car' refers to some essential and separate entity. 'Car' is the name we give to the collection of car parts, just as 'person' is the name we give to the collection of life experiences. Where bundle theory is concerned, *the number of persons is none.*

In the alternative social theory of persons, I am proposing that persons are both bundles and egos. The social view takes it that who and what we are is related to other people and the way they treat us: those that know us; those we are dealing with; those that we are remembering – including ourselves in younger form; those

Social Theory : ego + bundle - who and what we are is related to other people and the way they treat us.

[Handwritten annotations at top: "Bundled by others → person formed → established — To be conscious ⟹ ego/person in own right."]

[Handwritten left margin: "O persons / brought about socially / ↓ / I persons"]

that we think about; those that we have relationships with; that
what we are is the sum of those relations, ties and networks. This
standpoint makes the person extended across all that social activity
like an internet and an individual cannot therefore be bound by the
skin; rather, a person *is* a dynamic network of relationships.
A person is formed from a collection of persons that engage with
a child in early life. The person is made from other people before
a person acts in their own right. A person is given or 'gifted' person-
status, so that, over time, they can take responsibility and be
that person.[3] So we are bundled by others who bundle us according
to their ways. We become a person like them and of their kind.
We are thus made from persons who do this for us. *Thank you.* Once
established we can be said to be egos or persons in our own right. In
captivity, the person is all there is. Solitary confinement can be
personally devastating. Solitary confinement over an extended
period may cause the person to lose psychological integrity: in the
absence of what collects us together, we may disintegrate. From
a social theory standpoint such as mine, *the number of persons is none
at first and then one that may be brought about socially.*

Also, at the end of Chapter 1, we concluded that it is what
collects us together that makes us persons. Two ways this can be
done were introduced briefly: first, the way in which we are collected up by remembering or 'recollecting'; and second, other
people collect us together. This chapter will say more about this
through a wide-ranging discussion of how persons are made.

The idea of *positive and negative space* was introduced in
Chapter 1 and what follows develops this idea as part of the framework of ideas that form this book. We can hang various discussions
from this framework as we go along.

Negative spaces, shapes and contours

Much of what we have learned about our world has shown
us that we cannot simply trust that the way things ordinarily

44

seem to us is always reliable. It may seem as if the person that we are is enclosed by our skin or exists inside the frame of our head and body, such that a line can be drawn around the form of the body – as introduced in Chapter 1. In the arts, this is known as a 'positive space, shape or contour'. It is conventional to draw an outline around an object and to imagine the object contained completely within the outline. The positive contour highlights a belief about the world and about persons that makes it seem obvious that the rest of the scene is just background, backdrop, unimportant. This is the conventional assumption we need to unravel. As mentioned earlier, all experiences have shared contours; this is particularly obvious in the shared world of infant and caregiver.[4]

In this section I want to turn around our familiar world and engage with a different standpoint. Doing this will in turn make the familiar seem strange and thus stand out more, much as living in another country makes our original home country seem alien to us on our return. We are positive and negative spaces, shapes and contours. And we need to take both standpoints seriously.

In the classic Rubin's vase illusion we are faced with two alternatives for positive and negative shape.[5] If you were to draw an outline of talking heads such that all you could see were the two black profiles and a white shape between, you would be imagining Rubin's vase. If you looked at the white space, you could see this *as* a vase; this would in turn mean that the black profile shapes would flip and become background to what was now the central figure, viz. the vase. I would liken the social view to negative shapes in drawing. The negative shapes are those parts of the image that the positive shape makes that we would normally call background. They are all the bits between figures or between figures and objects or between objects and other objects. The great thing about the Rubin vase illusion is that we're not sure which is which. Positive and negative shapes are alternative, complementary ways of seeing; it's not a matter of deciding which is best. We need all the genuine alternative standpoints if we are to understand life and living.

How artists use negative and positive spaces, shapes and contours

In his later life, the painter Henri Matisse made collages from paper cut-outs; these were forms derived from both the positive shape cut-out and the saved negative shape sheet.[6] What follows involves two exercises that you can try and a commentary on what these exercises are about.

Exercise 1: Cutting out shapes

Find a picture of an object such as an apple and then cut out around the outline of the image. The cut-out apple is the positive shape and the cut-out shape left in the paper is the negative shape. The cut-out shape and the shape left where the cut-out had been are both perfect descriptions of the apple.

An artist will often draw the negative shapes in order to achieve the same outline view. They might use this as a technique for drawing a person in a life class. Importantly it will be an outline made from everything but the person; it will be made from the impact the person has on our view of the room in which they sit. The negative shapes are all the new shapes made by the presence of the person in the room, the way that they hide parts of objects and make new shapes of these.

It is very difficult to draw the body as an outline by itself, but it may seem obvious to do this. If asked to draw the human figure, many would try to draw it as the outline of an object that the line encloses. In drawing classes it has been shown that if a good likeness with the figure is wanted, it is much better to draw the negative shapes. It is important to look at things differently if we are not to try to draw what we think a person should look like rather than how the body appears, which may have distortions such as foreshortening. Of course, it is also true that features of the body, such as the face, can also be drawn as negative shapes.

If I turn outwards, I am shaped by all and everything around and about me. If I turn inwards, I am shaped by the enclosure of my skin and all that it contains. Clearly, we are both. But I think we have over-determined the inwardly directed and under-imagined the outwardly directed.

Rachel Whiteread's work gives many good examples because she is the artist probably best known for working with negative shapes. In sculpture, the negative spaces and contours make the point very eloquently by making what is normally invisible visible; by making it stand out. Have a look at her work *House* for example.[7] In this work, she casts the inside of a Victorian house so that, for example, a fireplace seems to project out at us.

How different our standpoint is if we view the human figure entirely as a product of its setting. Draw the setting and the human figure appears from it. We have another way of approaching what it is to be a person.

I believe that I am the impact I have on the lives of others. I am part of their negative shape. I am part of yours right now.

I believe that most of what makes me has come about through the impact of the lives of others on my basic early life. We are constituted by the active engagement that takes place between people.[8] I am made from the lives of others. I share more than I own. I am unique, but I am unique as this particular collection of experiences while knowing that even my experiences are mostly shared experiences and as much other people's as my own. I think consciousness is also like this.

How can you get to see your negative shapes? Be someone else for a while. Alter your stride and meet a stranger.[9] Test the familiar. Suspend belief.

Exercise 2: Drawing positive and negative shapes

Find a plant. Sit in front of it so that you are able to look through the leaves and stalks, stems and other parts of the plant. Place it in front of a plain, preferably white wall.

Draw the positive shapes of the plant. Draw an outline of the stems, branches, stalks, leaves and flowers.

Now take another sheet and draw the spaces between the leaves, between the stems and other stems, between the branches and leaves, between the flowers and other flowers, or between the flowers and other parts of the plant.

I hope the exercises, together with the ideas that go with them, will help you get the idea of differences between standpoints, such as those between ego, bundle and social theories of persons.

The making of persons

In Chapter 1, there was a short introduction to this topic and the following section goes into details. The idea that we go through changes as we develop is not new and many in developmental psychology have argued for seeing ourselves transformed through the various developmental changes.[10] Some developmental features are uncontested; others are still disputed. Some would argue for development as a natural achievement, that our human potential is naturally realised in developmental processes. Alternatively what we think of as normal development may say as much about our ideas of, for example, childhood as any natural development. If this has truth in it, we would expect to see historical changes in our ideas about childhood and that childhood today would reflect our modern world. There are historical influences evident in the differences between people born in the 1930s and those born in, say, the 1980s.[11] Becoming an adult is as much about becoming part of the modern world in which we live as it is about developing our bodies and our brains. Growing up is as much about our upbringing as it is about our physically maturing. Moreover, our bodies and brains show the signs of modern life and living in their development or the lack of it through mistreatment such as neglect.[12]

It could be said that as our bodies change, so do we. If development is not a series of stages, how does it work? It could be brought about by a continuous process, which, as it acquires a certain complexity or intensity, becomes something else, just as a chain reaction goes critical. It could be discontinuous in that social life intervenes in ways that transform the child once and for all. It could be a bit of both as well as other factors.[13] We need to know more about how we become part of our world. Experience might mean that a major change is the result of incremental changes, but it is not entirely clear when it is a change that is conceptual. If we go from having no standpoint to having one, it makes sense to say that our life has a discontinuity in this limited sense. We are simply incapable of conceptualising early life; it's like being conceptually closed.[14] We went from a dog that fetched the newspaper to a dog that reads the newspaper. And we do not know how this trick was done.

There are developmental changes that suggest as we grow we become 'blinded' to our early life – unable to see it at all; this has recently been evidenced in adolescence, but it is likely that similar 'blinding' occurs as a consequence of other developmental changes.[15] It may be that we simply do not remember what it is like to be an infant because we carry none of the stigmata through our bodies' development. Only highly stressful and traumatic experiences are etched deeply enough to show through.

It is uncontested that major developmental changes take place during the period between birth and five years old. What is disputed is the kind of impact these changes have on us, particularly where sense of self and mind is concerned.[16] That we can know something with such familiarity seems to be the very source of our uncertainty. How can we not know our own developmental history? How can it be that we could be wrong about what we are: surely we are what we are, and we went through our early life, and therefore we must know it? Surely the way things seem to us to be must also be true for us?

This is a particular kind of problem: that we are the object that we seek to have unravelled, the subject who unravels the object, and the very means of unravelling. This is a problem for anything in the field of psychology. The object of enquiry – what we want to know *about* – is also the *means* by which we carry out the enquiry as well as the enquiring *agent* or *subject*. This is usually known as the *problem* of reflexivity, although I think this is only part of what it means for us to be reflexive. I think reflexivity goes to the heart of the matter where questions about the nature of persons are concerned. The term 'reflexivity' is also used to categorise this problem. I will increasingly through this book use the word 'minded' to refer to a reflexive act of turning this way or that – turning towards, away, inwards, or outwards – because I suggest that it is the development of mind that characterises early development and it is being minded that characterises everything that a consciously knowing person does subsequently. But I need to go slowly through this.

I will try an example. When I talk to you, it could be said that my speech is directed towards you (although I may listen in to hear what I say). Talking to myself is a reflexive act that turns talking back upon itself. Where talking is normally received by someone else, I become 'the someone else'. I treat myself as the listener. I know how to do this because of the years of practice I have had in being on the receiving end of other people's talk. In terms of human history, the minded reflexive act may have been practised for no reason other than a human becoming isolated from the group. We will never know for sure. It might have been the case that an early human spoke aloud a question without another human present and chose to answer it for themselves.

In just such a way the advantages of treating oneself as a resource could have been fashioned; but I am not saying this is how it got started. I don't know. I don't know whether anyone knows how what I am calling being minded gets started. The simplest would most likely be that others make us in their image; that persons are built from the outside in a social process of interaction, exchange and engagement. But it is likely to be a two-way social deal. We, as infants, reach towards caregivers as they reach out towards us.[17]

In our early infant life, we use and exchange gestures and these come to mean things for us and for our carers, but our initial use of gestures is not reflexively minded. We do not know what we do: we simply respond with what we have built in. We go from reflex activity to reflexivity in about five years. As we become minded we develop the skill to withhold what we are doing, to do it privately. We become able to keep secrets.

We come to be able to treat ourselves as an object through a process of learning how others are independent from us and have an independent point of view of their own. Others have minds independent of ours that we do not know directly, but then other minds cannot know our mind directly either. Because a person can only see the world from their point of view, someone else can deceive them, lie to them and know that the other cannot know that it is a lie or that something is withheld.

George Herbert Mead was working on the social psychology of development in the 1930s; there has recently been a reawakening of interest in his ideas. From Mead I take the importance of the symbolic in all the forms of human interaction. Symbols have meaning for us according to how they are used and this can be different in different places in different periods and for different people. Symbolic meanings form the cultural code in which we feel most at home.[18] He suggested that not only do we work against one another in acts of deception, but we also take part in acts of co-operation (such as through the social practice of child rearing). We work with others co-operatively as well as against others competitively. Mead suggested that it was through co-operative and competitive acts that minds are made. Such co-operative and competitive acts as found, for example, 'in the care of the young ... or even in fighting' and 'what we term "minds" arise out of them'.[19] When I engage in symbolic interaction with a person, such as when I get a response from others, I also get a response in me causing me to become an object for myself. For Mead this was consciousness because 'the individual can then indicate to others what he is at the same time indicating to himself'.[20]

> Reflection, then, is a type of action in which the individual in conversing with others is conversing also with himself and is able to call out in himself the same sort of response which he calls out in another.[21]

And this is exactly the reflexive sense that I want to further examine. For example, if I play a musical instrument, I can play it *for* you. But I can also play it and listen to what I am playing. I may wish to do this to help me tune the instrument. So I both produce the sound and reflexively listen to the sound produced and use this to decide whether to change the tuning and which way. When playing an improvised piece as part of a group I can both produce my own contribution to the sound and listen to whether the contribution works. I can listen to the sound I produce together with all the other sounds. Or I might listen to just one other instrument in the group. And I can change what I produce in response to this in an ongoing musical piece. I can use your contribution as a counterpoint to mine. This is what is meant by reflexive.

Whatever it means to have this reflexive activity, my consciousness following development rests on it. Minded consciousness is a reflexive turning back upon itself much as the voices we hear in our heads privately seem to be based on the necessary practised acts of conversation carried out publicly. Imagination and thinking 'are an inner conversation that goes on in terms of the outer conversation with the groups of which [we are] part'.[22]

52

With the help of speech children, unlike apes, acquire the capacity to be both the subjects and objects of their own behaviour.[23]

Lev Semyonovich Vygotsky was another to highlight the importance of social action in the making of minds. We learn how to do privately what we once learned how to do as a public social action.[24] For example, Vygotsky stated that imagination is private play. We learned to play with others and through this developed the skill of private play that we usually call imagination.[25] Vygotsky works through the example of a child playing with a stick that they treat *as if* it were a horse that they were riding; this is a vital transitional stage.

> A child first acts with meanings as with objects and later realizes them consciously . . . [He] knows how to do things but does not know that he knows, i.e., he does not realize or master them voluntarily. In play a child unconsciously and spontaneously makes use of the fact that he can separate meaning from an object without knowing he is doing it.[26]

Vygotsky commented that 'in play it is as though the child were trying to jump above the level of his normal behavior'.[27] He argued that 'Play is the source of development and creates the zone of proximal development.'[28] This 'zone of proximal development' is how Vygotsky described how a child can do more when with others who can also do more than them; that this 'zone' is how we develop many of our psychological skills. We develop them because others help us to be able to do so; they 'scaffold' us. Scaffolding was a term used by Bruner to describe a similar process to the 'zone'.[29] By scaffolding he borrowed the idea that, first, we help others put in a framework to support their developing abilities until, second, they can sustain them without the scaffold. Through the social action of play we develop the psychological skill of imagination. So imagination is not an innate ability that brings about the public performance. Rather, it is the other way around.

The old adage that children's play is imagination in action can be reversed: we can say that imagination in adolescents and schoolchildren is play without action.[30]

Imagination is a skill that once developed allows us to slip the bonds of place and time because we do not need the object of our imagining to be present. I can be here and imagine what it might be like to be somewhere else. I can think how things might be in the future or might have been in the past. I can turn a scenario over in my head. I can play out what will happen when I next talk to you. I can imagine what may happen when I move into a new place to live. I can imagine what you might make of any writing I do whilst in captivity. Consciousness and freely acting are as much about what I will not do as they are about any public action. As one reader said, when I 'bite my tongue' – that is, when I decide not to speak – you cannot know what I might have said.

All manner of things follow from this. I can write this sentence as a writer and then read it back as a reader. If I were to be without pen and paper, I might write a sentence in my head and later read it back to myself, and thus entertain myself with my own creation.[31]

Senses of self

There may still be a feeling that we are a single unified self and that even though there may not be an actual entity called 'self' living within our bodies, there still may be a *sense* of self, a feeling of continuity and unity, and this needs explaining.

Viv Burr put it very well:

But we still feel (at least some of the time) as though we are a single, unified self, and we need to be given some explanation of this feeling. One suggestion is that our feelings of consistency and continuity in time are provided by our memory. Memory allows us to look back on our behaviours and experiences, to select those that seem to 'hang together' in some narrative framework (literally the story of your life) and to look for patterns, repetitions and so on that provide us with the impression of continuity and coherence.[32]

A *sense of* self is usually characterised as the first-person perspective of being a person. So I am using it here to distinguish that sense of who we are as if from the inside. I know I have just argued against this, but I have reason to keep the term in the restricted sense given: as referring to the *sense* that most people seem to have of leading their life, of being responsible, of making the world about us navigable, and having personal individual experiences. But I am deliberately casting this as a *sense* or *senses of* self to distinguish from the view that there really is a being that inhabits our positive shaped body. I do not believe such an entity exists, but I do think most of us recognise that it *feels as if* there were an entity.

I do not believe that we are an essential, independent, transcendent entity that can produce grounds for its own justification and support for the conviction that we are who we say we are. We have other grounds: other people, institutions, artefacts that give us our sense of identity and help to support and sustain it. We take these and use them *as if from the inside* to sustain our own identity once founded. Nonetheless, this sensibility merits a name so that we can discuss it and help us figure out how the whole thing is put together and how we might use it. The crux of the argument here is in the respect, compassion or humanity by which we treat others of our kind because not only do we have a sense of self, but we assume others do too.

It seems to me that my sense of self came upon me; that I came to feel the world and sense of self as something distinct and real, but I have no reason to suppose it was always like that. That I cannot imagine not feeling this way – feeling this way is just what it is for me to say that I'm alive – does not mean that it was ever so. It seems likely to me that my early life would have had a universal experience about it and a basic embodied sense that defined me and not me as it does with other species. I could move my body as an infant and know 'I am this body.'[33]

Can an infant suffer? Yes it can, but so can a chimpanzee. Does an infant suffer as an adult person suffers? No, I don't think so. The kind of suffering a person has may have about it all kinds of things not incorporated in the infant, such as the way we can incorporate meaning into suffering. We might, as an example, think that we are suffering as a result of an injustice and seek to set the record straight. I cannot see how this can be an infant's experience, but I can see a burgeoning sense of injustice growing in the child if it is badly treated; at least, once the child witnesses or has some experience of being well treated.[34] Some of this difference could be accounted for in the difference between being natural and being educated; this is an age-old argument to do with innocence and experience. One problem with this argument is the assumption that being natural would somehow be idyllic in some romanticised notion of what it might mean to be closer to the natural world. Feral children afford us a glimpse into what an uneducated wild child would be like. Although other factors may have a bearing, such as issues in mental health and well-being, the natural human appears to be simply like other social animals such as dogs and wolves. The wild child is simply wild. They are not wild in a civilised romantic fashion like some innocent child of nature.[35] Wild things change with experience too: there are consequences for the wild child from living a wild child's life. Some have taken experience as the corruption of innocence such as, say, with sexual experience. But this raises questions: why is experience necessarily corrupting? Why is innocence more virtuous than experience? Is it better to be ignorant or educated?

We might want to extend this treatment to other species that seem also to have at least the raw materials of a sense of self and have this help us treat those species better too. Other species as well as ours distinguish 'me' and 'not me' particularly in relation to the sense of 'my' body. Other species may have a sense of self; they might even be minded in the sense of having a Theory of Mind, that is, they have some ability to know what another can see from their position.[36] When a chimpanzee looks in the mirror and recognises its own reflection as itself, we can say that it has a self-concept; that it knows that the chimpanzee in the reflection is them.[37] But as we shall see when we come to Part III, this intuition is never fully developed into the reflexivity that humans usually develop.

To be reflexive is not just to recognise one's own reflection, but to turn this intuition to one's own advantage. Chimpanzees learn, as an example, to look inside their own mouths, to examine their teeth and gums; this is a first reflexive step because it turns a simple recognition into consciously knowing how to use the mirror as a tool to do something it cannot normally do: look inside its own mouth. Researchers have interpreted responses to others by orang-utans as mimes to prompt a particular action such as opening up a coconut.[38] But humans continue to develop. From recognising the intuition that 'I am this', we develop this intuition into a Theory of Mind. We have a sense of ourselves as 'being here' and of 'sticking out' into the field of experience as well as being the subject of that field. The complex intuition, for Tallis, opens us to the idea that another individual, embodied as we are, also has a viewpoint and it is a different viewpoint from our own.[39] We will discuss all this further in Part III.

One reader wanted to understand how the social theory of persons differs from the bundle view. Surely the social theory is a kind of bundle theory? It is true that the social theory incorporates the bundle view – we are collections of various kinds collected together by various means; these include collection by personal memory and collection by the part a person plays in social action. Nevertheless, the social theory also incorporates ego theory – a person may be produced by social action, but the product acts in its own right. The difference is this: a person once established is active in leading their life and is responsible as a person in the social world in which people live. By close analogy: a child is the offspring of an egg and sperm, which are organic elements and parts of other people; however, even though always organically based on their parent, there comes a point where we take it that the child is responsible for their own actions. They cannot claim that their parents remain responsible as it was their cells that started the process off. The product of a social process can be a social entity in its own right, recognised as such by their parents and by the law.

The same reader also asked about the case of an Indian sage who spent more than twenty years meditating in a cave in South India.[40] The sage's approach to meditation was simply to ask himself the question 'who am I?' When a thought came to him, he would mentally repeat to himself 'not this, who am I?' and be back to where he had started. Arguably, his was an entirely non-social life for many years but his reports, during the latter part of his life, documented how rich an existence his life of solitude was. I do not think that the sage's life was a non-social life because I think this muddles up what a person does as an adult with what happens to the child that brings the adult person about. You cannot go off to be alone because you take other people with you into isolation. You are the virtual society of mind that makes you up. So someone spending time in isolation may be cut off from society but still have taken the social experience that made them persons in the first place into isolation with them.

The reflexive process is itself a social act made from our exchanges with other people. We confuse our individual ability to act with the idea of being ourselves independent of others. An individual ability to act stems from our encounters with others, exchanges we make and how this makes us persons both in our own right and entirely existent because of others. As Cooley stated, individual and social are two aspects of the same subject: human life.[41]

As I have argued earlier, it is the social engagement of others already persons that gets a person started. From this

I suggested that we are, at the outset, made of people. Social life is part and parcel of our ongoing psychological life. We are already social. We are not alone and nor could we ever be so because we are already populated. Solitude is a rich experience but not because there is an absence of people as such, but rather because of an absence of distractions.[42] Solitude allows a quietening of the busy world and thus a burgeoning of what we usually call our inner world. But I believe this is the social world that made us making its appearance as if it had always been on the inside.

A social view is always about groups or groupings and therefore incorporates both positive and negative spaces, shapes and contours, giving each equal importance. If you ask me how it feels to be me from this standpoint, I would say that who, what, which, where and when also extends out from my skin in all directions enveloping other positive shapes. I feel I am neither solely inside a positive shape, nor solely outside in a set of negative shapes; rather, it feels that I am sustained, that I am spread out across place-time.[43] I do not feel the skin as a boundary, but as a permeable membrane.[44] Borders are places where exchanges are made as well as being enclosures to some extent.

The reason we have to come to know ourselves is because we have to come to know other people; the mistake is to view this act as an interior journey when 'finding one's self' may be accomplished by facing outwards, meeting others and coming to see oneself as they see us. As Robert Burns said:

> O would some power the gift to give us
> To see ourselves as others see us.[45]

Cooley's idea of the 'looking-glass self' is helpful here.[46] A 'looking-glass' is an old term for a mirror. As discussed earlier, we have the idea of an actual mirror to test whether an infant can recognise itself in its reflection, so here we take this further and imagine other people as virtual mirrors. Cooley suggests that we come to imagine how we appear to others, how we are judged by others and how we act with others in mind. If we become minded this way, we can act reflexively entirely as an act of imagining. We would hope that at least some of those who see us recognise our actions as in keeping with what they know of our character. When someone challenges authority, we may judge it as an act of consciousness for a person who freely acts knowing how their acts may be viewed. What Rosa Parks did was a free act of conscience that others knew was such.[47] She knew the consequences of her actions even though they were unplanned. She knew how others on the bus would see them even as she remained in her seat. She knew that other black passengers moved to the back of the bus and that she could have done likewise as she would usually have done. We'll discuss this further in Part III.

Our negative shapes, spaces and contours are formed from social situations in which our skills are expressed, have meaning and have an impact. We are symbol users and it is the social world about us that provides the symbols. We become minded through our development. Minding is not something an infant can do. It may be more useful to do as George Herbert Mead and others did and think of mind as *activity*, as something we do.[48] Mind in this sense is brought about by our becoming a member of the world about us. The world about us comes first and is prior to us in every sense: we become members of a pre-existing set of social relationships such as families, local communities, schools, work-places, etc. through the most basic fact of human life: the social practice of interaction with others.

We arrive at a point where we have a sense of self, but we do not know whether or not it's been there all the time; it may seem as if it has, but this could be an illusion. We assume it's been there in the background – building and changing all along – but from when? The sense of it having been there all along may itself have just arisen. How would we know that we'd just had our first conscious thought? The changes happening in the early years are turning us into a particular kind of contemporary modern human.[49] It may be that upbringing, schooling and other kinds of socialisation are responsible, but these are complex institutional factors not easily set up as testable variables.

Analogy. We need to be wary of an easy tale of cause and effect that suggests the brain unfolds like a tulip bulb. We used to think that all that was the tulip was inside the bulb as if some kind of essential tulip was simply coiled up inside the bulb awaiting the opportunity to unfurl itself. But we now know the importance of sunlight. Without sunlight reaching the bulb no growth starts. Unless the bulb continues to have further sunlight, it will not continue to grow. The brain does not develop on its own. Society is the sunlight acting upon the brain and making it develop in what we think of as its characteristic form; this form is as characteristic of our people, period and place as it is of our biology.

Social identities

A person's social identity is composed of their place in society and what defines it. We define ourselves as members of various social groups to which we have a sense of psychological belonging: we are members of families, friendship groups, partnerships in various relationships and staff in a workplace. In a sense we carry around with us the virtual presence of other people. We do not exist in isolation. We compare our situation with persons in other groups. We strive to stand out but also to fit in. We can see ourselves as the same as a group with whom we share characteristics or different from those groups with whom we seem to share none. We may seek to maximise our differences to make ourselves more distinct. We may struggle for power, status and reputation. We may challenge the superiority of some groups of people. We may challenge the status quo – the agreed-to and existing state of affairs that places groups into some kind of hierarchy or pecking order – and try to bring about social change if our group is not valued.[50] Our situation is not fixed and we need not think of it as set in stone: we create the situations in which we find ourselves.[51] Our social conditions are made even if we sometimes act towards them as if they were natural. The way things seem may be a matter of how we live today and the shared conventions and customs during this period of history. As Czesław Miłosz said:

> Man tends to regard the order he lives in as *natural*. The houses he passes on his way to work seem more like rocks rising out of the earth than like products of human hands.[52]

It is the status quo that needs challenging. Much of what we take for granted can be seen to have been brought about socially, culturally and politically. Consciousness is as much about what happens between people as it is about any particular person's life and living and, importantly, these can only be two standpoints on the *same* subject and not two different subjects. It is the familiar, the commonplace and the status quo we need to turn over. I believe accounts of what it is like to be held in captivity can help us do just that. Some of what we take for granted can be seen to have been brought about and we might wonder why it was that we have simply played along.

In apartheid-rule South Africa, Steve Biko challenged both blacks' identification as inferior and whites' assumed superiority. It is as important to understand domination as it is to understand resistance if we are to understand what happens when the status quo is challenged.[53] The Black Consciousness movement Biko helped to lead first challenged the identification as inferior that blacks took upon themselves. He encouraged black people to value themselves in their own right as persons and not in relation to anyone else. Biko himself was unbowed and did not show fear; however, this caused whites to become frightened. They could not understand why Biko was unafraid. Being unafraid, he would cause some whites to question their previously unquestioned superior position.[54] What Biko and others did is what I mean by acts of consciousness and conscience. This does not mean that all acts are political – although there are many political examples – but I believe they highlight the main features of consciousness for us. They make the collection that composes consciousness stand out. Conscience refers more directly perhaps to our reflexive nature. With conscience, we come to a position or standing, after having entertained alternative standpoints on matters of importance for us. We may *conscientise*, as Biko and others did, by making others aware of social conditions before challenging them.

Consciousness is about what is important to us as people; what we think about, talk about and do something about. Consciousness is about individual members of social groups acting with others in mind. It is the world about us, the psychological world we could call place-time. Place-time is a joint production: we put together our situation as much as we put together what happens in it. We bring things to a situation that make the situation what it is.[55] We are composed of other people and it makes sense to try to unravel our composition.

I believe that we are composed of patterns. It makes sense to talk about how we are made rather than any idea of a simple copying process. We may be able to copy information, send and receive information with certain kinds of equipment; but we would still need to remake the person at the end of their teleport. I am reminded of Ernst Gombrich's line of thinking in his book *The Story of Art*, which I would recommend. Gombrich is reflecting on Picasso's work and comes up with a question that he supposes Picasso might have asked:

> Why not be consistent and accept the fact that our real aim is rather to construct something than to copy something?[56]

The deliberate removal of point of view from Picasso's Cubist canvases draws attention to how the painting is constructed instead of creating the illusion of a painting as capturing a scene as if viewing through a window onto the world.[57] We should not be concerned by the use of the word construction. We have always thought of composition in painting and the arts generally. We may think that a construction or composition is not real. The car made of its car parts is a construction, but we really can drive it up the road, which was also constructed.

The idea of composition is helpful because it is the arrangement of cells and chemicals that is us, not any single organ. Prediction: if we were to build a conscious machine, we would most likely succeed if we built the equivalent of a child in machine form and set it free to learn from its environment as we do. The answer to the who and what we are is the composition of our living, imagining, knowing and acting. Others recognise us by the arrangement of how we look, the things we say, how we say them, the things we do and how we do them; these constitute the orchestration of our lives. These patterns are also networked such that recognition of us as persons takes place in the context of conversation or other ritualised practices. We are constituted by the patterns of characteristic exchanges. It is then down to our common human dealings with each other to determine how successful we are in carrying off the presentation of ourselves in everyday life. We do not wish to lose face so we take steps to ensure we are not disrespected or discredited. Our validity stems from the integrity of our exchanges. I am the pattern of performance and presentation you witness me to be.[58] And these are the negative shapes, spaces and contours of my life. It would take something out of character to make you examine me more closely; otherwise you would take me as who I said I was, just as most of the community do in the case of Martin Guerre.

What collects us together?

Other people: the stories of feral children

The idea of feral children was introduced earlier when we discussed the sense of self. Feral, or wild, children may have grown up with little or no interaction from fellow humans. If you were to have been born and grown up away from a human social community, you would not have become a person. If you were to have been kept in isolation, or severely neglected, or to have grown up with animals you would not independently have developed minded consciousness. Even if you were to have successfully grown up on some magical desert island, you would not develop into a person. You would have grown up more alike in kind to the local fauna with which you shared the island. Feral children growing up with pack animals such as dogs and wolves exemplify what happens. There has been much written about children growing up in isolation or with animals, much of which may be myth. This is a highly contentious area.

Some of the feral children may show signs of autism and make it difficult to distinguish whether we can learn anything else from them. Others clearly show signs of neglect and this in itself may be sufficient to adversely affect their development. Nonetheless, a child deprived of human contact does not become a person in their own right. And I think that it is this that is the most significant aspect of the stories about them. Where there are substantive details, the information is telling. We seem endlessly fascinated by the wild child of nature, the seemingly innocent child free from corruption, the so-called *Noble Savage*.[59] Books, documentaries and films have been made.

There are numerous examples, some better documented than others, of which some may have been made up. Nevertheless, they are all still interesting cases for what they say about even a supposed solitary upbringing. There was Victor, known as the Wild Boy of Aveyron (from eighteenth-century France). Victor was documented by Jean-Marc-Gaspard Itard.[60] François Truffaut also made an extraordinary film loosely based on this account, which I would recommend watching.[61] Kaspar Hauser is another (from nineteenth-century Germany), for whom the film *The Enigma of Kaspar Hauser* directed by Werner Herzog is well worth watching.[62] There is the true story of Genie[63] – not her real name (from twentieth-century Los Angeles, USA). I would urge you to read Michael Newton's book *Savage Girls and Wild Boys* as this is by far the best source I know of for its analysis and evaluation of feral children.[64]

I don't think feral children are persons. Nevertheless, I believe there are good ethical grounds for treating these children as proto-persons because they could have become persons. We do not know how they might have developed were they to have had the opportunities we take for granted. Being loved and cared for may be sufficient to bring about some development not thought possible in other ways. It is interesting how feral and isolated and neglected children respond to being loved and cared for. For example, Itard's documented account of Victor, the Wild Boy of Aveyron, reveals the love he had *from* and showed *for* Itard's housekeeper, Mme Guérin, with whom Victor lived for the remainder of his life.[65] There seems to be something about consciousness that is universal and fundamental; this is shared across humanity and possibly beyond and likely to be continuous throughout life as part of our composition.

We cannot become persons on our own nor does becoming a person develop of itself from within an individual body. Brains do not develop in a vacuum; they are not developing in isolation even though they develop inside a cranium. All kinds of interactions influence and help bring about brain function, organisation and activity. Once again, a brain in extreme isolation – as evidenced in severe neglect or incarceration – tends to show signs of poor development or disintegration.[66] This is all evidence for the co-operative basis of conscious life. Other persons are necessary so that we can become like them. Once we take seriously the idea of how others are implicated in our development, we can see how others constitute us; how we are made from other people.

As with mind, sense of self is also brought about in the process of social experience and action.[67] Mead thought that 'self' is what happens when reflection is focused on one's own actions. We acquire a sense of self through becoming reflexive. If we are acknowledged by those around us, we gain the status of person. Feral children would still be persons in this regard. On ethical grounds, we may treat feral children as persons because they *could* have become a person. Were we to have had their experience of growing up, we would not have become a person either.

So if we are drawing from the same features of consciousness, why aren't we all alike? I think we are very alike. If you look at persons and the community in which they grew up you can see how they are very alike. Differences are made much of but these can be few and quite minor, although we may attend to these more than the likenesses. What collects us together as persons is other people.

Other people: the story of Martin Guerre

I want to return to the discussion of the film *The Return of Martin Guerre* as a way of discussing all the matters above. Warning reminder: if you want to see and enjoy the film independently of this discussion, I suggest that you do that. What follows gives away a great deal of the plot.

As mentioned earlier, the film is supposed to be based on a true story from sixteenth-century France. A man returns from war. In the story, many years had passed since Martin Guerre left his village, perhaps as many as ten years. The story of his arrival is told by stages as the village becomes aware of his return. He tells those that he meets that he is Martin Guerre. He seems to recognise some of the people he meets and they seem to recognise him. Over so many years we would expect some established patterns to change both in Martin Guerre but also in those who remained in the village; thus we have two ways we might fail to recognise someone. We fail to recognise because we have changed and view the world differently. The world and my place in it may appear differently to me. But also Martin Guerre has been away from the village and to war and we know war changes people and simply going to other places may also change a person. He is changed as many were by the ravages of war. He fails to recognise some former friends, but then they have changed too. He is welcomed as the returning member of the community he purports to be. Such an incident is thought to have happened and the returning man did bear a resemblance to the villager who left about ten years before. He looks sufficiently like the original Martin Guerre to be mistaken for him by those that knew him. He makes mistakes. He mis-remembers events. He fails to recognise some people and places, but he is also spot on most of the time such that he convincingly carries off being Martin Guerre. He is even taken back into the family home by his wife (although it is likely his wife always knows he is not her returning husband; she may have accepted him because he was much kinder than her husband). The returnee fits back into life in the village, but he is different from the one who went away. But then those returning from war were different. The villagers see what they expect to see, so they may endow the impostor with the original's identity.

Families have often had to adjust to the returnees who are of course many years older, have perhaps witnessed many terrible events and those that remained are also changed over time. Sometimes changes are too great either way: the returnee cannot settle back, but also because the ones at home may have changed in ways that have remade them almost to the point of being different people. Meeting up after long periods has been described as like meeting a stranger. Each person has carried their sense of the other unchanged from their last meeting. The shock of the changes amplifies the trauma of the encounter. You might think it would be impossible for an impostor to return home and take up another person's life, but given the above and what we understand a person to be on the accounts given so far, it is not implausible in such a world as that of the sixteenth century. We might rely

on other forms of identification: the kinds that are official, author-
ised, institutional; such as birth certificates, passports, driving
licences, etc. But much of what constitutes identity is formed from
our relationships with other people. It is other people's reactions
to us, their treatment of us and the way they accept or reject us
that makes us who we are.

Even if other people recognise me as Martin Guerre and
I know that I am an impostor, still I may turn slowly into Martin
Guerre. When does occupying a role become simply how I act and
who I am? I become the collection of actions that I act out. What
happens the other way around? What if I am a faithful copy
of Guy such that from my subjective point of view I really am
Guy, but no one recognises me as such because I have teleported
to another planet where no one knows me? I will change and
become the person that the exchanges I make now fashion me to
be. And this may be quite different from how I was in the original
version. In part I become the collection of interactions I have with
others. If I were then to return, would I be thought an impostor?[68]

Remembering and recollecting

As introduced earlier, one of the key ways in which we
are collected together is through acts of remembrance: through
remembering or recollecting.

The kind of remembering skill we have makes it seem as if
there really is a continuity of experience. In Chapter 1 we discussed
John Dean's testimony and how this revealed various features
of the unreliability of recollection. From this and other research,
we know that memories are unreliable; part of the problem is
that memories are invariably selective and partial. Even if it is
our memory of an event that happened to us, it will be partial
because it is only from our point of view and selective often because
it puts us at the centre of things and often gives less importance
to other contributions. We need always to ask, whose recollection

To be conscious

is it? Events really happen but our memories of them are more like 'negative shapes' because the shape is our configuration, it is our relationship to an event. Others will hold different recollections, a different set of negative shapes that pick out an event.

Sometimes films use elision to keep the film to a reasonable length. Elision means leaving bits out. We see a plane take off in a film and then the film cuts to the plane landing, but we don't see the flight. We accept that the take-off and landing are a short cut to convey the idea of a flight. We get used to a film's language such that time passing can be conveyed by a very short set of images showing, for example, changing seasons over a year. We get the idea that a year or more has passed. We bring to the film the wherewithal, gained from watching other films, to understand the use of such devices.

Sometimes, as mentioned earlier, films fictionalise actual events by putting more than one character into a single role in order to simplify the plot or make it fit into two hours' screen time. We do this too. In the filmic autobiography of our own life, other contributions can easily be ascribed to our own or to just one other person as we simplify our memory of any given experience in the telling and retelling to ourselves and to others. There are elisions in our own life stories; periods when nothing much happens, but we do not necessarily feel this as a gap. There isn't a gap for us unless another draws our attention to it by virtue of the fact that they recollect what we do not. We live in both a physical and a social world. We can live with both of these even when sometimes this produces contradictions. I would advocate that it is necessary for us to be contrary because we are different kinds of collections of elements without the need for each to correspond with each other.[69]

Remembering is a social activity and is one of the ways in which we are collected together as persons.[70] Recollecting might be a better word to use. Memory does not copy or record what happened to us. We framed what we took to be the event in the

70

first place. Memory actively constructs what happened and our place in it, and continues to do so each time we recollect. Some of what we recollect was present at the time, some was added or elaborated, and some of what was present is absent.

Do we reconstruct our early life's events in keeping with our current experience of how things are? We know that we have a tendency to update recollections every time we remember so that there is no longer a memory of the way it really was forged at the time of an event. There is but the last recollection. We elaborate on our last recollection. We use recollection to try to collect our life's experiences back together again. As we change in our development, it seems likely that we would gradually come to remember that development in terms of what is now possible for us to remember and therefore we are likely to fabricate and elaborate in ways that would at least overwrite previous stages.

I can look at photographs of me as an infant, but I have to say that I recall nothing of that time. I have one in mind as I write this. It is of me aged about eighteen months on a beach somewhere. There is virtually no background to make out where this photograph was taken and with both of my parents dead I do not have anyone to ask for details. But the point is that I have no idea how I felt at that time. I have no recollection of it at all. It could be a photograph of someone else for all the good it is in my recollecting. Whereas when I look at a more recent photograph – from about twenty years ago – also taken on a beach, also with no real background, I can fill in all sorts of details about the time, the place, what I was doing, where I was. It does seem important and strange that I can look back over my life and go so far back and then nothing. I know some claim to have early childhood memories that are not simply of the intense flashbulb kind, but I do not.[71] Ask the five-year-old about their early childhood. They are closer to it and their memories of, for example, the day before may be far more detailed than ours. They are closer to their early childhood, so they should remember those early years, but do they? How much of the personal is present to colour their recollection and how much is the matter-of-fact colourless telling of events? How much do we scaffold a child's memory and then assume that the supporting work we did was all there in the child's own storytelling?

I do have recollections of childhood, but I'm caused to wonder about these and by how much these too might have been elaborated in ways that mean no vestige of any original memory is held. And there's a further problem. Memory is not a digital video copy like a digital camera's recording of an event. The camera's record can be replayed and someone who was there could confirm that that was exactly what happened (albeit only what was captured in the camera's viewing angle). But our memory is not like a recording.[72] Memories are compositions and partial in the same sense that all supposedly factual events are interpretations simply because they are not somehow events speaking for themselves. The word 'partial' is useful here because it is ambiguous. Partial means both not the whole thing, so only a part of it, *and* inclined to favour one point of view, so a preference for a particular standpoint. We'll discuss further the various meanings of 'partial' in Chapter 4. Interpretations only ever offer limited appreciations of what is going on; limited because an interpretation necessarily takes a particular standpoint *and* limited because only part of the picture is included in any interpretation.

Interpretations are worked up with what the interpreter is familiar with. World is that with which *we* can register and explore and interpretations are necessarily bound by our capacities and current technology that extends them.[73] Writers often talk of narrative simply because this interpretation is most familiar to them. It does not mean that life *is* a narrative, but life and living can be brought about and interpreted in that way. There is a difference that makes a difference and I think it lies in the distinction between interpreting consciousness as social and showing how the social makes consciousness as it does.

When we remember we put elements back together again, but this does not mean that those elements were bundled for others similarly. In any event, we experienced the episode from our point of view so even the original perception is distorted, selective, poor, lacking in detail and biased.

It is not that the factual event did not happen, but that there are so many ways in which the event happened for any of us. Memory is more like a painting than a photograph or video: it is a composition. After all, even with photographs and videos you have to stand somewhere. You have to point the camera at something. We construct the scene selectively and partially, ignore those parts that do not interest us, enhance those that do, leave bits out. We exclude features others might include.

We always have a standpoint on events and this means there are alternative standpoints not shown or depicted. We focus in. Try an exercise the next time you are out and see a view that you would like to capture as a photograph. Take a photograph with a digital device such as a camera phone. Look at the photograph and ask, 'Does it capture what you thought you saw when you looked at whatever it was that you wanted to photograph?' If not, what's not there? What's there that you didn't really notice when you took the shot?

As mentioned earlier, one of the peculiarities of memory over recording is that our memories are selective: we tend, as an example, to remember those elements that were important to us or for which we were the centre of the action.

Exercise: Try this out if you dare: sit down with a partner, parent, relative or old friend and recall an incident from many years ago at which both of you were present. Start asking each other questions about what you can recall from your different points of view. Unlike a recording, we cannot scan the image to answer the question. If we haven't selectively remembered something, there is no record of it; it's as if that element of the event never happened. Will this mean that those with heavily recorded lives will have a very different view of their past? Yes, I think so but they will perhaps find it easier to understand how selective and constructive their memory is for unrecorded events. In any event, a recording does not record how someone felt or what they thought and these can be amended or elaborated later. A photo depicts and we confer meaning on it. We add this in or bring it *to* the photo; it's not *in* the image. I look at the adolescent me and I think, what was I thinking when this picture was taken. I recall that I was often angry. I look like the standard angry young man, but I don't know this. I have no way (back) to have the sense of self I had then. We need a different conception of personal time because it seems to me that I do not pass through time and nor does time pass through me. It may be more like a palimpsest.[74] A palimpsest is a manuscript in which what was written has been partially erased and new writing written over the part that has been rubbed out. The idea is that memory might be like this. Nothing is actually erased, but everything is partly rubbed out and written over such that it is only the latest writing that is easy to read. Each rewriting, each remembering partially overwrites our last recollection of the same event. Just because all of my memories endure in this analogy, doesn't mean that I can get at the original writing. There is no *way it really was*.[75] Parts of my life are so overwritten that none of the early writing (memory) is detectable. Some parts are so deeply etched as to be indelible; they always appear through any overwriting that takes place after the event.

I was amazed to learn that one of my childhood memories couldn't have happened as it did simply because I wasn't at the incident. I assume now that I could only have heard about it from other family members. I must then have fabricated the same thing from my own point of view. This doesn't mean I was making myself important to the scene in the way that we might do as we grow more self-conscious. It was a very standard case of how we turn some episodes in our life into an episode recollected from a first-person perspective, as if we were the central character in a film.

In our early life, it is likely that we are building a first-person perspective. We put ourselves in the central role and have the action go on around and about us, much as was shown in John Dean's testimony discussed earlier. During the actual event we may have been only a spectator, but in our retelling and in our remembering we may switch our perspective.[76] We may do this for some events at which we were not even present. We confabulate – invent stuff that helps to turn the event into a story – as we do often when remembering dreams. We make bits up that act as linking passages joining together what may be weirdly separate images. It is unsurprising that a memory of my childhood turns out to be a memory taken from someone else and put into the first-person view. I'm sure when we are children, and have few memories of our own, we are even more likely to fabricate an incident we hear about such that we imagine it as if we were present. Our imaginings and our rememberings simply become one and the same after a few acts of recollecting.

Our memories: the life of Clive Wearing

What happens if we suffer memory loss as, for example, in cases of amnesia? In common forms of amnesia, a person may retain recall for parts of their life.

The situation for Clive Wearing is very different. His amnesia is such that he can only sustain a brief window of memory of his interactions with others (although some recent developments suggest there may have been further improvements on this).[77] He's a person for a brief duration and relies on improvised habitual repetitive patterns of communication to engage in the lives of others. His wife Deborah declared that Clive died for her when a virus killed off cells in his hippocampus such that he could no longer acquire new memories in the way most of us take for granted.[78] Some might think this would be a wonderfully innocent world where everything is always new, where everything is always just beginning. For both in different ways their life together has been made maddeningly difficult and impossibly frustrating. His ability to act is constrained and limited, as are the possible interactions that Deborah can have with him. Although it seems that Clive has some kind of emotional memory of Deborah, indicating perhaps that some kinds of memory are embodied in non-cortical brain regions, recognition even of his wife is not instant under certain conditions. Clearly intelligent and to some extent partially aware of his condition, Clive attempts to be the person we expect persons to be: articulate, funny, asking and answering questions, generally and genuinely interacting.

Clive Wearing is forever awakening such that he truly believes that at this time and today he has awoken, that he is conscious for the first time, that he is now awake for the first time. For his wife, Deborah, it seemed that for Clive it was always 'Forever Today', which is the title of the book she wrote about her life with Clive.[79] Deborah told the story of their life together, particularly the lives they led as they were monumentally transformed following the viral infection that destroyed major parts of Clive's brain, including his hippocampus, a brain structure that is so important to our ability to recall episodes from our lives.

It might be that in the future we will be able to replace parts of the brain such that an artificial hippocampus, as an example, could be transplanted into a person whose own had been damaged irreparably. Extensive damage to the hippocampus is likely to result in amnesia, particularly problems making new memories of episodes in that person's life. If it were possible to replace a damaged organ with a new one, might Clive Wearing be able to live again as an independent person? Would he regain the ability to make new memories? Would the result of the transplant still be Clive Wearing? He would not get his old memories back, but it is likely that he would be able to lay down memories from the transplant operation forward, and thus keep his episodic experiences from this point. With scaffolding from others that knew Clive's history, he might be gifted back his past, which he could turn into first-person memories.

Clive Wearing tries to respond in the way he thinks others would expect him to. So he has a repertoire of responses. This repertoire might seem like fluent conversation to an outsider, but, as Oliver Sacks suggests, the responses would be revealed as repetitive and held together by 'superficial associations', which enable him 'to re-enter the world of human discourse'.[80] But he isn't really able to do this and the act shows itself to be a sham over time. What Clive Wearing pulls off for those who don't know him gets him into the regular person club. Unfortunately, because the repertoire is limited and repetitive, he gives himself away, but the effort of the attempt must be monumental and all to do what? Be treated as a person like others. Clive is no longer in place-time and he is not leading a life in the sense that the rest of us do, but he does find continuance in music and in the love for his wife, Deborah, who reports in Sacks's book that there is evidence that Clive has extended the moment in which he lives to some fifteen minutes.[81] Whether what this allows him to do can also lead to greater social skill, who knows, but let's hope that it does. Clive's love for and recognition of his wife Deborah is itself testimony to his continuance as a person.[82] A note sustained albeit for a short time is still a note sustained: like life and living, it has duration.

Sacks makes the analogy of awaking in the morning and refers to Proust. It is as if we have to 'catch ourselves on' or get wise to our yesterdays.

> But for me it was enough if, in my own bed, my sleep was so
> heavy as completely to relax my consciousness; for then
> I lost all sense of the place in which I had gone to sleep, and
> when I awoke at midnight, not knowing where I was,
> I could not be sure at first who I was; I had only the most
> rudimentary sense of existence, such as may lurk and

flicker in the depths of an animal's consciousness; I was more destitute of human qualities than the cave-dweller; but then the memory, not yet of the place in which I was, but of various other places where I had lived, and might now very possibly be, would come like a rope let down from heaven to draw me up out of the abyss of not-being, from which I could never have escaped by myself: in a flash I would traverse and surmount centuries of civilisation, and out of a half-visualised succession of oil-lamps, followed by shirts with turned-down collars, would put together by degrees the component parts of my ego.[83]

For Clive Wearing, it is about performance rather than recollection. When he stops playing the piano, the thread is broken and he falls once more into the abyss.[84] Without reliable memories of what has just happened together with the continuity of connection going back into the past, Clive is cut adrift. The person has to be anchorable in time or we cannot act as persons (or we can only act in a highly constrained or limited way). As persons, we may be able to collect ourselves as well as be collected together by others that care for us.

Chapter conclusions

I think we are egos in the sense that we are individual members of our society. I have been fashioned as a singular standpoint. I can understand yours and mine will be much like yours in so many ways, but you cannot have my standpoint nor can I have yours. In the end I can deceive you if not myself. You cannot check whether I am Guy *from my standpoint* but only from yours. All the evidence suggests that this is quite sufficient for our social lives to function.

I think we are bundles because of certain conventional ways we have of telling our lives and events and experiences as if part of one life. Many lives makes just as much sense but may seem fragmentary to us. We are *polyphonic* people with many continuities running simultaneously like a musical score. Captives I have spoken to tell me that consciousness under captive conditions is like this. We simply assume that consciousness is singular or has only one channel when polyphonic consciousness in positive and negative contours is a possibility. We'll have further discussion about *polyphony* in the next chapter.

In the ego view, there is some sense that the person is 'inside' the body as a vehicle and separable from their environment. In the bundle view, no such thing as a person exists at all. From the social psychology standpoint I am arguing that there is no such thing as a person at birth, but a person may develop under the right conditions. I think there is a sense in which I am held together by my relationships with other people: a different kind of bundle view: a social psychology bundle view. There is a very real sense of my being inside my head and of being alone and of having an existence, but the character of what exists is like the bundle idea in that I am a collection of elements at all times. The difference is that I believe the collection does add up to an individual standpoint, a subjective experience of life and living, of leading this life of mine, of having a standpoint, of knowing that I know what I know and that my actions have an impact in my world.

From a social theory standpoint your death will have consequences for those who knew you before you died. But your death has no consequences for you as there'll be no *you* to be there on which the consequences can act. The idea that you left, exited or departed is apt only in the sense that your absence is what is ever-present to those whose life continued.

As Gabriel García Márquez shows so movingly in *Love in the Time of Cholera*, what we miss is the presence of a person; this is what death robs us of. If the one that died figured in our lives, we will feel them as an absence that might itself feel like a presence.

When she awoke on her first morning as a widow, she turned over in bed without opening her eyes, searching for a more comfortable position so that she could continue sleeping, and that was the moment when he died for her. For only then did it become clear that he had spent the night away from home for the first time in years. The other place where this struck her was at the table, not because she felt alone, which in fact she was, but because of her strange belief that she was eating with someone who no longer existed.[85]

If we are also the negative spaces, shapes and contours of our lives in the world with others, these cannot be as easily categorised as discrete separable physical entities. We lose the idea of a self-contained body if we suppose that we are also the negative spaces between ourselves and others. We have negative contours that place us in our culture and make it impossible to say where Guy begins and ends. I may be continuous with other people's experience of me and this extends throughout my social world. And this in turn means that framing inside a skin or body or anything discrete is untenable. Any separation is artificial and partial. I am also continuous with your experience of me just as my memory of our encounter is continuous with yours.

Our bodies change over time. Most cells die and new ones are born. We are remade as we go along, and hopefully remaking works well and new cells resemble old ones. Remaking takes place in an environment or setting. We are a composition arranged in a particular setting. You cannot simply remake an element because an element is only an element because it is distinguished from its setting. But any setting has the potential to be turned into many elements all of which are distinguishable by someone or some process. Why one rather than another is made is not a simple one-for-one correspondence once we are dealing with an arrangement as complex as a person.[86]

The physical copying of me is not the same as copying my life, which is what is at issue here. You could clone me, but as soon as my clone and I have different experiences, meet different people, have different social experiences, we will diverge. The extent to which my social experience is different from my clone's would determine how differently we acted as adults. We talk of having experiences and not having been the same since. A captive may have been a certain way with themselves and others before captivity, but their experience of captivity brought out a different set of characteristics and played down others such that following captivity they may emerge as a different person from the one that was taken.

I think there are problems with the conclusions reached by a certain kind of discussion of what it is to scan and copy us, to teleport us to a new destination; these discussions highlight an assumption: that the ecology from which we are formed can be ignored, treated as background, or assumed to be relied upon. Just because a teleporter worked at our departure point, there is no reason to suppose living would be sustainable on arrival in the new locality. What does it say about who we think we are if we believe we are like a self-contained unit that can be cut from its situation and pasted into another without loss? Not only do we assume the ecology at our destination, we are also assuming a social life of being with other people, but this was not conceived of in our thought experiment. We take it for granted that we can simply start again. But what do we imagine ourselves to be if this is how we think? Do we imagine ourselves to be separate units, 'an island, entire of itself', separated from the mainland, distinct and enclosed?[87] But even our bodies are not like this. Yes, we can talk of inside and outside but only once we have conceptualised the body as distinct from the environment in which it is embedded. We talk this way not literally but metaphorically. We are so embedded in our environment but much of what constitutes us we simply ignore. The atlas idea of negative shapes, spaces and contours belongs here too. If we draw a map of an island – and it may help to imagine a familiar island viewed as if on a map – we may chart the land and its contours and take the coastline to be another contour of the land with outcrops and peninsulas. We see the island as 'figure' set into the background of water. But if we look at the same general area with sea charts, these show the texture of the sea and leave the land blank. The land becomes background and the coastline becomes a feature of the sea with its inlets and harbours. When water is surrounded by land – as with an inland sea – the sea becomes the figure that stands out. Think of the shape of the Mediterranean, for example.[88] The coastline is neither sea nor land and belongs to both. We are like the many pages of a geographical atlas: there are many ways of setting out who we are and none of these need be reducible to any other. Each map has its own merits and contributes to our understanding.

I am populated by social, cultural, historical, ecological, environmental and other features; they constitute me; they make me who and what I am. As Ray Tallis wrote:

> Self equals what I am conscious of, which is, roughly
> speaking, what is or what has become important to me.
> And before this, how the networks of relations, social and
> cultural and historical physical etc. have constituted me,
> long before there was a me there to address as such.[89]

I am treated as separately existing by my society and come to treat myself this way but this does not make this sense of self inevitable or natural. Any explanation of this sense of self would be temporary and local at best. If we assume this idea of sense of self is real and certain and make this our assumption in research, we bias both how the research is designed and how findings from research are interpreted.

If we are self-contained units that can be cut out from our surroundings, we are like the positive shapes discussed earlier. You may think this is how it is and that, as one reader commented, even if you were to be knocked unconscious and woke up in a hospital, you would still be able to come to your senses about who and what you are. But this neglects to acknowledge the way the hospital treats you as a person. The hospital is not simply a backdrop to your life; it is part and parcel of how it is to wake up in a hospital bed. If you are fortunate and you wake up with your memory intact, you know who you are even if you do not know where you are. If you had no identification and no one reports you missing, you would be like the teleported person cut adrift from the world and your place in it.

My father did not like being in hospital because others had the power to decide when things happened. He had lived independently and alone for many years and was used to deciding things for himself. Nonetheless, he appreciated the care that he got and how members of the medical staff were trying to help him. He was in a different society from the one he had left in his own home.[90] We have not the wit to describe a person without a setting; these are not two separate things, but part and parcel of the same thing that we might call 'the world about us'.

What do we consider to be identical? In a limited sense, unless we are exactly the same after teleporting, we would not be identical with what left. If teleporting involved a matter transport, it could be argued that you would be physically identical. The matter that makes you up and its arrangement could be teleported as it is to your destination. This would be ultra-fast travelling, but in principle not different from getting on a plane.

But everyday, normal living involves cells dying and being replaced such that over a seven-year cycle our cell make-up is entirely different. Of course, brain cells – neurons – are mostly not replaced, so most brain cells do have continuity, although neural networks may reorganise. Brains vary over lifetimes: new neurons are made, patterns of activation may change, neural nets may be reorganised. So normal living involves replication. In a very real sense we are not identical with the physical body and brain organisation we had, say, ten years ago. So, in what sense are we continuous over time given the discontinuity of cell replication? One answer is that cell replication always takes place in a context: your body and its current state. If you are an athlete, the musculature is replicated during cell replication.

You may believe that persons are entirely physical arrangements of bodies and brains. I believe persons to be social in character and that the social character of who and what we are needs to be considered along with beliefs about our physical make-up. If we want a more complete idea of identity, the social will be a necessary part of what it is to be us. We treat each other as social creatures and we need to examine this treatment and its impact on ourselves as persons.

If I am treated as the same person by others, this may be the most reliable fact that establishes my validity. You verify me by recognising and acknowledging me. Think again about what happens when I wake up in a hospital bed after an operation or an accident. You collect me up and hold me. *Thank you.*

I think we are social in character and this means that becoming a person incorporates the social psychological properties of life and living. I am not convinced that these properties can easily be copied, scanned and teleported because they do not simply exist in me. I am also what I am part of and therefore teleporting would lead to me becoming a greater absence than presence. I wouldn't be all there at my destination because some of what makes me who and what I am is when and where I am and with whom I am located. We are implicated in the world.

Our social lives are not another version of what happens to us physically; they are a different kind of relation altogether. When I look up from what I am writing I can both see a ship coming into port *and* write this sentence about it. There isn't a way that what I have written could ever stand in for the actual ship: no one is going to try to set sail in my sentence. And yet my sentence and the ship are related by me, here, now. The sentence is a social phenomenon; it is only an observable fact to a person educated with the wherewithal to read it. In order to write this sentence I need to understand all manner of conventions about my world and my relationship to it, and put into practice the conventions of writing about it. And you need to know at least one of the conventions of reading to follow what is written.

I don't think that we start out as persons. Persons are not present at birth and are social rather than natural kinds. Persons are brought about by social life experience with those already persons. Occasions for social experience are brought about by social institutions such as home and school, with family, peer groups, teachers, caregivers, friends and others close to you. I don't believe that a physical entity called person lives in my head or in my body, but I believe I am a person before the law and recognised as such by most nations. A person is not bound by the positive contour of the skin or the body or the brain or any other enclosure. I think that Mead was right to conclude that mind extends across our social worlds.[91]

I think the universal consciousness that gets going as we are formed up in infancy is similar to that of our closest primate relatives and that we might have remained like that had we not had the benefit of our community, our society and culture, our carers and families and the way that their relations with us make us transform into persons like them. Feral children are testimony to what happens to the child bereft of human company, for that child's consciousness remains universal and uneducable, as far from us as another related species that we can now recognise as part of the hominid family while also knowing that they are not like us. In a different way, being isolated from all human company may cause us to come apart, to fall apart, to literally disintegrate as people and become the fragmentary elements but without what makes them cohere, what holds us together. I believe that it is other people that hold us together. This kind of devastating isolation could also be caused by being shunned by those who know us, who act as if they do not; or by being in a place where nobody knows us, recognises us or acknowledges that we exist. William James wrote:

> No more fiendish punishment could be devised . . . than
> that one should be turned loose in society and remain
> absolutely unnoticed by all the members thereof. If no one
> turned around when we entered, answered when we spoke,
> or minded what we did, but if every person we met 'cut us
> dead' and acted as if we were non-existent things, a kind
> of rage and impotent despair would ere long well up in us,
> from which the cruellest bodily tortures would be a relief.[92]

In some ways this is the alienation of modern living where, in a city, we could pass thousands of people in the course of a week, and neither acknowledge nor be acknowledged by any one of them. This sense of alienation can cause a person to fall apart in the midst of so many others. This could destroy us as persons by causing us to lose our sense of identity because it was other people that made us persons in the first place and gave us our identity by giving us theirs. We may wish to feel anonymous and when I lived in London there were times when this seemed a boon to me, but we can also feel more alone when in a crowded place.

What helps many captives survive is the building of an imagined, virtual, social world. What helps captives is what makes us in the first place. We make a social world in which we live this life of ours. Writers get locked up more than most people. As dissidents, writers can create an impact from dissident writing, even when attempts are made to stop them.[93] They are particularly skilled at doing what a person needs to do to ensure their own continuance and integrity. To continue as a person in captivity, do what writers do: make up a virtual social world. We had this done for us; the captive (writer) has to do it over again on their own. We make a virtual social world *knowing it to be so*.

Example: If you lock me up I will be changed by captivity. As a person I can reflect and recognise that I am becoming lost in captivity and going down into an apathy and emptiness from which I am unlikely to personally survive. I will have become the tame animal your punishment is forcing me to be. Because I can reflect and know my situation, I can also change it and resist the outcomes that your actions are having on me. By resisting I will change my behaviour towards you and this in turn will turn the tables on you as you now have to face something different from what you would expect to find. I will take further courage from your reaction and use it to feed my resourcefulness. It will make me stronger. You may beat me but now you are forced to acknowledge that I am a person and I will know that I am free and you have become chained. I will know *that* I am and that my actions have consequences. And that you of all people have to acknowledge that I exist. I can take these into my life and how I live the remainder of my captivity.

In the next chapter, I will discuss some of the conclusions I reached from my reading of the genre of captivity and the interviews I conducted with former hostages and political prisoners.

3   To be captive

What can accounts of captivity tell us about how it is for us to be conscious? In this chapter we'll turn to a discussion about minds and captivity and look at what it is to *be* captive. You may recall that I researched imagination by investigating former captives' experiences of solitary confinement. And this meant reading about former hostages and political prisoners, and interviewing four of them. Some of that research is recounted here and related to consciousness more widely. From having reviewed so much material there is an obvious question: can you lock up a mind? Many regimes have wanted to and it is often dissident writers who are taken and held captive, disappeared or imprisoned. So, in this chapter I propose to discuss how it is to *be* captive *for* the captive *from* their point of view. And I will include some excerpts taken from interviews with former captives so that you can hear some of this in their own words.

I believe that where identities are concerned, we are only persons because of the exchanges we make and have made with the lives of others. We are made of the relationships we have with others; these are what make us who and what we are. When we are separated from other people, deliberately isolated or incarcerated, or put in solitary confinement, we may start to disintegrate. But we may also come through it and be renewed by it.

The stories of captivity take on an epic quality because they follow a classic epic storyline. A captive disappears from life, as if they had died – their absence is all there is; then much later the captive reappears as if reborn, reawakened or resurrected. The sequence is like nature's seasons: autumn time when the leaves fall from the trees and the land is barren, but everything is going on underground; then life returns in spring and the leaves return; there is renewal or reawakening. The sequence is also much like the story of the phoenix: the mythical bird that dies consumed by flames and rises again from its own ashes.

This epic-like quality seems to be one of the reasons why the stories of captivity related by former hostages and political prisoners are always, dare I say it, so captivating. In this chapter we will tackle what it is for a person to disappear into captivity. The idea is to set out the remarkable ways in which these accounts chart the human condition, what it is to be a person and how a captive sustains a sense of identity over and against the inhuman practice of solitary confinement. Before beginning let me first state that although I will not be discussing the brutality of captivity, this book is not intended to make light of the destructive power and cruel practices witnessed in the accounts of captivity. We should not forget those that have been destroyed by such an ordeal. It is one thing to survive imprisonment, but it is all the harder to survive if you are tortured or become ill. There are numerous examples of survival under the most extreme conditions, but there are also many who do not survive for one reason or another. The focus of this book is on what accounts of captivity can tell us about ordinary life. An extreme situation need not be different from our own except in terms of the intensity and magnification. Life and living is amplified rather than changed and easier to see because undisturbed by the usual distractions.

Research that put people into isolation, supposedly to study so-called sensory deprivation, highlighted some of the problems that prisoners would face in confinement and some of the ways in which a prisoner might survive intact. Many felt disoriented during the first part of their isolation. Participants reported how their thinking was disrupted in isolation; that they would lose track of what they were thinking about. Some reported that they could probably have managed to keep their thinking from being disrupted had they had someone present as a listener. They said that this might have worked even were they to have simply *believed* that they had a listener.[1]

Albie Sachs was a South African barrister who defended people prosecuted under apartheid laws. He was arrested, detained and kept in solitary confinement. He wrote a book on the effect of being deprived of all human contact and the methods he used to get through it; in it he reflected on what it is like to be captive:

> Being alone all the time, day in and day out, has had a disintegrative effect on my thinking, and I find it difficult to organise ideas and to sustain interest in them.[2]

A captive may be sustained by the knowledge that they are part of a political movement and that others are continuing their opposition to a ruling authority. Hostages may also gain great comfort from knowing that others are campaigning for their release.

Anthony Grey

The use of the word *Hostage* in the title of Anthony Grey's account of captivity in Peking (now Beijing) was original for the modern age. He had been referred to as under house arrest, but was determined on release to fully catalogue the cruelty and excesses of his two-year ordeal.[3] *Hostage in Peking* was later to be circulated among the families and friends of other hostages as a way of helping them understand what their loved-ones were going through. Grey set up the Charlton Foundation, a general charitable trust which, by means of an affiliated organisation Hostage Action Worldwide, worked to help the Beirut hostages and families between 1989 and 1992. He was a Reuters correspondent in Eastern Europe and it was in this role that he was taken hostage for two years by China's Red Guards during the Cultural Revolution of the late 1960s. He was born in Norwich in July 1938 and became a local journalist before joining Reuters in 1964. Since his release he has become a successful novelist writing historical works mostly set in Eastern Asia. His change of literary genre seems to stem from the short stories he wrote whilst in captivity which he concealed from his guards and managed to get smuggled out of China. These became his first fictional book *A Man Alone*, published in 1971.

When I interviewed Anthony Grey about his experience held as a hostage in China in the 1960s, he spoke of the importance of the support of other people. It is one of the most inhuman factors in the holding of someone in solitary confinement: to let them believe they are forgotten people; that nobody knows about them; that nobody cares. In recent history this has been shown up painfully in the practice of what came to be called 'Disappearances'. The Disappeared are those people taken, often literally plucked off the street, where no one admits responsibility for the action. And no record of the 'arrest' has been entered. It is as though they disappeared off the face of the earth. While I was still setting up the tape recorder, he had begun talking about the importance of social support, so I asked him to go over the same ground with the tape running as I felt this should be on record.

> The terrible thing about solitary confinement, and
> confinement of this kind, is the sense of total
> abandonment, the isolation factor; that you're alone,
> unjustifiably, and nobody cares. And that's a terrible
> feeling which I think reduces you a lot inside yourself. And
> to discover when you come back that people have written
> to you – although the letters haven't arrived – that they
> have campaigned; that they have gone to parliament; that
> there's been activity; where people have really cared

counteracts that and seems to be of enormous importance. Or at least to me it was. And I think it's generally true. . . . The 'No man is an island' idea is really true. And that we are all interlinked. And we all are in some way responsible for the rest of the human family.[4]

Brian Keenan

Brian Keenan was born in Belfast in 1950. He had taken up a teaching position in Beirut University in Lebanon because he wanted to travel. It was one morning when he was going off to work that he was kidnapped. Although aware of the dangers – teachers were being recruited because previous occupants of the positions had been kidnapped – he decided to go anyway, believing that as the holder of an Irish passport he would not be a target. It was a nuance lost on his kidnappers. He was taken hostage on 11 April 1986 and spent the initial period in solitary confinement before being held with John McCarthy, with whom he spent the longest part of his captivity. On his return he moved to the south and found sanctuary from the media in the arms of friends and people in the west of Ireland.[5] His book *An Evil Cradling* about his experience of captivity was published in 1992. It is a testimony to the spirit of fellowship that, although he was released in August 1990, he decided that he could neither sign a publishing contract, nor complete a manuscript until the other hostages held in Lebanon had come home. His story of captivity is in two parts: about a third of the book articulates his experience of solitary confinement, most of the other two-thirds is about his experience of captivity with John McCarthy. Brian Keenan promptly replied to my letter requesting an interview stating 'I would be delighted to help you with your research.'

Brian Keenan had often been asked about how he would have survived had he not spent most of his imprisonment with John McCarthy. The answers he gave during each of our conversations say much about what makes us who we are. He said:

> We're all made persons by our encounter with another and we need an encounter for that.

And also later:

> We only become valid – and have a valid identity and a valid meaning – if that's received by somebody else. And is understood. And is shared. So, I don't know how I would have reacted had I been on my own. But I certainly know the importance of finding my validity through the presence of someone else. And I think that's pretty frightening.[6]

There is a very strong sense that it is in being recognised and acknowledged by others that we are confirmed and verified. To subvert a well-known saying: 'Others think of me therefore I exist.'[7] One of the terrors of isolation is knowing that if our existence is not attested to by others, we may be personally destroyed; that our very existence is validated in the encounter with another – without that contact, a person has no integrity and may, literally, disintegrate. But many get through these periods of confinement intact: how do they do it?

We bring the wherewithal of our continuance into the cell with us if we can but recognise this. We are made socially and for me I would say we become social creatures through and through. Our minds are not confined because they comprise the whole of our social world. If we treat ourselves as such we can occupy the long boring eventless periods of captivity with an imaginary or virtual social world. Artists and writers have always done this and in some ways it is ironic that they get locked up by oppressive regimes when it is they who are most practised at how to survive such an ordeal. If you are held, become like an artist or writer and let go the reins of control at least some of the time to allow yourself the scope to play in an imagined virtual world. There will be a necessity for a disciplined occupation of an extended time. There will be a need also to surrender and to allow yourself free rein. You will need to do both. Normally, people are fearful of letting go, but in captivity you have to do some of this. Boredom and the endless round of days in a cell will make ordinary kinds of conscious control almost impossible to sustain. You would need to get a mind like a writer or an artist, or a contemplative's sensibility to fashion yourself psychologically in ways that would help you survive captivity.

If you are isolated, you will be forced to occupy yourself. In solitary confinement, the captive is the only person who is there to deal with the ordeal, so a captive simply makes someone up. We turn ourselves (back) into the social creature that we are. Becoming introspective, that is, tending to turn inwardly, does not necessarily make us insular. If we take the turning inwards and the many voices we find there, we encounter ourselves as a vast resource that was always there. We make of ourselves an imagined other with whom we can converse. For our sanity we need to recognise that these parts are all played by ourselves, but that we need not fear the interplay. In their simplest form exchanges are between the captive as a person imagining and an imagined person. Imagining could be likened to the first person, the ordinary sense of the continuous you. Your imagined person is like a third person, what Brian Keenan described to me as a 'third party'. He recognised this as 'just yourself as the observer'. During the time Keenan was held alone, he treated himself as a counterpoint much as a writer imagines someone as a reader. This need not be the kind of unhealthy split found in cases where a person dissociates and separates from the first person because the ordeal is too painful to endure. What I am trying to describe here is akin to writers' use of themselves as a vital counterpoint and to something we do all the time but little recognise because the scale of the action of ordinary living takes us out of ourselves in ways that are diverting and distracting from our psychological make-up.

Imaginer and the imagined observer are both intrinsically you, but, as we all do to some extent, the counterpoint allows a reflexive conversation. And this counterpoint can become different people and as long as a captive always remembers that the many voices are all part of them and going on in the captive's head, all will be well.

Vladimir Bukovsky

Vladimir Bukovsky was born in December 1942 and first arrested while a student at Moscow University. He was expelled from the university in 1961 for organising a poetry reading in Mayakovsky Square. His first imprisonment was in a psychiatric institution (June 1963). Later, he was one of the first to get documents to the West regarding psychiatric abuses in Soviet Russia. Bukovsky had four stretches of captivity in different institutions lasting respectively 21 months, 8 months, 3 years and 5 years 9 months. He spent a total of 11 years and 2 months in prison between June 1963 and December 1976, at which point he was expelled from Russia as part of a prisoner exchange. The limit on solitary confinement was 15 days. However, by the expedient of simply starting another stretch, Bukovsky's longest period in solitary confinement was 45 days. The account of his experience, *To Build a Castle*, was published in 1978. He graduated from Cambridge University in 1981 and conducted research in neuroscience at Cambridge and Stanford. It was through the late Stephen MacKeith that I met Bukovsky. I contacted him and he readily agreed to a meeting and interview. Following my letter requesting an interview, Bukovsky promptly replied that 'As a former graduate student in psychology I sympathise with your effort' and had no objections to being questioned about his experience of captivity.

Whilst held as a political prisoner in Soviet Russia, Vladimir Bukovsky built an imaginary castle in which to secure himself from the worst excesses of interrogation and torture. He was first held in a psychiatric institution and then later in a series of prisons. Bukovsky's imaginary castle is populated with his friends, the 'guests' he invites to dine with him. In his book *To Build a Castle* he described his imagined virtual world. He was interested in architecture from childhood and he exercises his mind by imagining the architecture for his castle. The following passage from his book written after his exchange is suggestive of the use of imagination as what he called a 'sideways escape'. Anything that does not involve either the past or the future is a sideways escape. The attention to detail is important. The need to keep occupied when faced with the monotony and boredom of the punishment cell known as 'the box' is paramount.

> Knowing all this in advance, I would try, when sent to the box, to smuggle in a fragment of pencil lead, usually by hiding it in my cheek. Then I could spend my time drawing castles – on scraps of newspaper or directly on the floor and walls. I set myself the task of constructing a castle in every detail: from the foundations, floors, walls, staircases and secret passages right up to the pointed roofs and turrets. I carefully cut each individual stone, covered the floor with parquet or stone flags, filled the apartments with furniture, decorated the walls with tapestries and paintings, lit candles in the chandeliers and smoking torches in the endless corridors. I decked the tables and invited guests, listened to music with them, drank wine from goblets, and lit up a pipe to accompany my coffee. We climbed the stairs together, walked from chamber to chamber, gazed at the lake from the open veranda, went down to the stables to examine the horses, walked round the garden – which also had to be laid out and planted.

We returned to the library by way of the outside staircase, and there I kindled a fire in the open hearth before settling back in a comfortable armchair. I browsed through old books with worn leather bindings and heavy brass clasps. I even knew what was inside those books. I could even read them.

Bukovsky might be suddenly taken for interrogation. He would remain in his imagined castle to answer the questions.

Idiots! They didn't know that I was returning to my friends, to our interrupted conversation before the fire. How were they to know that I was talking to them from my castle battlements, looking down on them, preoccupied more with how to fix the stables than with answering their stupid questions? What could they do against my thick walls, my crenellated towers and embrasures? Laughingly, I returned to my guests, firmly closing the massive oak doors behind me.[8]

Although by the time Bukovsky was held, interrogations were not so serious, he still endured sleep deprivation and a number of periods in 'the box'. The imagined castle walls are both a structure of defence and a consolidation of his story in the face of any attempt to erase his narrative. The castle works as his strategy of independence and his ways and means of maintaining it. He sees the world with the fortifications of his castle, from his castle battlement.

Polyphony

It was Vladimir Bukovsky who used the word 'polyphonic' to describe the development of certain techniques when he was held as a political prisoner. I did not know the word and had to look it up. It means many sounds or many-voiced. In music it refers to a composition in parts each with its own independent melody. It is often used to describe choral music as having many (sung) voices as, for example, in plainsong. Polyphony can be used to suggest many sounds and the many possible ways that sounds are produced independently and together in composition.

Polyphony was used by the Russian philosopher Mikhail Bakhtin, who used many musical metaphors. He suggested that the many 'social voices of the era' can each be given their full due in a narrative, such as in Dostoevsky's *Brothers Karamazov* (one of the examples used by Bakhtin).[9]

Bukovsky used it to describe consciousness under certain conditions and I want to further elaborate that use to offer a fresh description of how it is for us to be conscious persons, to lead our lives, to have a point of view, to know and to be minded. I think we are polyphonic people and that consciousness could be described as polyphonic and that we are made like a self-playing musical instrument the multi-track performance of which amounts to the composition we call 'my life'.

Initially for the captive there is a shift from a conventional view of consciousness as single track to at least one other. And these two go on along together and also act as counterpoints as they would were they to be independent melodies in a musical composition. It may be that the change is brought about by the need for the prisoner to let go of the reins of conscious control. The kind of conscious control we associate with freely acting in the world may not be sustainable during confinement where nothing happens and we are unable to engage in events. Some hands-off, letting go with some idea of directing towards or setting the limits seems to be necessary and desirable. The following exchanges are taken from our conversations.

I have used certain transcript conventions in the quotations from transcripts below. Speech patterns do not always easily fit standard written grammar and punctuation. In places I have used two dots '..' to signify a change in mid-sentence, where a speaker started saying one thing and then went off on another track without finishing the first thought. Three dots '...' are used in the standard way to show where I have omitted part of the transcript for the sake of clarity. Bukovsky was born in Russia but speaks very good English; however, he may use an idiom that seems strange. I have kept to Bukovsky's own words as, with a little reflection, it is not difficult to see what he means.

As far as the hands-off kind of control was concerned, Bukovsky commented on his use of imagination:

> BUKOVSKY: Well that was inevitable. That's what happens. You have to. If you want it [imagination] controlled then you have to be of two minds – one is imagining and another is observing.[10]

This makes the observer an imagined position to see *with*. In Bukovsky's first experience of being imprisoned he was placed in a psychiatric hospital. The idea here is to have political prisoners observed so that if they exhibit behaviours thought to be indicative of psychosis, they can be kept in a psychiatric hospital indefinitely (on the convenient basis that, at that time in Russia, it would take an authority to state that the original diagnosis was wrong, and this was not going to happen). Bukovsky acquires the ability to watch himself as if from outside and describes this as having 'several activities' in his mind going on at the same time. This was vital to Bukovsky. Why?

> BUKOVSKY: Because when you are locked in let's say with twenty madmen, you start questioning yourself. You lose your point of reference. I mean, are they mad or is that me who is mad? So that is a pressure. And therefore you develop very early, very keen techniques, very interesting techniques for checking on yourself, constantly checking on yourself.

Did I do anything? And then it becomes your second nature. You constantly observe yourself.

SAUNDERS: So that just happens, the checking just starts to happen? It's something that you don't really decide about it, you just find yourself doing it?

BUKOVSKY: No. It's just because you are frightened, you suddenly..

SAUNDERS: You don't want to..you don't want to become like them.

BUKOVSKY: Exactly. You're just frightened you may lose your mind. Or perhaps you already lost it. Scary proposition huh? That came in psychiatric hospital, the first time. And then you develop these keen techniques of observing other people ... But you do live in a high tension environment. And you are very quick at assessing people, quick at understanding what's going to happen. Also observing yourself. It's a kind of a state which is difficult to describe because it's kind of a balance between several activities going in parallel.[11]

In the heat of the moment I didn't pick up on this. So, the second time I spoke to Bukovsky, I asked him about these 'several activities':

BUKOVSKY: In general, I believe – and there are some theories in physiology that it's true, but theories – that we do work in parallel in many activities. At the time simply we are not aware of it because the channel of conscious activity is one. The others are kind of suppressed, but they go on along. Now, in

situations of high intensity, you suddenly
become aware of several activities in your
mind going on at the same time. Now it
doesn't mean that they got mixed up, they are
not. It doesn't mean that. But you can switch
over. No you cannot mix them up together.
That doesn't happen and you would be
frightened of that ... But you are aware of
certain things going at the same time, you
know, probably because of the lack of
excessive information, excessive sensory
input. Since you are feeding on yourself. Since
you are using more internal information,
rather than external, then you suddenly
become aware of these things.[12]

Quietening down the cacophony of everyday life – the way
we are drowned out by the deluge of what is going on – could lead
to an intensity and attention to detail not possible in normal life.
Bukovsky elaborated these ideas into a musical metaphor.

BUKOVSKY: Certainly, you do know that you are
              polyphonic. And if you are in jail for a long
              time, you perceive it as an advantage, the
              polyphonia. And you use it as an instrument.
SAUNDERS: In what sense, way do you use it?
BUKOVSKY: Well, first thing you try to have all the
              channels uncontradictory.
SAUNDERS: Right. Okay.
BUKOVSKY: It's a symphony, you see. It's supposed to be
              somewhat harmonical. For example, if you do
              have a problem and you can't cope with it,
              you relegated it to one of these channels.
              Right, and you just let it grow, let it develop.
              If you're pursuing something on another

channel, something pleasant and harmonical, the chance is that the problem will be solved there and you will get the answer.

SAUNDERS: So what are you saying?

BUKOVSKY: It's a set of instruments. It is like ...

SAUNDERS: Are you saying that there is a crossover in that sense?

BUKOVSKY: Somewhere very deep. Yes, somewhere very deep. It's probably something to do with rhythms. I would imagine, I mean I do believe there is a certain rhythmic nature in the work of brains. There must have been something. If the rhythms are not contradictory then they are supplementary.[13]

And it may be just this that leads to all the following: the increased sensitivity, the acuteness of insight; and changes in consciousness that allow the multiform consciousness spoken about by Bukovsky.

SAUNDERS: So these..the parallel activities in some way can feed off each other?

BUKOVSKY: Right.

SAUNDERS: Provided they're not in that sense contradictory which is going to ...

BUKOVSKY: The funny thing about this is well, for example, you play chess, you want to win. If you do win, you might suddenly trigger off a decision, a solution of a problem, which you relegated to that hidden channel. In other words, what I mean to say, the successful resolution of one problem in one channel very often leads or coincides, whatever might be, to a successful resolution of another problem or another, so these things must be

related. They couldn't be sheer coincidence.
I don't think it is. There must be something
in our inner mechanism which is not quite
clear, not studied properly, which is
connected. I don't know. I mean you end up
by experimenting with yourself. You
suddenly realise an important thing (in my
view): you are an instrument. And you have
to learn how to play this instrument. And if
you play it well, you can perfect your own
performance. And if you play it well, you
know, you would achieve better results. So
you certainly become aware of yourself as an
instrument. A polyphonic instrument. You
know, an interesting thing.[14]

There is an experience *of* a performance and not an experience *and* a performance. If we think of the qualities of an
experience as properties of persons rather than mental states,
there is no need to divide the world into two. If what we are is
like a musical performance, our experience of our performance
is part of the performance and not something that is separate
or separable from it. We will return to this in Part III of this
book. By getting away from explanations that seem always to
involve either visual metaphors or an emphasis on language or
both, we can have an alternative appreciation of consciousness.
For Bukovsky, this kind of performance is drowned out by the
cacophony of ordinary living.

SAUNDERS: The awareness of it or the consciousness of it
is much more under that sort of heightened
condition.

BUKOVSKY: Yes.

SAUNDERS: Does that mean you don't, you wouldn't now
at all, or wouldn't be able to reach that?

BUKOVSKY: That's the problem. Once you start
unwinding, you lose most of these abilities.
Well you probably have some of it still going
on, but you don't ...

SAUNDERS: But you're not conscious of it.[15]

Without a point of reference, particularly poignant during his first imprisonment in a psychiatric hospital, there was a fear of exploring.

BUKOVSKY: Most of the people don't go into these things
precisely because of fear, they are afraid that
they are treading dangerous terrain. And they
might just lose track, lose the reference point
here. But when you're alone and inside the
cell isolation, that's the only thing you feed
on, so you have to and then you become
hooked on it. It becomes fun ... You
experiment with it. You experiment with
your own instrument. And therefore you go
with it. Although some voice will tell you,
always that there is a danger, I mean
particularly in the conditions that you are,
with no reference point. There is a certain
apprehension living, whatever you do,
concerning our mind. But you tend to go and
experiment much more easily in these
conditions simply because of boredom.
I mean there's nothing else to do.[16]

This is the part that often gets overlooked: the sheer boredom of being captive, often without books, pencil and paper, or indeed anything to relieve the seemingly interminable days of captivity. You have to use yourself as a resource. The prisoner is reflexively turned back upon themselves to use themselves as a resource, to be resourceful. With nothing else to do boredom is greater than fear. And this is the crux of it for me: to experiment with yourself, to play yourself as if you were a musical instrument; to find out about the sounds you produce; to tune yourself against others and the world about you.

Brian Keenan and polyphony

Something of the polyphonic is evident in Brian Keenan's expressive account. As with Bukovsky, this challenges many of the conventions in psychology about identity, the sense of self and what it is to be a person.

Brian Keenan had his briefcase given back to him in the first cell. In this he had a stub of pencil and some paper (in the form of textbooks). However, he hadn't used them to begin with, fearful of becoming dependent upon them. He reasoned it was likely they would be confiscated if discovered, or, as did happen, not be moved when he was moved. Then, he got to a point where he no longer cared, and it became important to 'repossess himself', so he simply wrote down everything that was occurring to him. He was concerned about the discovery of these writings, but decided to make use of the resource nonetheless. He wrote some of it in poetic form so that he could defend it as poetry if it was discovered by the guards. On reading over what he had written he was shocked to find he recognised no part of it. This is what Brian Keenan wrote in his book *An Evil Cradling*:

> Eventually it came to me that here in these pages there was something I could only dimly perceive, some threads running through and holding it together like the veins that carry blood to the living heart. Here in all this confusion some veins of life held everything together. I don't fully know what it was, yet remember feeling that in these strange pages was a whole human being.[17]

I asked him about this passage and what it meant and whether he could tell me more about the written notes he made on the textbooks from his briefcase.

> KEENAN: And maybe that's another important thing for your research is the need, when I think back on it all, it's always imagining presents you to the different persons that you are. It's like all the written notes. In a way, ten different persons writing one long, longhand.[18]

In a similar way to Bukovsky's polyphony, Keenan describes a company of persons, a manifold make-up that in 'one long, longhand' makes for a composition.

As expected, when he was moved, he never saw the briefcase or his books again.

Others in the cell may be felt as presences but known as intrinsically part of you. Keenan argues that this is what some captives associate with God, because 'It's all the language has to give us.' There is a knowing 'I'm not alone', but this doesn't have to translate into religious language. Talk of presences in the cell came from asking Brian Keenan about the arrival of the bowl of fruit. His first reaction is to glory in the colour. He had been on hunger strike and one time when he removed his blindfold following one of his guards coming into his cell, he discovered a bowl of fruit with an orange in it. Most of the food hostages were given was grey and bland. He refuses to eat the fruit but marvels at its presence in his grey cell.

> The colour orange, the colour, the colour, my God
> the colour orange.[19]

Others commented on how anything that stands out from the grey has intensity and a vibrancy that renders it vitally alive. He came to feel this as a presence and an emblem of what was seemingly present in the cell with him, although known at the same time to be intrinsically part of himself. And the presence became different things for him:

KEENAN: The presence became my father. We never had a close relationship. We were from different sides of a kind of cultural divide. But yet a sense.. what always came to me as him. You would be feeling pretty awful ... I think most people who go through it find it pretty hard to talk, though you'd be talking to yourself ... You'd be saying to yourself, Brian, 'catch yourself on'.[20] Be careful. You're also here. You know the words are inside your head ... They're coming from somewhere else. And that somewhere else is always, I think, identified in the human imagination with a person. And that person becomes different people, but what seemed to predominate all the time was my father talking to me ... He died a couple of years before I 'disappeared' and I was an only son, with two sisters, but I was the only boy. And maybe, in a way, all the guilts come to you. When the imagination starts working. It's one of the great compensations – to meet people at distance. And it's an opportunity. It's a given opportunity. But that bowl of fruit seems to symbolise this was being given, and had a life of its own. When all it was, was a bowl of fruit that was going mouldy. But it seemed to speak to you about other things, and huge reassurance, something was being given. That there was a presence of home, and that you weren't alone.[21]

Hinted at in this section is the difficulty of bearing memory in the confinement setting, for it is so easy to be drawn down by guilt.

> KEENAN: You remember an incident in a more profound
> way than you ever actually have. And you
> could understand all the things around it which
> you didn't do when the thing was actually
> happening. But in captivity, it's much more
> profound. Because you begin to think, well why
> didn't I? And guilt is the hardest of memory
> and imagination's reinvention of the moment.[22]

Nonetheless, it is important to 'meet people' in this virtual social world we call imagination, and to have an encounter with others. It is necessary to transform the meaning vacuum of the cell into an outpost of the familiar and known, to occupy oneself. There is a need to populate the emptiness of the cell with what would normally be given by the culture from which the captive has been torn.

At one point his captors give him metal cutlery and he chances on his reflection in the spoon. He is struck by the reflection such that his voice cries out, 'That's not me':

> KEENAN: [T]hat there's me – conscious, present, me
> saying, 'That's not me'. And there's also another
> me that has in some way gone through a
> transforming process also speaking at the
> same time, saying, 'This is not me'. That, the
> identity that I was trying to forge for myself, to
> survive, was no more me than the transformed
> image I was seeing in the mirror. So it was a
> kind of interior voice, another me saying,
> 'This is not me'. And the image that you're
> trying to survive by here isn't here either. It was

kind of.. I didn't sense like that as I said it, but
afterwards – and I thought about it long
afterwards – that it was two voices in harmony.
By saying, 'This is not me', it was the Brian
Keenan that was locked up and who has had his
beard shaved off, saying, 'This is not me'. And
then there was another me saying, 'This is not
me'. There's a process of change has occurred . . .
It was very much like a counterpoint in music
to that . . . It was the same thing only.. You'll
understand as an artist. It was a different hue,
and a different shape, and a different colour, and
a different tonal value to it. So it was a kind of
counterpoint to that third party, that objective
observer. And the kind of saying 'This is not me'
was more, more unemotional, direct and
honest. But it didn't. It had the sense of the
objective dispassionate that the third party
observer had. Something more immediate and
direct. A voice coming from you. That was part of
you . . . It was almost like two voices. I was
unaware of it though at that time when I said it.
But afterwards I thought that that's the
significance.[23]

The two voices are nothing to do with pathology. We all
have voices in our heads. We assume one voice, but multi-voice or
polyphony makes more sense. Often it is the attempt to suppress
or the fear of the many voices which can lead to pathology, not
simply the idea of existence as many-voiced; or else all writers are
mad. There are myths to do with multiple personality; that the
many voices are really people in our heads. Much of the treatment
now focuses on coming to accept these voices as inherently part of
ourselves. The idea is for all parties to accept that the voices exist

and go from there; to help a person to work with the many voices that make themselves up and not to feel they have to fight or suppress as this usually simply makes matters worse.

Returning to the notion of voice as voice to write from, to listen to and the voice in the text, Keenan's account has echoes of the polyphonic:

> KEENAN: And the strange paradox that that kind of imprisonment is – it releases all these persons, or energies, or interests or whatever they are, that, unless you have been living a religious life – there's no way that.. That imprisonment is a fearsome and awesome liberation, which is all these other persons, or other interests, or other energies. We're all there and a vast resource.[24]

It is so easy to label this romantic and to scoff and suggest that we mock those afflicted with mental illness by this treatment of subjectivities as anything other than pathology; but this is unjust and merely polices what we can say about subjectivity. We are not taught to think of using our own resources; we are taught to rely on others, others who are experts or specialists. And this division of labour is what is pathologising such that we cannot treat ourselves as other than separate, idiosyncratic and incomplete. I am arguing for the use of ourselves in a free fashion that might liberate our resourcefulness. In terms of human rights, the safeguard here is conscience. If we relate to others in a spirit of fellowship, we will always consider others' freedom when expressing our own.

Terry Waite

Terry Waite became a negotiator over the plight of hostages in Iran and Libya and finally with the kidnappers of the hostages in Lebanon until eventually he was also taken captive.

He had been the Archbishop of Canterbury's envoy. He was released in November 1991 after being held for almost five years, almost four of which were in solitary confinement. He published his account of his experiences in 1993.

The structure of Terry Waite's book telling of his period as a hostage, *Taken on Trust*, was made to 'recreate the experience' of confinement, and his experience of 'how my mind worked in those days'.[25]

What is salient here is the notion of recreating the experience and the difficulty of doing this with any conventional literary style. Waite tells two stories in juxtaposition – as counterpoint: his own story – his life and times, and the story of his captivity – his memories, dreams and reflections. Terry Waite's solution is one borrowed from John Fowles's book *The French Lieutenant's Woman*. Although writing a very different book, Waite considers the structure of Fowles's book to be insightful about the character of consciousness in his days of captivity. The following is also suggestive of a polyphonic conscious experience.

> WAITE: I got really the clues to the construction of *Taken on Trust*, interestingly enough, and I haven't said this in the book, I got clues for that, from the novel *The French Lieutenant's Woman*.
>
> SAUNDERS: That's interesting. That's very interesting.
>
> WAITE: Do you remember that?
>
> SAUNDERS: Yes, because it's got the two things going on at the same time.
>
> WAITE: Exactly.
>
> SAUNDERS: Yes.
>
> WAITE: And I thought that that the writer of that book has got it exactly. He's got it exactly ... And that's how I knew then how to put the book together. It wasn't in any way copied.

I mean, because it's an entirely different
book ... And I think, I think it's possibly one
of the reasons why *Taken on Trust* has been
so enormously successful. Because somehow
in the writing of that book in my head – and
I'm speaking about writing it in my head. I'm
not now speaking about putting it on paper.
In the writing of that book in my head
I wanted the structure of the book to recreate
the experience.[26]

Waite relates the structure of his book to how consciousness was during captivity and particularly to constructions of time.

Anthony Grey on polyphony

I discussed these ideas with Anthony Grey. For him, the
seeing *with* the imagined made all seeing different following captivity. He was involved in a project:

GREY: And I made a TV film. And I can remember filming
        in Oxford Street and so on. And I felt that what had
        changed in me was that I saw everything through
        the eyes of an artist, which I wasn't before. I was
        just a reporter, an agency journalist, always
        rushing, always getting the story, getting it, filing
        it, getting it in the paper, looking in the paper the
        next day, going off, a new story. I felt I'd been
        stopped dead in my tracks, put on the spot for two
        years ... And that I now saw everything in an
        artistic way; that I saw things in a creative way.
        And just walking down the street: there wasn't
        just a billboard from an advertisement, I saw the
        colours. And I saw the creative beauty in what the
        artist had done with the billboard, if anything.

And that even people in the street and the flow of them was something .. I saw things in a different way and I would always do that.[27]

The significance of the polyphonic is suggested in the fore-going in that the idea of simply recording is troubled. Seeing *with* the imagined can mean seeing the possibilities or seeing the limitations, but all seeing is putting things together. We can put things together *as* a reporter or *as* an artist or *as* a scientist would do so. Rather than see parts or wholes as having properties, we might see polyphonic possibilities.

As I said earlier, it is ironic that writers often get locked up by regimes as they are probably the ones most prepared to survive such an ordeal. A writer must spend time in a self-imposed solitary confinement, often the same space day after day with just the made-up virtual world of imagination for company. The virtual world can buoy the prisoner's spirit, but there will be bad days when a kind of apathy or numbness – sometimes called 'accidie' – sets in.[28] The not knowing if or when or how captivity will end has been called living a 'provisional existence'.[29] But then this is how it is for all of us in a way. We may be able to divert ourselves with a plethora of all those things that need to be done, places to go, people to meet, but unless we are never alone, we will face days like these.

When I discussed what I was researching with friends, they would often say that it must be sad talking to these people and I said, no, quite the reverse. These are the strongest people I have ever met. If I were to have to choose people to be on my side to take a stand, I would choose former hostages and political prisoners. To survive such an ordeal makes a person realistic about themselves and able to withstand many of the normal shocks that serve to shake most of us. These survivors are just like us; that is why their stories are so uplifting. They are not a special brand of specially trained people. I was asked were these special people. I asked

Bukovsky what he thought. He said 'no': all kinds of people survive solitary confinement. We may only know the few that came to write about it, but there were many who could have written accounts and for whom survival was also their experience. What their accounts tell me is that when stripped of all the modern cultural baggage we are all persons like this; that we are all too human and much the better for it.

Chapter conclusions

I want to hold some of the thought patterns from this part as we start another line of composition in Part II to run alongside this in Part I. Part I is about life and living and what it is to *be* conscious. In Chapter 1 we asked questions about continuity, what it would be for us to travel using a teleporter and whether or not the replica on Mars would be us. We need to think about continuity because I think we take it for granted that life is continuous, that it starts from birth (or conception), is continuous from there on until we die. By treating our lives as single separate continuous streams, we are faced with the question of what happens when we die (or are teleported). Does the continuity of us simply end? In which case, we started and had a lifespan and that's that. We could be egos or bundles, social beings, all three, none of the above, or something else. If we continue after we die, it might also be natural to think we *entered* at birth and were in existence before this. If we continue, how would this be for us? So much of this life of ours is based on our situation. It is the social world that makes us. It is the world about us that gifts us ourselves such that we would be much impoverished without it. What would the continuity of life after death be like without all that we have come to accept as part and parcel of our life and living?

The thought experiment tends to make us assume that as long as we are intact then all will be well at our destination. From a social standpoint this is unsustainable in so many ways.

If the world at your destination is unlike that at your departure, your life and living may not be sustainable. It may be too hot or without an oxygen-rich atmosphere. It might be that all of the flora and fauna is inedible. Oh, and worst and most vital of all even if you survive the local climatic conditions, you're alone. Even if you survive the new ecology, you lack the social climate of other people. You might endure this, but you would have to transform yourself to do so and would no longer be the person that entered the teleporter cubicle and pushed the button.

CONCLUSIONS FOR PART I

So, what does the discussion in Part I say about persons, senses of self and identities? We are made from interactions we have with others, the ties and bonds we have with others; the networks; the settings and situations we share with others; and the language communities and communities of all kinds, such as my university. What these features have in common is that they are all social in character. The social character of us is to do with the ways we as persons are set in the world about us, the period in which we find ourselves, the place where we are located, the community or people to which we are joined and by whom we are accompanied. We are made of others such that from a social psychology standpoint it makes no sense to talk about persons as individuals in isolation. For a person to be established, social interaction is a necessary condition. 'It's impossible to have a personality immune from human contact.'[1] We are persons brought about socially by the action of people already persons. We are made persons in this place, during this period, by persons already situated in the world about us. They make us like them. They turn us into one of them. Only a social explanation will get at this. No amount of other kinds of explanation could ever explain our social character.

We need to be willing to entertain alternative worldviews. I have held a belief in various kinds of forces and presences. I have also believed in none. I believe that becoming a person fashions for us a very definite presence that acts and has an impact, but one that is social in origin, can be explained by social factors and is a social kind of being. Whether anything fashioned in this way survives the death of the physical body, I do not claim to know. I believe our continuance is in other people, but I'll come back to this later.

So, is the teleporter ultra-fast travel or dying or something else? What is at stake here are the basic beliefs we hold about who we are and what makes us human. What are persons made of? Are we simply the material facts of our existence? Will all our explanations be of the physical kind? It may be so, but if it is, this will be the kind of physical material world that incorporates features not usually thought of this way. The physical will have become stranger than it is normally made out to be. Nonetheless, it is persons that think, remember and imagine. It is persons that are conceptual and psychological in kind.[2]

Would anything with a body and brain like yours also be as you are? Would they be a person? Would you say they had a mind? Would they be likely to have a sense of self and identity? What would it mean to be able to scan and copy the information that is you or me? Would scanning and copying the brain be sufficient? Would copying brain function or all the brain networks be sufficient? Would copying memory be sufficient? In fiction, there's no need to go into details about how someone is teleported. We go along with the idea that the person appears at the new destination unharmed and entire.

There need be no 'as it is' because the world for us is brought into being by us in acts of consciousness. Similarly, there is no way it really was in the past, not even in our past, because our past is only the way it is because we stand towards it and address it as we do. How could such standpoints be reduced to something in any particular brain? It is likely that most of the features of psychological life are brought about as a result of people in interaction rather than brains in isolation.

Being a person is more than the sum of any individual's parts. History cannot be so easily replicated. A memory of an event, as discussed earlier, is partial, selective and from a first-person point of view. Experience is always shared experience given how we are minded. Being a person is being a part of society, social groups, historical moments, 'place-time'. How could these be scanned and replicated? Robotic engineering would work in the end, I assume, on the basis that robots could learn from their environments, including the idea that they could learn from human and manufactured environments in which sensory information is necessary but not sufficient for learning. Are we going to arrive at the conclusion that the only way to get consciousness like ours is to build something that can do what we do? Isn't that what engineering is *in principle*? This doesn't make the engineered product identical; rather, it is sufficiently similar that it can stand in and perform the same function. The visual world I see is not brought about in the same way that a camera's is, but the camera can stand in for my eyes when, as an example, I want to observe something out in space. The camera can stand in for a feature of my visual system even though it emulates rather than replicates it. When we take a photograph of a view from the point at which we stand the image seldom captures what we thought we saw. Why not? The scene only appears to us as it does because of the patterns of looking we have made. We actively compose and frame the world such that we enhance some features – those that interest us – and diminish others. It is only *because* we actively look in certain habitual ways that the outside world seems to us to be as it is.[3] The idea of an 'outside world' is another seeing habit and convention, much like seeing positive rather than negative shapes. We cannot see the whole scene because there isn't a scene 'out there' to be captured and framed. The image cannot stand in for what we thought we saw because there is no such thing as an image independent of our interpretation of it. Only a person can 'read' the image and turn it into a 'scene'. We do not so much view the world but see *with* a worldview.[4]

Ernst Gombrich described fellow art historian Kenneth Clark 'stalking' an illusion concerning how the effect of a painting was brought about:

> Looking at a great Velázquez, he wanted to observe what went on when the brush strokes and dabs of pigment on the canvas transformed themselves into a vision of transfigured reality as he stepped back. But try as he might, stepping backward and forward, he could never hold both visions at the same time, and therefore the answer to his problem of how it was done always seemed to elude him.[5]

Of course, it is not really about the canvas; it's about the person looking at it; it's about what the person is looking at the painting *with*. What a person sees depends as much on the viewer as it does on the viewed. In social theory terms, it's the worldview a person brings to the canvas.[6]

In Part II we will examine what it is *to have* conscious experience: the sense of having a 'point of view'; the feeling that we have location in *this* body; and the feeling that we *own* the experience we have; that it is *our* experience. I will introduce the theme of *Cubism* and the idea of what I came to call a *Cubist Psychology*.[7]

Part II

To have consciousness

INTRODUCTION

In Part II, we will ask: 'How is it for you?' We will unravel what is meant by the phrase 'subjective conscious experience' and address why subjectivity is important to us as persons. I will set out a *Cubist Psychology* standpoint on human experience. Experience is always 'shared human experience' that is only private when we do not reveal how it is for us. Any explanation of consciousness that leaves out the way things feel to us must fail to fairly address the subject. It is only by asking about 'how it is' to be a person that we can examine assumptions we may have made about our lives. Conventionally, there is a sense that we are completely separate from others, that we have our own personal private life and an essential self that lies at the very core of our being. I think we need to pull apart the familiar and everyday to get some idea of 'what it is like' to be us. As in Part I I will offer a social psychology standpoint, plus an added 'psychology and the arts' treatment in Chapter 5; both of these are written for you to try out *as if they were yours* or as a resistance against which to test out your standpoint.

Part II differs from Part I in the way that consciousness is tackled. In Part I, we took the verb 'to be' as the main focus: in Part II, we will take the verb 'to have'. One of the commonsensical and commonplace ideas we have is the idea that we all 'have experience'. We do something with someone else, such as go to see a film, and then ask them afterwards: 'How was it for you?'

Why? Because we don't *have* their point of view and the only way to find out anything about it is to ask them. Their report will help, but it won't stand in for 'how it was' for them. We know that the report isn't the experience itself from the standpoint of the person having it – it's another one of their productions – but it may be all we have available to us. When the phrase 'how it is' (or Nagel's 'what it is like'[1]) or the word 'experience' is used in this part of the book, it stands in for the longer expression 'subjective conscious experience' and refers to how it is for us to live through and witness this life of ours. Having said earlier in this book that I do not wish to define terms, I will need to distinguish between some terms that lead to misconceptions. As these terms come up, I will say how I'm using them.

How we treat experience

There is the sense in which we feel we *own* the experience we have and that this sense of ownership extends to our point of view, our place or position, our sense of being located or situated, the sense of self; that what I have is *my* experience, that this point of view is *mine*; that I have *my* sense of self, that this is *my* life that I am leading. I don't know how ownership is bound up in this, or whether this sense of 'to have' is implied in all languages; but however these two ideas are related, it is the connection between them that is important. There cannot be two separate things going on. There isn't 'me' and 'my experience', there is only '*experiencing*'.

Experience may be treated in different ways. I may treat it as if it were happening to someone else and create the virtual standpoint that makes it seem as if I am witnessing experience from an outsider's point of view. I may treat experience as if I had privileged access – a backstage pass – to my own experience. This may make it seem as if the experience, or at least some part of it, is unavailable to others; that it is private and personal to me and available only to my introspection. But this mistakes conceptual treatment for facts of the matter about a supposed interior life. In the arts, similar experiences may be had in a virtual sense through a gifted writer's portrayal of what we think of as the inner experience of a character (such as the anguish of Raskolnikov in Dostoevsky's *Crime and Punishment*).

My experience is not 'in my head' so it makes no sense for me to look for it there. If I were to look for my experience introspectively, with what would I do the looking?[2] In psychological terms, the way we turn this way and that – including turning inwards – should be interpreted as a standpoint. We could see this turning towards as a way in which we treat ourselves and our lives, a convention that's useful when it comes to describing how it is for us. But it's not a conceptual map of an actual inner territory. There isn't actually an inner world in which to carry out our inner lives; although there is such a virtual world, as evident in accounts of captivity. The virtual world imagined by captives in solitary confinement offers us a way of speaking about how it is to be minded, but it would be a mistake to take the manner of speaking literally. Nonetheless, there are consequences of our imaginings and some of these may, literally, have an impact in the world about us. Turning the tables on guards is one such example.[3]

We can have the same experience but not the same standpoint towards it. If you and I go on a protest march together, we both share the experience of the march. But you may be delighted to be taking part in a protest for the first time, whereas I may be feeling cold and tired and wanting a coffee. Others can see our marching, but they cannot see the different standpoints we have on our shared human experience.

In English, experience can be either a noun or a verb and it is this that conveys the two ideas. First, the idea of *having experience*; this implies that the person has a standpoint, a situation from which they witness with their point of view. Second, the idea of *experiencing*; this implies living through, feeling or undergoing something. Both of these ideas together suggest that whatever is experienced is necessarily first-person. Nonetheless, I don't think that there is an actual separation between 'me' and 'my experience'. There is only one thing going on and that is how it is *for* me to have an experience *from* my point of view. I think the idea of 'having' comes about from the particular subjective point of view that a person has. Experience is always *from* a location. Without a standpoint – a turning towards something – we would not consciously experience anything.

Subjective conscious experience

When we ask someone what an experience was like or how the experience was for them it is because we cannot know how it is for someone other than ourselves. We expect a reply that talks of how the experience seemed to them, how they felt, how it appeared to be from their point of view. We are asking about something quite intimate, personal and subjective and we are asking about it because although we may have an inkling of how they might be feeling, we do not know. We understand that a first-hand experience can only be had by the person *with* the first-hand experience. We know that what we get second-hand by way of inkling is not the same thing.

We can read someone's first-hand report of their experience but that does not mean we now *have* that experience ourselves, although we may at least be more knowing about it. We can turn over their experience in our imagination and see what that experience might feel like from our first-hand point of view. We can watch a film that puts us in the position of the hero or protagonist, where the camera lets us see what we would see were we to be in that position ourselves. The camera stands in for the subjective point of view and we may learn to take that subjective point of view from watching such films.

As I will be drawing on the genre of captivity throughout, I will use an example from the accounts of captivity given by former captives.

The first time a political prisoner is locked up they are likely to feel disoriented. Experienced prisoners recognise the signs in new prisoners and are often able to mitigate the worst aspects of the experience by helping them make the adjustments needed.[4] 'Sensory deprivation' researchers looked at what happened to people when placed underground in bare rooms and with a reduced sensory stimulation. They concluded that the situation caused disorientation in participants and that this was a reliable finding of what it was like for a person to be so confined.

But then along came a Turkish student to confound the research conclusions. He did not experience disorientation. He fared so well that he asked to carry on. Eventually, he told researchers what he was doing.

> He had used his confinement time in a very meaningful way by practising what he was sure was going to happen to him later in life. He was from Turkey and was in the United States studying politics. He was convinced that when he returned to Turkey he would get into difficulties over political matters and probably end up a political prisoner in solitary confinement at some time in his life. Thus he was practising an adjustment to this in Sensory Deprivation. I think he was enthusiastic about Sensory Deprivation because he was relieved to find that he could easily endure such a test.[5]

Up to that time, many researchers believed that it was the extreme situation that caused a person to behave as they did in response to it. They also believed that disorientation was a real property of a person's situation, of how sensory deprivation affected a person and how it was for them. Since then we have had to recognise that it is also what a person brings to their situation that makes them have the experience that they have. This makes the experience social because now it is a question of how we create the experience. An experience does not just happen to us.[6]

An experience isn't in any one person. In any event, many experiences are obviously shared because we take part in activities with others. Experiences cannot be either 'in here' or 'out there'; they are constituted by particular people in particular situations of their particular making. To understand what it is for someone to have a particular experience requires that we look for properties of people and not free-floating mental qualities that get attached to things.

Event / experience

I want to distinguish now between an 'experience' and an 'event' and say how I'm using these terms. An event can be depicted in various ways – such as spoken or written narrative, photographs or films – but what an event is 'about' for someone who experienced it cannot be simply depicted – a reader, listener or viewer must do some work. The viewer must bring something to the depiction to get at how it would be for someone to experience an event first-hand, such as being put in solitary confinement. When we talk about our experiences, these are usually couched in terms of an event.[7] It may seem simple to record events – about which there may be widespread agreement – but it isn't clear where an event ends and a person's experience begins. Memories may be based on actual events and others present may be able to testify to the accuracy of a person's recall of an event; nonetheless, there's a difference between an event recalled and what actually happened. Sometimes all those present agree on a particular interpretation and there are no dissenters present who could contest it. But this means still that the meaning of an event is negotiated. Films make a different take on what may be thought of as actual events, but those present may not recognise the version that is produced. Conventionally, we tend to agree on certain ways of seeing things. It may be that where we find the greatest level of agreement is where we need most to examine what is apparently all too familiar, unproblematic and taken as read.

Experience / experiment

Both of the terms 'experience' and 'experiment' are derived from the same word root and were at one time used almost inter-changeably.[8] They convey something of how it is to try (out) and to test (out) our life and living.

I want to use the expressions 'tried' and 'tested' to convey some of this ambiguity. We talk about trying things out and may wish to convey that we are *both* seeking to experience how it is to do something *and* testing ourselves and the situation. The Turkish student mentioned above brings both of these meanings to his participation in the sensory deprivation studies. He was 'trying out' sensory deprivation because he wanted to find out what it would be like to be put in solitary confinement. He was seeking out the experience of solitary confinement to get a feel for how it was for him to live through such a situation. He was also 'testing out' the situation in order to experiment with how well he could adjust to such a situation – to test his ability to survive such an experience. We can ourselves *be* the experiment we are testing out. Without the two meanings together we cannot make sense of what he is doing in the sensory deprivation event. Any empirical project needs to recognise both. There is an event and it does have 'facts of the matter' that describe it, but an event *for a person* always includes what a person brings to the event that makes it into their experience *of* an event, an experience that is necessarily always *about* their point of view.

If *I* am locked up, it may seem as if it is only *I* who has to deal with being in solitary confinement from *my* point of view. But a person does not exist in isolation. We are who we are because of other people. It may help me survive the experience if I can draw on myself as a vast social resource. We can be resourceful under such conditions because we know others have survived such an experience and that we can too, even if we've never read about them. When we are put into isolation, we take our social world into the cell with us. We bring all the people that make us who we are to bear on what happens to us in the cell. Paradoxically, experience of isolation highlights how we are social in kind. Our experience or 'how things seem to be' are social phenomena. I regard 'phenomenal feels' or 'qualia' – what I am calling 'experiencing'– not as uniquely personal and internal properties, but as social properties of how it is to be a person.[9] From this standpoint, conscious experiences are properties of people and not separable from them. We would need to say 'my experience' or 'their experience' because when experience is used, it makes sense to ask 'whose experience is it?'[10]

Phenomenal feels / qualia

There are some obscure terms used in writings about subjective conscious experience and I will discuss these briefly here. The intellectual problem of how things feel for us and how this is bound up in a person's unique experience is often referred to as the problem of 'qualia' or 'phenomenal feels' (these terms refer to the subjective qualities of our conscious experience). Both terms are unfortunate because they are not in common usage. 'Qualia' is the plural form; the singular is 'quale'. A phenomenal feel, or quale, includes such experience as what it is like to feel different pieces of cloth, to touch them or to run the cloth through your fingers. Qualia are often thought of as properties that objects have that are sensed, such as the feeling of cloth just mentioned, or the taste of your favourite drink, or smelling a wildflower, or seeing a sunset, or the feeling that comes from listening to certain music, and so on with our other senses. These examples tend to have something to point to, some quality of an object that is available to the senses, providing an easily pointed-to example for a particular sensory experience. We can agree on a certain experience when feeling velvet, for example, because we can find some velvet cloth and compare notes of how it felt to run it through our fingers. But to describe the feel of velvet as subjective is of a very different order from, let's say, the subjective experience of how it is to feel fear. Fear cannot be pointed to in the same way as cloth, but it clearly exists for us. Where experiences are concerned, the latter will be more useful to this book. Because fear is an example of how experience is a property of us as a person: how it is that we stand towards those, for example, who oppress us. More will be said about this in Part III. So both qualia and phenomenal feel are terms we use for our subjective conscious experience. As stated earlier, I will use mostly the term 'experience' as shorthand for 'subjective conscious experience'.

Point of view

Even if your experience of solitary confinement is similar to mine, I still do not have your experience of being in solitary confinement from *your* point of view. I cannot verify your experience as true because I cannot have your experience as my experience.

If you are my jailer or interrogator I do not want you to know how it is for me as your prisoner. I am going to keep that to myself. My experience will be private because I withhold it from you. I can keep it to myself because it is only *my* conscious experience. You cannot know how it feels for me to be a prisoner. As a guard you may expect me to be in difficulties with being imprisoned. You may expect me to be angry, depressed, but almost certainly you expect me to be suffering, to be having a hard time of it. After all, would you not suffer if you were in my shoes? If I can convince you that I am doing all right, I may turn the tables on you. You may think that things are not going as they should. I can do this because you cannot know how things are from my point of view. Paradoxically, if I were to do this even when I'm not doing all right, my turning the tables on you also switches *my* standpoint. I may come to feel that I'm doing all right having caused *you* to doubt what is happening to me. Vladimir Bukovsky described to me how this worked when I asked him about using imagination when he was imprisoned.

BUKOVSKY: But you also play with imagination in different things. For example, if you find something oppressive. And you find it unpleasant and oppressive. You always play with your imagination in order to change your own feelings. For example, if some person is threatening you, like a bad prison guard who has a nasty habit of trying to bully people and frighten them. You consciously try to find funny side in what he is doing and you react to that as if he is comical. Oddly enough it not only helps you to relieve the tension of him being aggressive, but it actually puts him off. And he stops. Because it's laughable. He suddenly realises – not being capable of looking at yourself from outside like we do – he suddenly realises a discrepancy between what he is trying to achieve and what he achieves. He sees that people start laughing at him and that you do quite conscientiously. For example, I've noticed very early, I must have been twenty-one; a way to cope with fear is to become angry . . . I just found something repulsive and angry in that person and became angry consciously. And there was no fear. So you do these things. I can imagine hundreds of combinations of these things you can do. But you do these things quite deliberately. I mean I'm sure people do it all the time in many situations.[11]

Instead of the prisoner turning inwards – and being oppressed by the guard – the idea is to turn the guard's action back upon itself. This may result in the guard turning inwards instead, reflecting perhaps on why the prisoner is not weakening as would be expected in their situation. It is this 'turning towards' action that is characteristic of how it is for us to experience anything.

In the arts (which we will discuss later in Chapter 5) it would be impossible to tell a tale in film, play or novel without characters that have standpoints; we always have a take on things and we have to make a take in order to tell a story.[12] With novels we ask: from whose standpoint is the novel written (or which ones if more than one)? Who is the central character? What approach is taken to a historical moment in order to characterise it on screen or on stage? When we start to write anything, we have to manufacture the standpoint from which the written account or story takes place. The action must be shown from a point of view. We have to put the camera somewhere. We have to turn it towards something we make out.

We adopt a 'willing suspension of disbelief' if the characterisation is sufficiently compelling.[13] We can entertain an alternative standpoint if the art form sustains a secondary reality we are willing to believe in temporarily. Conversely, it is only by suspending belief in our familiar worldview – the primary reality that we sustain – that we can entertain alternative viewpoints.

One after another and one next to another (*nacheinander* and *nebeneinander*)

I was reading James Joyce's *Ulysses* and struggling with all the allusions that I didn't get, when I stumbled across the two German words *nacheinander* and *nebeneinander*. I was struck by their use and by the notes that accompanied them.[14] *Nacheinander* means 'one after another' and *nebeneinander* means 'one next to another'. Life and living are like both of these. We may be more familiar with the 'one after another' simply because writing is the form that dominates many standpoints: one word after another in sentences;

one sentence after another in paragraphs. Painting and sculpture highlight the 'one next to another' as these media allow the viewer to see any particular feature in relation to other features at the same time. For example, we may look at a painting such as *Guernica* and see different forms next to each other all at the same time.[15] We may initially not make sense of it as a painting, but when we do, we may continue to see some of the composition as a set of relationships between forms and not as separate elements. Of course, books are like this too if we think about it. We could not follow what was said unless we read any word *with* other words, and any sentence *with* other sentences. And so on. Books require a different kind of organisation, and this does entail turning pages to find things. But painting may call for a viewer to have already seen Cubist work before in order to make sense of *Guernica*. We would need to see any particular painting *with* our painting viewing history and thus *read* this painting from a history of having *read* other paintings.

Cubism / Cubist Psychology

Now this is why I think Cubism is so important and how I believe a Cubist Psychology might give us the wherewithal to tackle complex issues.[16]

The first big idea of Cubism in modern art was that of having more than one point of view depicted on the same canvas. This was important because it made art conceptual and no longer representational. Instead of trying to 'fool the eye' with a painting that looked like it was a view through a window frame, the idea was to paint a conception of the world.[17] To paint 'how it is for the artist'. And this in turn highlighted how perspective painting was simply another convention, another way of seeing, and not a view of the world as it really was.

Cubism in painting marked the end of creating the illusion of depth on canvases. In traditional perspective painting, the viewer looking at the canvas is positioned by the painter as if they had the same viewpoint as the artist. The artist chose to set up the easel at a particular position and painted the scene or the person (or the objects) *from* that position. When we looked at the painting it was as if we were in that landscape and looking at it from a particular vantage point. We would expect that if we were to go to that vantage point we would recognise the view.[18]

In Cubist painting, the idea was to paint a canvas as if from many possible viewpoints at the same time. Cubism in painting gave the painter the freedom to move around an object and combine various views of it into a single image. For critics, this was the central feature of the Cubist style.[19] Various sources suggest Cézanne's painterly investigation of, for example, Mont Sainte-Victoire – see cover illustration of this book – was the first move in what became *Cubism*.

The analytical Cubist way of seeing does two things: first, it allows us to take many angles from one conception; second, it makes us think of more than one way of conceiving any one object.

In the first case, we simultaneously see more than one viewpoint at the same time. For example, our ways of conceiving a guitar in Picasso's Cubist painting: the multiple images of the same object, of what a guitar looks like when viewed from different angles.

In the second case, we get more than one conception of any one thing. For example, Antony Gormley's body-cast sculptures do this. They are from one object – Gormley's body – cast in many different cases. There are many different forms that the cases take because of the position of Gormley's body. Referring to his Turner Prize-winning sculpture show, *Testing a World View*, Gormley described what he was doing as a kind of 'psychological Cubism'.[20] Psychological because in Gormley's work there is evidence of many different conceptions of the one object.

If you have many planes intersecting, you get many surfaces on a single canvas, none of which is selected by an artist to *be* the viewpoint for the artist and thus the viewer; rather, all of the viewpoints are painted in an assortment on one canvas. It's like having many surfaces on one surface highlighting the canvas as just that: one composition of standpoints among many possible such compositions. We look at an object, such as a guitar, and see it as if from many points of view. We can conceive of the guitar in many ways and, with the advent of Cubism, painting moved from the art of depiction to that of conception. I'm calling for a Cubist Psychology for much the same reason. I think psychological life is conceptual (not representational) and that we therefore produce the viewpoint from which we view the world. As persons, we *are* the compositions – the Cubist manifold – producing our view of the world.

What appears to be a single standpoint is a manifold. The standpoint does not comprise a set of things *in* the individual; rather, it comprises the consequences of the set of positions that a person has taken up with others in social, cultural and historical times and places. The individual is the end of all this activity, not its creator; nonetheless, by being the end the individual can act as an agent of change by choosing the standpoint to be taken now, or from now on, or the standpoints that will no longer be taken. Not that this is as simple or easy as it sounds. It is because we are a collection of the lives of others that we can lead this, our life in a different direction. It takes only minor changes of combination, framing and activation to achieve quite different results. We decide 'what goes into the frame' and by inclusions and exclusions we derive the palette that colours our character.

We are educated in the ways of viewing. When we read a novel (or are read to as a child) we take in *how* viewpoint is put together *with* the viewpoint presented. We view films in the light of other films of a similar genre that we have seen.[21] We are practised in the art of watching a film. Films have their own language and we can pick this up just as we pick up other languages. As we do this, we also learn what the conventions mean, although much of the time this is tacit knowing and, unless studied, not something we know consciously.[22]

I am trying to do likewise with this introduction to Part II: setting out various conceptual notes that I hope you'll carry forward and bring to the rest of your reading of this book.

The story or thought experiment that we will focus on in this section deals with the problem of explaining much of the above. How is subjective conscious experience explained? Some of the conventional ways of seeing illustrated above highlight how easy it would be to fall into what is known as dualism. Dualism is the belief that there really are two things going on: that there is a separate mind that somehow lives in our head and looks out at the world that is really 'out there' rather like the artist looking out on the scene they are painting. There is an age-old philosophical debate that is related to this and it is usually called 'the mind–body problem'. I will sketch in some of this problem before discussing Nagel's question, 'What is it like to be a bat?'

The mind–body problem

The mind–body problem is one of the common ways in which discussions about consciousness begin. It is the problem of how mind (or mental processing) is related to the body (or physical processing). Of course, the assumption that we are asked to allow is that there really are two distinctly different kinds of stuff – mind stuff and body stuff. But are mind and body separate things in any meaningful way? They may seem to be different kinds of stuff, but we may be led to this conclusion from their conventional description. In any event, why do we assume mental and physical are polar opposites such that the terms are mutually exclusive? If I take an alternative standpoint and talk of our physical and psychological features, most people would see these as two characterisations of the human condition that not only exist simultaneously, but are related in a multiplicity of ways. Just because talk of distinctions may lead us to assume that there are divisions, this does not mean that there really is a dividing line between the two features.

Our psychology students may talk of psychological characteristics as determined by nature or nurture as if these were polar opposites, but none can say where nature ends and nurture begins as we would expect if there really were a divide. As students learn more they may come to recognise that explanations involve many different kinds of characteristics and these do not easily fit into dual frameworks of either this or that. So, for example, it is likely that *identity* has to do with the physical body and the genetic endowment of an individual, but it is equally obvious that identity has to do with a person's development. Human development necessarily involves not only a maturational process – our bodies mature – we grow up, but also a social process – we become persons. Our personal development depends as much on how we are brought up as on how we grow up such that upbringing will offer a social explanation for such conditions as neglect. We grow up as part of a culture such that we bear the marks of our time and place: we are twenty-first-century people characteristic of where and when we grow up. And there are very many other ways in which psychologists characterise identity.

Why would it be a problem if mind and body were made of different stuff? Most commentators would reply that dualist explanations are problematic because it is difficult to work out how two different things could ever interact with one another.[23] If a ghost goes through a wall – because it is not physical – how do we suppose that it is also capable of moving physical objects? Most would argue that dualism is solved by either identifying mind with brain and thus relating each as entirely physical or entirely mental, or by arguing that although mental and physical need not be identical, a functional analysis will show how seemingly non-physical processes are indeed physical.

I want to argue for an alternative characterisation. From my social psychology standpoint, mind is social in character and can be understood through an analysis of the mind–person–world view that I am outlining in this book. Mind is not simply the physical processing of individual brains because these could never explain the different circumstances in which I may carry out the same actions, such as signing my name.[24] The assumption that we are asked to allow is that there must be only *one* thing going on and that all explanations need therefore to be physical-type explanations. I want to contest that assumption and put forward the idea that there are always *many* things going on at the same time. So, in much the same way as we can be located many ways simultaneously – and these all contribute to our standpoint – we are persons in a polyphony of characteristic forms: social, cultural, historical and, yes, also physical. If we are to understand persons, minds and worlds, we will need, as some have already acknowledged, a multidisciplinary and interdisciplinary programme of research. We will need to acknowledge also that the different kinds of things that exist – and the distinctly different ways in which what exists for us can be characterised – need not be reducible to something more basic without losing what that distinction was meant to offer to the explanation as a whole.

I want to take Nagel's article 'What is it like to be a bat?' and turn towards a social psychological explanation for point of view and conscious experience. In the following chapters I will set out what it means to say that we have subjective conscious experience and points of view. I think these features are brought about over time and are not fully present in the infant. In so doing I will discuss the consequences of certain kinds of development. I will need to introduce a social idea of 'mind' and I will use material from interviews with former captives to help get a discussion started. Mind and what it is to be reflexively minded will be further developed in Part III. So, Chapter 4 directly deals with Thomas Nagel's question 'What is it like to be a bat?' In Chapter 5 we will examine treatments of subjective conscious experience in the arts by looking at depictions in films such as *Being John Malkovich*. Chapter 6 returns the examination of experience and point of view to the subject matter of captivity, and here we will examine *a captive mind* and how it is to *be* captive.

4   'What is it like to be a bat?' (Nagel)

I'm going to discuss Nagel's wonderful question,[1] but first I want you to try to imagine what it is like to be someone else.

'I wouldn't be me if I were you!'

What is it like to be someone else?

Ask 'What is it like to be someone else?' Think about someone you know well and report what it is you end up doing. Make notes on how you set about the question and on anything you did to try to work out how it is for them.

How did it feel to *be* them? Could you imagine it? What were the difficulties you had with the exercise, if any, and what did you do to overcome them? You may have turned the question around and asked another related question: 'What is it like to be *me*?' You may believe that you have experience and that there is something it is like to *be* you. What follows is a brief synopsis of Nagel's key points asking 'Why did Nagel choose bats?' After this there is a commentary on Nagel's article; and this, in turn, is followed by a discussion about how his question – and the question in the exercise – relates to this book. All quotations in the following commentary are from Nagel's original article.

Why did Nagel choose bats?

Nagel illustrated the connection between subjective conscious experience and point of view with a telling example: the bat. Nagel assumes that we believe that bats have experience; that there is something it is like to *be* a bat. Bats are mammals like us, so why would they not have experience as we do? They are not such a simple creature as to cause us to doubt that they have experience. But also he chose bats because they have a very different way of finding their way around called *echolocation*. They have sensory apparatus so different from us and it is this that allows Nagel to pose the problem of point of view and experience so vividly.

Bats are not blind, but, as they hunt at the end of the day and at night, they do not use their visual system very much. Echolocation means that bats use the 'clicks' they generate to bounce off objects and so find their way around and find prey in much the same way as other species, including our own, would use vision. But echolocation is not really like any sense that we have and 'there is no reason to suppose that it is subjectively like anything we can experience or imagine'.[2] This appears to create difficulties for the notion of understanding what it is like to be a bat.

As Nagel suggests, it will not help us to simply imagine that we can fly around at dusk using sound to locate insects or to try hanging upside down in caves (as bats do) in order to imagine what it might be like to be one. If *we* imagine what it's like to be a bat, we only get to see what it would be like for *us* to behave as a bat behaves. We could close our eyes and pretend to be blind. We could tap a cane and listen to the echoes the cane-tappings make, but this does not get us any closer to what it's like for the bat. It wouldn't work any better for someone blind-from-birth even though they are likely to be experienced with cane-tapping and listening to the result. However well we imagine what bats are experiencing, we would be getting at what it was like to be a bat from *our* point of view – not the same thing at all. If we leave the subjective point of view out of our explanations for conscious experience, our explanations for consciousness will be incomplete. As Nagel suggested, we will have sidestepped the problem. It would be a human take on what it's like to be a bat.

So is the problem similar to the one we have with other people such as our friends? When we try to imagine how it is for our friends to experience something, we find we are imagining what it would be like for *us* were we to be in our friend's shoes and having *that* experience. Instead of experiencing the world from their point of view, we have interposed *our* point of view on *their* situation: we are still seeing with our eyes even if what we are seeing is something that – like being colour blind – we are ordinarily unfamiliar with. We are more like another viewpoint that our friend could entertain. Thus, we are no nearer to understanding our friend's point of view. We are only learning how it might be for *us* to experience something that our friend is experiencing. What we are not doing is experiencing what it is like to *be* our friend. Nagel says:

> Insofar as I can imagine this (which is not very far) it tells me only what it would be like for *me* to behave as a bat behaves. But that is not the question. I want to know what it is like for *a bat* to be a bat ... Even if I could by gradual degrees be transformed into a bat, nothing in my present constitution enables me to imagine what the experiences of such a future stage of oneself thus metamorphosed would be like. The best evidence would come from the experience of bats, if we only knew what they were like.[3]

I want to know how it is *for* the bat to do what a bat does. But I cannot do this by adding to, subtracting from or modifying my present experience. Even if I were slowly transformed into a bat – as Nagel suggests above – nothing that I know presently helps me to imagine what the metamorphosis into being a bat would be like. Once I was transformed I would no longer have my point of view as a person and therefore I would have lost any point of reference. I would simply *be* the bat and no longer me.

We seem to have struck some early difficulties in understanding how it is for the bat to be a bat. If we cannot use the ordinary way of working things out from our own experience – or at least use our imagination based on what we know to try to conceive what the bat's experience is like – we will need to find alternative methods to understand the bat's subjective standpoint.

Even if we were to be able to converse with bats, we would still have a problem. We would still only get the bat's report of how it is for them. The same problem can exist between one person and another. The subjective experience of people born deaf and blind is not accessible to me, or mine to them. Nonetheless, we would believe that the other's experience has a subjective character like ours. Nagel turns the problem back on itself: 'We will have as much difficulty understanding our own experience properly if we approach it from another point of view as we would if we tried to understand the experience of another species without taking up *its* point of view.'[4]

And this is the crux of it: reports of our experience *would not on their own* help us understand our own experience. If we were to approach our own experience as if from an objective standpoint, we would have difficulty understanding it. Our report on our experience from an objective standpoint would be a different kind of production and not an insight into our world. Reports offer further conceptual versions of our lives and not a mirror held up to our supposed inner lives.

We may go to see the same film but have entirely different experiences of it. Although the film is a shared visual event, the experiences we have of it are not shared. We are *both* our subjective personal experience of how it is for us *and* our shared experience of our common humanity. And each contributes to each form of production. Nagel says:

It is difficult to understand what could be meant by the objective character of an experience, apart from the particular point of view from which its subject apprehends it. We could call both approaches different kinds of subjectivity. After all, what would be left of what it is like to be a bat if one removed the viewpoint of the bat?[5]

Our explanation could tell us all about bat behaviours but nothing about its experience, which is what we wanted to explain. If we removed our friend's viewpoint of the film from any description of it, we would be no longer including how watching the film was *for* our friend.

In a psychology laboratory, we may run an experiment and have people participate in it. We may record what happens to participants during the experiment. But we also need to take into account what participants bring to the laboratory – their conception of the world and of psychology, for example – and what they make of the experimental set-up; these, and other factors like these, will affect the outcome.

Nagel concludes that we need a better understanding of subjective and objective 'otherwise we cannot even pose the mind–body problem without sidestepping it'.[6]

From my viewpoint, I think that *subjective conscious experience* is (social) psychological in character and is a social *kind* and is therefore not reducible to a purely physical type of explanation. Subjective experience is an *act of consciousness*; it's about how we constitute our world and not simply a partial view on it. But I'll say more about this later.

Commentary on Nagel's article

Nagel complains of a 'general human weakness'[7] whereby explanations offered for what is currently *not* understood are couched all too often in terms of those things that *are* understood although entirely different. We may have been led to believe that a book was going to give us an understanding of consciousness only to find what we are given looks like 'awareness' instead. The switch from consciousness to awareness is similar in kind to a 'bait and switch' move. The bait is the offer of something we want to have explained; this is what draws us in. Once caught, a switch is made. We are offered an explanation of something else. There is a tendency for all of us to do what the best illusionists do: switching something we cannot work with for something with which we can work. Nagel complained of this tendency in his article. I'd agree with him. But isn't consciousness simply awareness by another name? No, I don't think so. What has gone missing is the person, the subject, someone who acts consciously in the world about us, what it's like to lead this life of ours *for* the person doing the leading. The very idea of a person with their subjective conscious experience is not explained.

The problem that Nagel suggests we would like an explanation for is 'conscious experience' but what is offered always seems to fail to explain 'subjective point of view', which is a central feature of conscious experience. A point of view must have a subject: persons have points of view. Thus conscious experience is what it feels like *for the person*, the 'how it is for the subject himself',[8] how it is *for* them. Conscious experience seems to be widespread but it is still 'difficult to say what provides evidence of it'.[9]

Testing for an absence of subjective experience is easier said than done. The history of dealing with what we now call 'locked-in syndrome' details this difficulty. When deciding whether a person has conscious experience, has locked-in syndrome, is 'minimally conscious' or is in a 'persistent vegetative state', we may use technology to help us.[10] The patient may be unable to help us with any kind of speech, gesture or movement if completely paralysed. Unlike Jean-Dominique Bauby – discussed in Part I – they may be unable to make any voluntary muscle movements. But they may be conscious, have conscious experience from a point of view and know that they know their situation. We can use certain kinds of brain activity to stand in for the normal 'yes' and 'no' when we ask the patient questions. But the brain imaging doesn't tell us that the person is conscious; it provides only a system of coded communication, the code of which is agreed person to person. It is the person that is conscious, not the brain.[11] We can establish that the 'yes' and 'no' are in meaningful response to questions by first checking them against the existing family knowledge of the patient. Those treating the patient can check for consistency of reply. What determines consciousness is context, the meaning framework into which yes and no answers are put, and not the brain-imaging scans on their own.[12] Once a communication link is established, we can ask all manner of complex questions. We can ask about their subjective experience and how it is *for them* to be a person with locked-in syndrome. Nagel's basic argument is that 'the fact that an organism has conscious experience *at all* means, basically, that there is something it is like to *be* that organism ... something it is like *for* the organism'[13] – so, something it is like *for* the patient with locked-in syndrome.

By 'something it is like' Nagel is referring to what we call the *subjective character* of experience; the way that experience is always an experience *for* someone *from* their point of view. If the feature of subjective experience is left out of an explanation, the problem of explaining conscious experience will be 'falsely posed'. Nagel goes on to say that 'every phenomenon is essentially connected with a single point of view, and it seems inevitable that an objective physical theory will abandon that point of view'.[14]

If we took the report a person gave us of 'how it was' for them, we would not assume that this was equivalent to having their experience from their point of view. We know that our own reports of our experiences are not the same as our experiences. Reports can be shared, but our first-hand experiences are necessarily ours and ours alone. There is a feeling that we are alone in our heads; that our singular standpoint cannot be had by someone else, and that we develop this along with other senses of self.[15]

When we ask the question 'What is it like?', we are not looking for what the experience resembles. Saying it is like this or that does not get us any closer to understanding what it is to have the experience the bat has. Hence, it may help to think of the question as equivalent to us asking one another 'How was it for you?' – as we have been doing already in this chapter.

Point of view

How do we acquire point of view? How do we 'get it' or come to understand that this is how it works? What makes the penny drop? How do we wise up or catch ourselves on? Does something suddenly click into place and as if by magic we have point of view? It is more likely that we go through a long developmental process that finally reaches its conclusion.[16]

Why does it matter? Because the way it seems to us may be a misconception. There may be kinds of conceptual and empirical work that could help us unravel some of the conceptions we have for the familiar. If infants are different from us – perhaps because they have a more limited use of capabilities – then we as persons are not on the scene yet. If we're not there at the beginning, we may have different things to explain. If persons are constituted – made – we need to explore how this is done and what it is we are made from. As an example, although I believe we are 'proto-persons' as infants, without a social engagement with us by those already persons, we will not simply unfold as a person on our own. The cases of feral children and those of neglected children attest to the importance of other people in getting a person started. This is further discussed in both Part III and the Conclusions.

This process of development may be like transforming into a bat in that we would not know beforehand what it would be like from the transformed point of view. Even if we were to have had some kind of conscious experience prior to developing point of view, it is doubtful that this would have enabled us to anticipate such a shift. How do feral children react? Do we have examples of older children going through this critical development period later and thus remembering something of the process or of what it was like prior to it? So how does it work? I don't know and I don't think anyone does.[17] I think further study in social developmental psychology will help to explain how point of view develops; but also that we will need to include an understanding of convention in the arts as well.

We conclude from this that we cannot get to the experience of the bat from our experience. We know this of each other too. I do not know how it is for you from your point of view. Even if you tell me what it is like from your point of view, I still do not have your point of view on what you have just said; I have mine only. As we have just said, this does not get us any closer to the under-standing of subjective experience we want to have. Nonetheless, we continue to believe each person's experience *has* such a subjective character and that there are facts about experience that are bound up *with* a particular point of view; however, this is not the same as the idea of having a private life.

For something to be private, we would need to withhold it from others, much as political prisoners do.[18] The distinction between private and public becomes very important in the circum-stances where a prisoner might not want to reveal how they are coping with their captivity. Private is not a separate world of our own making, it stems from prior social action.[19] Acting privately is a skill: the skill of doing 'in our heads' the same thing we learned how to do socially. The only difference is whether or not others know what it is we are doing. There isn't an inner world as such and no person inside to which this inner experience belongs; these are only true in a metaphorical sense. There are two different standpoints on the same act of thinking: revelation or concealment. I can say what I think or I can withhold it from you, but there isn't an extra inner experience of private thought only available to me that still remains unspoken.[20] This would highlight the same problem we discussed in relation to the ego theory of persons in Part I.

Reading books, novels in particular, helps us to understand the standpoint of others, to develop an understanding of alternative standpoints from ours, and to populate our developing minds. Points of view are had by all of us and we can shift them and take up the point of view of other people. We can be conscious of more than one thing at the same time. We are polyphonic people. It is because we can know of more than one thing at the same time that we consciously know that something, for example about our point of view, has changed. To notice something has changed we must know *both* something as being the same as it was *as well as* something having been changed at the same time. As Wittgenstein said:

> The expression of a change of aspect is the expression of a *new* perception and at the same time of the perception's being unchanged.[21]

If I can entertain an alternative viewpoint, I could know this only because I also entertain my original position. I am a free person once I can shift from one standpoint to another. When I shift, I have both old and new standpoints *at the same time*. The 'new' position may feel alien to me at first such that I may suppose that it isn't me.[22] But a new or developing viewpoint becomes ours through our use of it. We practise shifting like this as children: we may, for example, have practised how it is to be an adult as part of our play activity.[23]

We can perhaps more easily imagine two things going on at the same time in the hearing modality; for example, when listening to music. A vocal harmony is known because I can hear two notes *as* two notes as well as hearing them together as a resultant. I can shift between different points of view and entertain more than one at the same time. I can simulate what I think is your experience from your point of view and know it to be different from how I might have the experience from mine. I can hear myself as a polyphonic instrument and play versions of viewpoints. I am arguing throughout this book that the freedom to shift is more evident in the stories of captivity simply because, as Bukovsky said, 'there's nothing else to do'.[24]

We understand others often to the extent to which we can identify with their standpoint. The more different another person is, the greater the difficulty we have in understanding their standpoint; it seems to be inaccessible to us. In our own case, with our own experience, we occupy the relevant point of view. It is transparent for us unless we shift to another.

This is the crux of the mind–body problem. If facts about experience are accessible only from one point of view, then the mystery lies in how these could ever be revealed through our current methods of understanding. Some parts of enquiry in psychology may need to be closer to the arts and humanities than to the sciences. Other facts about the world are not connected with a particular point of view and so these features differ in kind from conscious experience. We can have a particular point of view about lightning, but we could still understand lightning as a feature without needing to understand a person's point of view on it. If we want to understand conscious experience, understanding the point of view connected with it is essential. Understanding lightning through the experience of someone struck by lightning would never be available to us from an objective analysis of lightning.

In an interview with Susan Greenfield for *The Psychologist*, the point is made about drugs and drug-taking:

> [W]e know how [they work] at a molecular level, but we still need the phenomenology – people telling you how they experience them.[25]

Where Greenfield uses the phrase 'we still need the *phenomenology*', I would simply say instead that 'we still need the *psychology'*. After all, Greenfield elaborates after the dash by saying *'people telling you how they experience them'*. I believe that psychology should be the study of people. Interestingly enough, the British Psychological Society website now states just this.[26] In terms of getting at knowledge of a person's experience, one of the only ways to find out about their experience is to ask them about it, to ask how they conceive their experience and what they make of it. How would we get to the side effects of prescription drugs were we not to ask people on drug trials how it was for them to take a particular drug?

If there is not an objective nature to subjective experience, then the subjective cannot be had from different points of view.[27] It would mean that experience cannot be classed with other features of the world whereby observation of physical and functional characteristics adds up to a complete understanding of that feature. In general, the standard objective view has it that the less connected with a single viewpoint, the more objective is the description of anything. But having all the objective starting points in the world will not get us any closer to the subjective point of view of another person. Experience simply does not fit with the objective view. 'The idea of moving from appearance to reality seems to make no sense here.'[28] If subjective experience is only understandable from a single point of view, any move to greater objectivity, i.e. less attachment to a particular standpoint, takes us away from the real nature of the mind–body problem.

Our psychophysical reality is about *both* our psychological life *and* our physical life (among other kinds of life). Psychological concepts, such as 'person', should not be treated as if physical concepts, such as 'body', can stand in for them without loss. The same activity on the physical body underlies many different activities associated with the psychological properties of persons. Without knowing the circumstances of the person, we could not judge *from the physical activity alone* what a person was doing and why.[29]

150

Subjectivity and a particular point of view

A person is conscious and experiences the world from a subjective point of view. In the longhand way of putting this, we say a person has 'subjective conscious experience'. It is the word 'subjective' in this phrase that we most need to unravel.

Where point of view is concerned, experience is always *from* a standpoint *for* a subject. To put it in terms of the main theme of this section, 'what it is like' is how it feels *for* the person concerned. When we talk of what we think and feel, and of what happens to us, we necessarily talk of *our* experience. Ordinarily, subjective experience simply is what we think and feel and what happens to us as people. So, subjective experience is a person's experience; it is their life and times. This is likely to be more obvious if you have experienced hard times.

In everyday use, the word 'subjective' means many things. Three related meanings will be discussed here as these seem to me to be helpful where acts of consciousness are concerned. It is these three meanings *as a set* that I will use from here on when using the term 'subjective'. The set of three meanings hang on the term 'partial' and the many ways this can be understood.

First, subjective refers to a *particular* point of view. What makes it subjective is the particular person: it is *my* subjective experience, for example.[30] It is *partial* because my part is one particular part among many parts played out.

[handwritten margin note: Partial / impartial]

Second, subjective refers to a *partisan* position. What makes it subjective is the position the person takes. We may have a stake in something or an interest that makes us subjective, that gives us preferences, makes us biased or leads us to make certain interpretations rather than others. It is partial because being partial *to* something *is* to have a preference.

Third, subjective refers to a *partial* or incomplete viewpoint. It is partial because it is incomplete.

Acts of Consciousness is an example of these three meanings:

- This book is written from a *particular* point of view: mine. It is a *partial* understanding of consciousness because this is one book among many books offering viewpoints on consciousness.
- This book is written from a *partisan* position: a social psychology standpoint with an interest in the arts – what I have called a *Cubist Psychology*. The interpretations I make are in keeping with these interests and preferences.
- This book is *partial* because it does not offer a complete view of consciousness. It is *partial* because it is a personal selection of matters broadly covered in the field of 'consciousness studies', but does not offer a comprehensive survey of that field.[31]

Importantly, only persons have standpoints and therefore subjectivity is an inescapable feature of what it is like to be a person.

A subjective standpoint always affords us only part of the picture. We have a partial or subjective idea of what is going on because we are only part of the action and can only see part of what takes place – the part available to us. A camera may record what takes place: a person reports their part in the action and the parts of action that were salient *for* them.[32] Nonetheless, our reporting need not be biased: we may report actions that are not in our interest to report. We may faithfully report what we recall. We may not withhold anything from our report. This does not make us *impartial*.

When we think of someone being impartial, we think of impartiality as a value, something a person, such as a judge, may strive to be. When we talk of 'objectivity' in an everyday sense, this *striving to be impartial* is what we mean. We hope that a judge will put their particular, personal, partisan views on one side.

We hope they will try to see the whole picture and not just a version put forward by witnesses and lawyers. But we know that this, at best, is an attempt only and that no particular person could ever be completely objective. So, objectivity is a value and the person holds subjective positions too.

An attempt to be impartial is what is meant by being objective; nonetheless, this means that however impartial we may be, we will always also be partial. We can be both impartial and partial because these are different positions we hold and not mutually exclusive frames of mind. We can see *both* alternative explanations for evidence *and* advance a particular explanation. Understanding persons as subjective means we are all partisan in one sense: we are historical beings and therefore place-time is a factor. Place-time was discussed in Part I and refers to 'time as a person experiences it' and 'our familiarity with places'.[33] Our development, including our development as persons, takes place in the circumstances of our time and place. We are persons of our time and place such that place-time constitutes our subjectivity, our place in the world. We cannot, for example, escape a misconception about our world that is a given fact of the matter today, but may be shown to be wrong in the future. For future generations, the new conception about our world may seem just obvious to them.

When a community strives for objectivity, this can minimise the partisan element. An appeal judge may overrule another judge's decision because they recognise that the first judge's decision was partisan with respect to part of the case that was put, for example. So, subjectivity and objectivity are not opposites. They are two, of very many, subject positions a person may take up. When it comes to evidence, a person's report might not be biased; it may be simply a person's particular view on what happened. Their report may be faithful to their recollection of what happened. All points of view are particular and partial, but not all are partisan.

Ways of knowing[34]

Subjectivity and objectivity are two out of very many standpoints or stances towards evidence. What counts as an object-ive standpoint is when a person tries to put their beliefs and values to one side when interpreting an event. The person shares their work with others with different standpoints and asks for their views, although this may mean consulting a particular com-munity and thus fail to note assumptions held by that community that will limit both what counts as evidence and how evidence is interpreted. So, a standpoint comprises what a person brings to evidence and is thus always partial in the senses given above.

Where standpoints are concerned, we come to see *with* these positions rather than from them. We use point of view to imply opinion or belief or simply 'view' or 'viewpoint'. It seems that we cannot simply view the world; our view always implies a viewpoint with which we see the world. The word 'see' or 'seeing' is often used figuratively to convey the idea of 'knowing', as found in the words of a song: 'I wish you could know / What it means to be me / Then you'd see and agree / That every man should be free',[35] where 'you'd see and agree' is a shorthand for 'see what I mean' or 'come to know'. A point of view is a standpoint that we take to see *with*. And we always do this. John Berger said:

> The relation between what we see and what we know is never settled. Each evening we *see* the sun set. We *know* that the earth is turning away from it ... The way we see things is affected by what we know or what we believe.[36]

We always have a standpoint. A standpoint is brought about *both* by being physically located *and* by social experience.

We don't so much view the world, we see *with* a worldview.[37]

Our memories have standpoints: we do not remember an incident; we remember an incident *from* our point of view *with* the standpoint we had. John Dean's testimony, written about in Part I, is an example of just such an incident.[38] We shouldn't assume that there could be a view that wasn't so positioned. I think that all standpoints are fictions. As stated earlier, as persons we cannot have the simple facts of the matter, but only an interpretation from a given standpoint. And an interpretation is a kind of fiction – a reading of events and not a simple one-to-one rendering of them. As soon as we start to articulate the facts of the matter, we necessarily make an interpretation.[39] We have to put things together to make an interpretation. There will always be other compositions that could have been put together. It is a similar story with taking things apart. Unless we've put things together in the first place, there isn't a straightforward way of taking anything apart. And this is why some refer to subject matter as constructed.[40] There are always a variety of ways by which we can put our conceptual world together and still make sense of it. The Cubist painting may use a different set of conventions, but it is still possible to make out an object like a guitar.

The subjective standpoint is what constitutes our world and is not merely a point of view on it. The world about us is brought about by certain conventional ways of seeing we have learned. If we take the conventions for granted, it is as if we didn't have them. If the subjective point of view is a social phenomenon, a property of people, you will want to see the workings out for this claim. It may not be immediately apparent how social properties of people *are* subjective experience. Unless we suspend belief, we take as read that our world is as it seems to be. These issues will be addressed in Part III.

When considering subjective experience, it does not make sense to ask what my experiences are *really* like as opposed to how they appear to me. Our descriptions of how it is for us are *real*. The mistake is to think that simply because social worlds start in a different way from physical worlds, i.e. they are brought about or made by us as people, they are not real.

The historical battle that took place on a particular field is a historical event that archive evidence can show took place. But there need be no physical remnants of the battle at the site. The field itself does not attest to its history, whereas people do.

The map is not the territory.[41]

A line drawn on a map showing a national border may run along a river for part of its length. But a political boundary is not the same as a natural boundary. Crossing the river is not the same as crossing the border. Were the national boundary to be moved, the river's natural boundary would still exist.

Whatever is for thinking or saying exists for us.[42]

So unicorns exist for us but they are not of a kind that exists in physical form. Many things exist for us and there are a variety of forms that characterise existence. When we ask about what characterises existence, we need to include the psychological – our conceptual world – and so social, cultural, historical and other forms that are not covered by physical form (the world of representation or depiction) are all important in the project of understanding the human condition.

Nonetheless, properties of people are real *for us*. We recognise the character of a person as those ways of describing them that are consistent. If we are fearful *as a person*, we will act differently from the way we would act were we to be fearless. *How* we act has an impact on our lives and the lives of others – whether, as an example, we act *thoughtfully* or *thoughtlessly*.[43] How we act towards other people, other things and other situations is part and parcel of what makes us persons. Minded action may be best expressed with an adverb that qualifies the action.[44] Acting *freely* expresses how it is to act in a minded fashion.

There are objective facts about imprisonment such that it is possible to describe the physical features of a cell. But nothing in the cell's physical features will *of itself* tell us about the subjective experience of the prisoner in the cell. Guards may not know how the prisoner is experiencing how it is to be captive, particularly if the prisoner deliberately hides this.

Wider discussion of subjective conscious experience: the bigger picture

There is nothing as unique as the subjective experience had by a person, but there is also nothing as shared as our common humanity. We share what is often called the 'human condition'; this includes ideas such as a search for meaning in things. Rather than think of ourselves as essentially private and arriving at things from the inside, it makes more sense to see us as social, cultural and historical beings (among other kinds) getting their sense of who and what they are from upbringing, schooling and place-time. From this standpoint, the search for meaning is a cultural given not an essential personal discovery stemming from any individual. Your experience is only yours, yet everything about your experience is made from the common ground of all human experience. And this to me is what is meant by the human condition. We are condemned to be separated but that which separates us is also what joins us together. It's like the walls of a captive's prison cell: the walls are both what separates the captive from the lives of others and what joins the captive to them. Walls are neither inside nor outside. Nevertheless, there is a wealth of difference between being a prisoner inside and a free person outside; and this would be a difference for all of us were we free to choose between them. It would be a difference of standpoint. It would be a psychological difference that makes a difference to how it was for us either to be a captive or a free person.

Do we wish to deny the reality of subjective experience on the grounds that it is difficult to describe or understand? Nagel considers whether our inability to conceive what it is like to be a bat means that there could be facts that exist which are inaccessible to us and about which we will never consciously know. Just because we are finding it difficult to build methods to investigate conscious experience does not mean that conscious experience does not exist or we will fall for another fallacy: 'absence of evidence' does not necessarily mean 'evidence of absence'. We may simply lack the right approach or method, or worse, assume that approaches already taken – for example in the arts – are not valid as evidence.

The facts supposed in Nagel's article are facts 'that embody a particular point of view'.[45] Nagel makes clear that this is not simply an argument about privacy; rather, it is about the type of thing we call point of view. We cannot have another person's point of view, but we can hold different points of view. Our attempts to see something from someone else's point of view are essential to social life. If we were never able to adopt anything like another's point of view, we would be totally stuck with ours and have no idea about the lives of others.

Our ability to imagine 'what it is like to be in someone else's shoes' lies 'at the heart of our humanity' and what we might call our social conscience.[46] Conscience need not be a matter of individualised guilt or shame or socialisation into the moral order of a particular society; it lies at the heart of our humanity and, although codified in various institutions, precedes organised moral codes. All social groups come up with codes of conduct for living together. Acting towards one another in a spirit of fellowship is a matter of conscience that is a principle enshrined in the *Universal Declaration of Human Rights*. We'll come back to conscience in Part III and in the Conclusions.

We can hold a variety of subjective positions and it is a matter of convention or received wisdom that the most objective of these is thought to be better, but better for what? We should not privilege any particular position in relation to arguments and evidence. Often only the subjective experience will do as nothing else will stand in for it. The problem then becomes how to interpret the evidence, but this problem is apparent in all kinds of evidence derived from a variety of standpoints and discussed in a variety of communities. We need a psychology of persons.

I'm arguing *for* a particular position: that the psychological is different in kind from the physical such that no reduction to, or explanation from, the physical is necessary. Subjectivity, or how it is for us to be persons, is part of the (social) psychological character of how it is for us to be the persons we are in the world about us. Instead of taking the way things physically feel to us as being emblematic of all experience, I'm arguing that the subjective conscious experience of how it is to be a person is best described by looking at what is important to us as persons, as people. Moreover, as others have suggested, many experiences have no way it feels to have them.[47] What is important to us (or for us) has a subjective dimension because persons do. Persons are made of what is important to people. As reported in part of an earlier quotation, Ray Tallis wrote:

> Self equals what I am conscious of, which is, roughly speaking, what is or what has become important to me.[48]

I would use person rather than self but I think the point is the same. The qualitative feel is not an attribute of an object or mental state; it is a quality of what it is to be human. It feels like something to be free; there is a 'how it is' to be captive *for* the person held. We'll return to the idea of 'what's important' when we discuss phenomenal properties as properties of people. But more on this later in Part III.

None of this should be taken to suggest that the subjective experience is not real; rather, the different readings may highlight how what we experience as real is made real through the variety of ways we characterise what exists for us and how this makes us social minds. We are sometimes looking for an explanation of the unique when a social explanation would fit. We will address this again in Chapter 6 when we talk about a captive mind. It may seem paradoxical but it seems to me that the ideal example for examining social explanations is solitary confinement. When a person seems most isolated, alone and solitary is when they are most obviously social and relational in character.

Chapter conclusions

When we ask the question given in the exercise at the start of this chapter, 'What is it like to be someone else?', we may see how another's subjective experience is like our own, but also not something we can have from someone else's point of view. We don't know what another is experiencing unless they reveal it to us. Tactical deception is based on the idea that a person cannot know for sure what another is doing, unless it is obvious. Deception highlights the subjective character of experience: if we were deceived it is because we could not tell by observing external behaviour what the other was doing. Expert illusionists might be able to read the micro cues, but even they would be fooled by someone who was equally expert in the art of deception. Deception is also part of the human condition and attests to the subjective character of a person's point of view.[49] Acts of co-operation and collaboration also attest to our subjectivity: if I can work *against* you in deception, I can work *for* you in co-operation. And I may carry out this helpful co-operation in ways that are not obvious to you.

I can treat my experience as if it were someone else's and have two takes on my experience: a first-person experiencing point of view and an imagined observer with a third-person observing point of view. These are two standpoints held by the same person on the same object and we are not limited to two. This highlights a particular problem with points of view. We may share much of what constitutes our experience, but we cannot share all of it because part of what characterises our experience is intimately bound up with our point of view. We could even say that it *is* our point of view. What can be said about our experience that would not also imply point of view? This is where 'to be' transforms into 'to have'. What it is to *be* me is what it is for me to *have* my point of view. The sense of ownership, of having a point of view, is what makes it mine and what it is to be me. It is my experience that I have both lived through and reflexively witnessed.

So, Nagel is both wrong and right. I believe that he was wrong to suggest that if we removed the viewpoint of the bat we would remove the phenomena of experience. Human experience is a shared social phenomenon. But he was right that a bat's (or person's) point of view could never be covered by an objective standpoint. So, there really is subjectivity for any particular person. Experience is *both* private and subjective *and also* public. It is private because it can be concealed. It is public because all human experience is part of our common humanity and therefore shared.

Reflecting on bats takes us to the conclusion that there are facts about our world that we cannot understand but which we have to recognise are facts that exist in our world; and these shape it in some way. There are many experiences available to inhabitants of planet Earth and many of these are closed to us. We have to recognise that we do not even know where to start with this kind of fact: how could we have the point of view of the bat without being the bat and therefore unable, because no longer us, to be reflective of just that point of view. Knowing the bat's point of view would be fatal for us as humans because we would no longer have any other point of view but the bat's. We would have become a bat. We need to accept *both* that there are some things about which we do not know *and* that we may never know about some of these.

Thomas Nagel has given us a wonderful way to approach the problem of subjective experience and point of view. By asking 'What is it like to be a bat?' we can address how it is for us to be us. Subjective experience and point of view are matters often sidestepped because they do not fit standard viewpoints. Nagel, among others, said that we will only sidestep the mind–body problem if we do not fairly address the problem of subjective experience and point of view. We fail to understand our humanity if we fail to address these issues. When we ask, 'What is it like to be someone else?' we can see how acts of co-operation and collaboration hinge on our attempts to understand the standpoint of one and other, much as they do when we wish to deceive the other person.

We see how what it is to *be* me transforms into how it is *for* me to *have* point of view. The experience from this point of view is solely mine. Only *I* can know it. There is a sense of ownership that makes this *my* point of view, *my* experience and *my* mind. What is *mine* is what I have lived through and witnessed. Were we to treat our experience as if it were someone else's, we would be as unable to understand our own experience as we are unable to understand the bat's experience. Having subjective experience in solitary confinement allows the prisoner, who is the public property of those who hold them, to retain a private life that is entirely theirs and that they need never reveal – and they can use this as the wherewithal with which to survive captivity. It is the social character of who and what we are that highlights that we are not solitary. When we seem to be most isolated, we are paradoxically most social. Much of what I think of as mine is our shared humanity. The Turkish student survives the sensory deprivation chamber particularly well because he brings the wherewithal into the room with him. If a person has at any stage been part of a social world, they will take their social world into isolation with them. Torture and brutality of different kinds may destroy me personally or may weaken me such that I can no longer call on the vast resource that I embody as a person. But the accounts of captivity attest strongly to the ways in which captives draw on the world they brought into the cell with them. They are not alone because they inhabit the virtual social world we call being on one's own. Being on one's own can be true physically – you can separate me from human contact – but not psychologically. You cannot separate me from my virtual social world because this is who, what, where and when I am as a person.

We'll come back to how it is to be captive in Chapter 6, but first we'll take treatments in the arts as a way to examine our psychological conception of how it is to be a person. We'll look at the variety of ways experience and point of view are treated through the lens of different conventions used in different kinds of artworks.

5 Treatments of subjective conscious experience in the arts

We can ask how artists and writers have treated how it is for us to experience anything. The idea in this chapter is to do just that. Clearly, ideas about consciousness are nothing new and people have tried to conjure our experience in ways that can be set down on paper or put on film. As Theo Sarbin said:

> Long before there was a science of psychology, men and women created and told stories about the efforts of human beings to make sense of their problematic worlds. Novelists, dramatists, poets, essayists, and film makers – storytellers all – have continued to provide insights about human motives and action, even during the hundred years that human conduct has been examined by scientific psychology.[1]

We'll have a look at film, television, painting and the novel as treatments of subjective experience in different media.

Let's start with how I'm using the word 'treatment'. I believe that our psychological life rests on the way we treat each other. What makes this a psychology book is that all the conceptual analysis concerns how we treat each other and by this I mean how we act towards each other. Treatment is what makes a psychological life: how others act towards us and how we in turn act towards others. Treatment is used here to convey also the idea of how we consider what it is like for someone else. We think about them and may play out, *as a presentation*, how we imagine their experience would be if it were to be ours.[2] And this is how I'm using the term 'treatment'.

As an example, we can reflect back by acting towards ourselves as if we were acting towards others. But this doesn't mean there is something inside us being reflected back *to*: there's just the reflecting back as a production in its own right. We treat ourselves as if there were someone at home. I think that we need to reverse the familiar conception: it is the most recent form of us that is the *core* of us; that leads this life of ours. When we turn inwards and act towards ourselves as if from an outsider's point of view, the turning inwards is itself the action.[3] We turn towards the life we have lived so far and look backwards across it. But life is lived forwards even if it is understood backwards.[4] These actions are like bodily inclinations: we can walk towards a physical destination such as our workplace, and we can turn around and walk *back* home. Directions in living may be thought to be analogous to physical movement, but they need not be. Our life so far is the product that brings about consequences.

Looking back – much like turning inwards – is a different kind of activity from walking to work and back. Hence we should always treat remembering as a kind of fiction. We cannot know in advance which moments are significant. Indeed, we can only ascribe importance looking back. We cannot know what the turning moments in our life are at the time we live through them; it is only afterwards that certain moments acquire significance *for* us. The psychology of memory is not equivalent to running a tape backwards or pressing 'back' on a digital device. Looking back is a different kind of 'acting towards' a life from the 'acting towards' we make when we lead our lives. Memory may also relate to events yet to happen, such as when I remember the date I am due to submit this book to the publisher.

In this chapter we will take a look at some of the treatments of subjective experience and point of view made by artists and writers. Those in the arts are often radical in their conceptions of the human condition. They have found and concocted all kinds of ways to portray and characterise the human condition and such features as point of view and *what it is like* to have conscious experience. The idea in this chapter is to fairly examine consciousness in the light of certain treatments from the arts and ask the question, does this treatment help us to understand our situation and to try out and test our worldview? We share the human condition that includes what we understand from *both* the arts and culture *and* psychology. Moreover, there are more understandings than these once we also accept the importance of all the disciplines usually embraced by the three terms: arts, sciences and humanities.

The only way to know what it is like to be a bat is to *be* the bat. Nonetheless, in our attempt to understand the bat's point of view, we succeed by what the attempt tells us about who we are. And this is why reading novels is so important. The better we are at putting ourselves in someone else's shoes, the better we will understand ourselves, other minds and the world about us. We cannot know another person's point of view *from the inside* and even if we did, we'd no longer have our original point of view with which to compare the person we have now become. But we can try out an alternative standpoint from our own so that we can test how it is to see things differently, just for a while. In the arts, we are always being asked to entertain an alternative standpoint. Writers write in the style of other writers or in a different genre. Musicians play things in a different musical style. Painters paint in the style of other painters. Artists may allude to other works in their own work and offer by so doing another standpoint on their own work, in their own work. Remakes of earlier work refashion a film and may take a different standpoint on the main action or move the action to a different place or period. Directors may offer a different take of a film: there are director's cuts. When we watch a film, we are invited to take a standpoint different from our own. We can treat the alternative standpoint *as if it were our* own. This idea is played out in the film *Being John Malkovich*, which has the tagline: 'Ever wanted to be someone else? Now you can.'[5]

Film

Warning! Plot spoilers. The following commentaries give away significant plot points and storylines for the films *Being John Malkovich*, *Blade Runner*, *The Return of Martin Guerre*, and *The Diving Bell and the Butterfly*.

Being John Malkovich

In *Being John Malkovich*,[6] a means to be someone else is treated as if this were possible. Much of the film is played out for humour, and very enjoyable it is, but I want to examine the way the film plays with conventions. I will look at *both* cinematic depictions of subjectivity, conscious experience, point of view and the like *as well as* how conscious experience appears to us to be.

The male lead character finds a portal through which it is possible to experience the world from John Malkovich's point of view. John Malkovich is a well-known actor, so another layer of absurdity is added. What we see is John Malkovich *playing* John Malkovich. After all, it is a film and the actor John Malkovich has to *act out* being John Malkovich when the director calls 'action'. The portal leads into Malkovich's head such that we get to see what it is like to see and be seen in the world from the standpoint of being inside John Malkovich's head. Only it doesn't.

Ostensibly, we are supposed to be John Malkovich in such a way that his body becomes this body of mine. On film, we are a fly on the wall in John Malkovich's head. It appears as if we *share* his view of the world and that we have privileged access to him, but what we are actually shown is an outsider's perspective on what it is like to be John Malkovich. The viewpoint may be from behind the eyes (as if from some kind of ego point of view), but it is not Malkovich's own point of view; rather, it is the visitor's point of view of Malkovich's life. The visitor is like an alter ego or double somehow inhabiting Malkovich, but as long as this alter ego keeps very quiet, Malkovich himself suspects nothing.[7] The principal way we get how it is to be Malkovich is through the way others treat him (and we are there also to experience how it is, for example, to be a famous actor).

In terms of film, if someone were to become John Malkovich, a viewer would see no difference between John Malkovich and John Malkovich playing himself. We would *be* him and view the world from his point of view and thus not have a viewpoint *of* his experience. The mask over the camera lens is a visual device for telling us when it is someone else being Malkovich; otherwise we wouldn't be able to tell. What we are given is more akin to the conventional view of being occupied by an alien presence. All these characterisations have in common the idea of what it might be like to have more than one ego in one's head, as found in conventional beliefs about multiple personality disorder.[8]

This visual device in John Malkovich plays to myths about multiple personality, where the voices in a person's head are thought to be different, distinct identities all living in the same head.[9] The idea of the ego as being like someone sitting in a movie theatre was called the 'Cartesian Theatre'.[10] It seems as if inside our heads there is a viewing room where what comes from our senses, and principally from our eyes, is shown to us. It's much like a movie theatre for one. We have art supposedly imitating life.

Art may imitate life that in turn might imitate art. Watching a film is like acting in the world. We view the world through two holes in our mask-like face as if looking at a screen. We are inside, in the dark, looking out at the 'big screen' that we call the 'outside world'. We are the single ego in the viewing room watching life outside go on through twin holes in our face. What if someone else could sit in our movie theatre and see what we see?[11] Some writers speak of their muse, the 'uninvited guest': the voice in their head that 'tells' them the story, or the voices that 'play out' the scene in their head. Is life and how it is characterised imitating art? Have we adopted what we have learned from art? Having adopted it over time, have we subsequently come to feel that this is how it seems to us to be? How often does someone doubt the familiar world of how it seems? The idea of a beginning, a middle and an end is a convention in storytelling, such that we consider the story of our life, our auto-biography, as telling it just as it is rather than through the lens of a narrative device. So, perhaps, has experiencing the world come to seem to be just what is shown on film: the looking out on the world from behind our eyes as if we are a viewer in some kind of movie theatre where the screen is a window to the world outside our heads and we are sitting in the darkness of our heads watching the show.

What we have is not a different participation but a more intimate form of observation: the viewpoint may be from inside the observed person's head, but we are no closer to actually being John Malkovich. We are a fly on Malkovich's inner wall allowing us access to his life, but still we do not have privileged access to Malkovich's own point of view. The tagline used for the film was the question, 'Ever wanted to be someone else? Now you can', but this is not really what's on offer. To further the problem, we have Malkovich being aware of another presence in his head, including the female lead character, which adds a sexual dimension. But we do not get nor could we get to be John Malkovich because that would simply be the same as John Malkovich being John Malkovich; this would not make for a great film. If we had Malkovich's point of view we would indeed be Malkovich but this would entail no longer being you. The film would be identical to a film about John Malkovich being John Malkovich.

What is it like to be *John Malkovich*? What is it like to be *you*? Can we play out conversations in our heads? Can we listen *as if* to someone else's point of view? Can we imagine what it's like to be someone else, or to have someone else's point of view? We cannot *literally* do this, but *nor can the person who has the point of view.*

169

Cinema resorts to the narrator and the idea of an interior life when something cannot be shown; for example, when we *must know* what is inside the head of one of the characters in order to reveal something crucial about the character or the plot. How does cinema do this? We *hear* the character's voice *as if* we were listening to the thoughts inside the character's head. Here's the point though: there's no sound when you're thinking. Your thinking isn't spoken in your head; it only *seems* like this. What would be the point of actual voices in your own head? What would be doing the listening? And we would be back to the familiar problem of how having a separate entity called 'you' makes for further problems that would need explaining and fails to resolve the issues under discussion. What's worse, we imagine that we are also some kind of fly on the wall for any experience; that we see 'out' through two holes in the face; that we have an inner voice in our head that is us. How conventional!

Film conventions

All ways of showing are conventions. New ideas break old conventions and may become the norm in the next wave of filmmaking and thus become conventions. Filmmakers expose the conventional view when trying to solve how to show what being someone else might be like. In so doing, they highlight implicit assumptions we make about what it is to be ourselves. Do you believe that you see 'out' from inside your head and simply look out upon the external world? Is it as if you were a camera placed behind a mask with two holes cut out for eyes to look out through? We may suspend disbelief and feel part of the action, but the way films treat problems of point of view and experience highlights the taken-for-granted ideas we have about experience, point of view, feeling and being. We are the camera turned towards the action and as such it seems we establish the convention: inner viewpoint turned towards outer view.

Voiceover in films may help us decode what is happening, but the voiceover need not represent what it is like to think or reflect. Whatever internal commentary we have – and this in itself may be like a kind of journalistic reportage – unless what we are voicing in our heads is well rehearsed it will not be the coherent one-sentence-after-another, grammatical reflections offered in many film voiceovers. If you hear an interview and then view a transcript, it becomes obvious how speech is 'cleaned up' in the process of setting it down. We do not ordinarily think or speak in prose sentences. We change tack, make false starts, repeat ourselves, hesitate, go one way then another then back again, and repeat ourselves. Sometimes researchers transcribing interviews try to capture the particular linguistic tics by using additional symbols to set down the way words are emphasised, drawn out or cut off and to show the pauses and silences that occur.

Conventionally, what is seen is what is 'out there' and does not obviously include what we bring to viewing any film. We watch films *with* what we bring from our film-watching history. We could never simply 'look' at a film.[12]

The classic 'shot reverse-shot' in film highlights the making of a standpoint. There is a convention in film that a conversation is shot in two parts; this might be because only one camera is available, but also from a desire to use close-ups of the stars' faces. Also, it requires only one actor be on set at any one time to shoot their half of the exchange. It has become the conventional way to shoot such a scene. A shot is set up with the camera facing one actor and filming their dialogue, and then the camera is turned to face the other way to film the other actor. Later the two clips are edited together so that we seem to shift from one actor to the other much as we might were we to be a third party sitting at a table with the actors and switching our attention to each speaker in turn as they speak. Often one character is shown to the right side of the screen and the other to the left, which further serves to enhance the sense of turning from one to the other. Sometimes there is a certain amount of overlapping, so that we continue to see one actor when the other has already started to speak. We can hear what is being said, but we also now get an idea of how the other actor is responding to what is being said to them. If the two are seated at the same table, it is as if we are sitting just behind them and looking over their shoulder. Intriguingly, we may be thrown if the director places the camera on a different side of the table for each actor because this would break a convention. We would become conscious of the camera work because it was unconventional.[13]

In films, we may get to know more about the hero or protagonist when the director gives us access to his thoughts by using a voiceover or by showing us what they are like in a back story that reveals features of their character that we do not have for other characters. In the film *Blade Runner*, the use of a voiceover, particularly in the 1982 version, highlights the problem of our subjective experience and how we portray what goes on in our heads. Filmmakers have had to come up with something and the voiceover has become the convention. Ridley Scott didn't want the voiceover and in his director's cut version of 1992, he removed it. Many directors want to retain the principle of 'show, not tell' and seek a visual solution to portraying subjective experience. Many would like to leave room for the audience to try to work out what's going on rather than always make it explicit. Some films, for example *The Road*, would be impossible to follow without a voiceover (or without having first read the book).[14] We may have mistaken this convention for how it is for us. We may assume that the inner voice is like this. The inner voice may have become more like this because this is what we think is normal and not mad.

We may identify with a central character simply because we know more about them than about other characters and can relate to them, have sympathy for them, care about what happens to them. But the problem is that this may simply make us biased towards other characters that are not given such a detailed back story. We may see the action of the film through the point of view of the hero, for example. Although if we have this standpoint, we usually come to see how the standpoint does not give us the external world, rather it gives the hero's viewpoint of what the external world is like. So we have a partial and partisan view that gives us an unreliable view of the world. When directors give back stories to many characters, we may shift our allegiances as we sympathise with characters that seemed nasty or unpleasant. We may come to regard them differently from first blush. If we were to see ourselves as polyphonic, as shown in many of the best dramas, we might be more realistic about who and what we are.[15] We might see ourselves as many voiced and peopled.

The Wire – discussed later in this chapter – was unusual in television because we got to see events *from* the point of view of numerous characters. This is not a view we have of real life. We have a partial view. We see parts of the picture and may be partisan in our viewing such that we favour some parts of the scene over others. Some parts of what's going on we simply do not pick up on. Our take on what's going on is not what's given in the footage. In films and television programmes, normally we are given a partial view too.

We watch films and we may adopt the 'willing suspension of disbelief', as mentioned earlier.[16] What is this? We know the film is fiction, scripted, made up, acted out and that it is not real. If we were to stick to this viewpoint we would remain detached from the story and not be moved by it. If it were a scary movie, we would not be scared because the special effects might still be seen as special effects. But most filmgoers, much as children when listening to stories, are willing to enter into a different reality and, provided it is internally coherent, we will go along with all sorts of strange ideas. We let go of our normal view of reality and go along with the film as if it were real. Why's this important? Because for all intents and purposes we cannot know whether those we are with – such as people at work – are genuine, deceitful, manipulative, helpful, or pretending, among other things.

Point of view

We treat each other as having a unique and separate point of view. We are different bodies and from this we accept that each person has a physical basis for having a different set of experiences from us. Does this amount to a point of view like a physical location? Can we have another's point of view? Can we imagine it? What does it mean to say that we imagine someone else's point of view? We use analogies here. We talk about walking in someone else's shoes as a way of putting ourselves in their position. Their shoes have been where they have been and have been moulded by the way they walk. To be in their shoes is like having their feet, sharing the same standing point, the same place, making the same footprint on the world like the lines of footprints on a beach or a trail, making the same journey. These are basic marks showing that a person has passed this way. These are the imprints of our deliberate steps. To sweep away these marks is to make it as if we were never there. Footprints are thus an analogy for the impact a person has on their world. To wear another's shoes is to understand the impact they make and what would be lost were that impact not to be felt.

I think it is possible to change one's point of view and fashion a new set of shoes. We need to walk in them a while and they will feel like someone else's, but we can wear in a new perspective to the point where it becomes our own. Of course, our old point of view will now feel as alien to us as the one we've now worn in. I think this is how it is for us and hence there's a certain fatality about life and living: having lived a certain way, we have moulded our shoes a certain way. Much as the way we walk becomes synonymous with us – we can recognise others from this feature alone, particularly useful at a distance or when we see someone walking away from us – our point of view will also become a definite holding pattern.

The Return of Martin Guerre

In the film *The Return of Martin Guerre*,[17] Gérard Depardieu's character says he is Martin Guerre. He seems to know Guerre's family and friends; they in turn, although uncertain at first, take him to be the person he says he is. As mentioned earlier, even his wife seems to accept him, but it seems she may have done so because her real husband was cruel and the new one is not. In the film almost everyone takes Gérard Depardieu to be Martin Guerre. There are exceptions, but these are plotted ambiguously so that they could have ulterior motives for showing him to be an impostor.

For Gérard Depardieu, he seems to know everything about Martin Guerre's life and society. We are who we are supposed to be: we are the person we are treated to be. It is because others think of me as who I am that I am who I think myself to be. In a very real sense one's individual point of view is granted scope only through the points of view of others *on* us. We are ourselves because of the impact we have had on other people's lives (and they on us). When we are not, it will be because we cannot *ourselves* have a direct impact on another's life (even if those who knew us still can). Without a direct impact from our point of view, we are no more.

Gérard Depardieu walks in Martin Guerre's shoes, works on Martin Guerre's land, and sleeps with Martin Guerre's wife, therefore he *is* Martin Guerre. There are moments when Gérard Depardieu is faced with those who knew the original so well as to doubt him. Gérard Depardieu can only do so much because of memory, although he can also explain his ignorance of things or hide his lack of wherewithal behind the effects of war; that he is only different from how he once was when they knew him because the war has intervened and made all soldiers a stranger to themselves and their own kind. There is a subplot that shows he was in reality a poor man from a neighbouring village. His own village is far enough away not to be known by locals – although some passing through recognise him – but also near enough for him to know the local landscape.

The impostor knows he is not the original. He does not know these local people. He does not love Guerre's wife. He shares no previous experience with them. It seems unlikely that someone could do this, but connivances of similar deception have been carried off convincingly enough for the closest of close partners and friends not to know or guess that something is up. Where someone plays out the roles of two people, there will always be questions over which is the original and real and which the imitation or impostor. Where questions of character are concerned, 'one man in his time plays many parts'.[18] It is because others think of him as Martin Guerre as they do that he exists as such a person. What then does this mean that a person is?

If we consider point of view to be made from who and what a person is, this would include both memory and the real experiences of life events that are the bases of memories. To be a person is to have both the memory and the real experience. But what if our memories were unreliable or in some way false?

Blade Runner

In *Blade Runner*,[19] the idea is that in a future world – 2019 as conceived from about 1979 – android replicants would be doing some human jobs and they would have been so well built as to be indistinguishable from people in the film. The new Nexus 6 is designed to artificially copy humans in every way except emotions. They are known as *replicants*. As emotions are thought to create a risk, the design has a failsafe: the *replicants* have a four-year lifespan. The *replicants* in the film have managed to hijack a ship and return to Earth from an off-world colony. So, what do they want? They want extra life. A Blade Runner is a futuristic cop that tracks down and 'retires' (kills) renegade *replicants*: Deckard, played by Harrison Ford, is a former Blade Runner asked to come out of retirement to track down and kill the *replicants* that are running amok on Earth.

Deckard doubts his existence and wonders whether he is in fact a replicant. It has been suggested that the name Deckard sounds like Descartes and that this was intentional given the idea of doubting one's existence.[20] He cannot be sure that the memories he has are actually related to real experiences in his past. Has he been 'gifted' a past in some kind of technological improvement to android design. 'How can it not know what it is?' asks Deckard. And finds he cannot answer his own question for himself. The latest version of android is 'gifted' memories of a childhood to cushion them against the ravages of emotions running wild. They even have photographs as cues to their memories much as we have for ours. He acts as if remembering his own childhood. 'You're talking about memories.' We hear children singing on the sound-track. This is then repeated at least three more times during the film to indicate Deckard's memories. In one of these he is looking at a set of photographs in one of the replicant's rooms. We wonder, are they like a set he owns himself? In an alternative version, we see a dream sequence of Deckard dreaming about a unicorn. An origami unicorn is left outside his apartment door suggesting that the dream has been 'given' to him and that someone else knows this.

Blade Runner's themes have been discussed at length.[21] The question 'What does it mean to be human?' addresses one of the themes. Rachael is one of the new generation of androids on which Deckard uses the invented Voight-Kampff machine (a kind of empathy detector). Rachael asks Deckard, 'Did you ever take that test yourself?' In a further allusion to Descartes, the android character Pris says, 'I think, Sebastian, therefore I am.' Sebastian is a genetic designer who works at the Tyrell Corporation, and is the principal person responsible for the creation of the latest generation of androids. Some have said that the film's main theme is how to remain human in the face of technology.[22] At the end of the film, the last surviving replicant, Batty, shows human-like sympathy for Deckard's plight. Batty expresses an all-too human shared sense of empathy.

It is said that 'it takes a thief to catch a thief', so is this why Deckard has been despatched to 'retire' rogue replicants running amok on Earth? Is Deckard a replicant? Ridley Scott, the director, assumed Deckard was a replicant but many fans and critics were not so sure. The question is, 'How could he not know what he is?'

And this is the question for all of us. How could we not know what we are? Surely we are what we are, what we seem to be, and therefore we should know it. But do we? Do we learn our conventional part in a familiar action drama and simply play it out without examining what it is we are doing?

The Diving Bell and the Butterfly

The film *The Diving Bell and the Butterfly*[23] was remarkable for its faithfulness to the original book, given that the book was dictated by Jean-Dominique Bauby from a first-person point of view. To recap, the film is based on actual events as reported by Bauby in his book of the same name. After a massive stroke he ends up in hospital with locked-in syndrome. He learns to communicate by blinking one eye, which is the only voluntary physical movement he has. It is comparatively straightforward in a book to set out a first-person point of view. In cinema it is thought highly uncinematic to use camera and voiceover to create such a point of view. But the film is compelling because it presents us with Bauby's situation and not a director's version of how being locked-in might be shown cinematically. Having said that, the very solution itself is a convention that we believe accurately depicts how it is for Bauby writing his book, when Bauby is himself using a first-person convention to set out his own position.

In the first part of the film, we are not aware of the camera as conventional shots are used to present the life and times of Bauby going about his business as editor of a magazine. At the end of the first act, we see Bauby have a stroke. During the second act of the film the director uses the camera to present us with

Bauby's view of the world. We are allowed to hear Bauby's first-person conscious state by the use of a voiceover. We see what Bauby sees because the camera stands in for Bauby's point of view. We are Bauby and share with him the distressing experience of being locked-in. We endure this experience with him up to the point where those treating him realise that he is conscious and able to communicate via the voluntary blinking of one eye. And then our viewpoint shifts again. Act 3 of the film is carried out with the camera once again as third party, fly-on-the-fourth-wall, but not representing the point of view of any particular characters. We see Bauby as others see him.[24]

Television

The Wire

As mentioned earlier, the television series The Wire[25] allowed us to see many standpoints on events rather than the particular first-hand view of a central character, such as used in the film about Bauby. There are it seems to me many alternative polyphonic possibilities available at any given time; it is when I say or write something or carry out an action that the multiplicity is (briefly) set into a single event. We are polyphonic people and the single narrative construction is a convention we use to simplify complex events. This idea is never more clearly evidenced than in drama depicting characters' different points of view on an event. Drama that relates these different points of view highlights how lacking in anything singular a single event is!

In the television drama The Wire this is evident. We get the back stories of many characters. We see their part in the unfolding drama from their point of view in their part of the cityscape of Baltimore. We witness what institutions do to people and how they help make and break us as persons. The characters are people from a variety of institutions from organised crime, to the police, the judiciary and the press, and so we see drug addicts, drug dealers, informers, police investigators, local politicians, judges, lawyers, journalists, among many others. Because we see the world from their standpoint our view of what's going on changes as our worldview changes with the change of standpoint.[26] *The Wire* does not show reality in the conventional ways we expect a television drama to do. And this highlights the conventions in television as just that. We could call *The Wire*, and other programmes like it, 'Cubist television drama' because it has many standpoints shown on any one event.

Painting

Guernica

If we were to view Picasso's painting *Guernica*, we would see a very large canvas with various forms painted on it. We might make out some people even though they were not depicted with photographic realism. We might be able to interpret the way some of these people looked, but even though it might seem to you that those depicted were in distress, nothing in the painting would *of itself* explain the painting and / or why it was painted.

How will looking at the painting *Guernica* help us to understand consciousness? I believe that artists ask and address questions in ways that we can usefully carry over into debates elsewhere.[27] An image made by an artist can do more than one thing at the same time.[28] An image denotes or depicts, connotes or carries meaning, and may also have cultural significance.

Denote, connote and signify

First, *an image denotes or depicts something.* An image can make something known by the marks used to render it. There may appear to be simply a one-for-one correspondence where what it depicted seems just obvious to a viewer. There are heads and faces depicted in *Guernica*. The image of a face looks like a face. I recognise the image *as* a face because it corresponds with the idea of faces that I hold. With *Guernica*, Picasso used an unusual convention derived from Egyptian art: depicting a feature, such as a feature of the face, by drawing it in its most characteristic form.[29] A nose is drawn in profile and an eye from the front rendering them 'impossible' bodies. But we can still see these uncharacteristic forms as faces. When we understand the principles of Cubism, we can see *with* this convention and make sense of what's denoted.

Second, *an image is also said to connote something*. In addition to what something denotes, there is what an image means, what the image is about and what it may be meant to imply. With Guernica, we read the faces and they seem to show anguish, distress, agony, among other things. We may infer from this that the painting is about some horrific event, but we may have no idea what this is.

Third, *an image may also have a cultural significance: it may be iconic*. An image can come to stand in for something, to say something about something. Picasso's painting *Guernica* is about a historical event. It depicts the horrific carnage caused in a terrifying aerial bombing raid on a village during the Spanish Civil War. It was sent on a brief world tour during that war as a protest against what was happening in Spain and to draw public attention to it. It drew attention to what today would probably be thought of as a war crime, and helped to galvanise support for those against fascism. It had an impact. It still does.

Picasso's painting *Guernica* survives him and will most likely survive as long as there are free people who recognise why it should be seen and witnessed and why a tapestry copy that used to be on the wall outside the room in the United Nations building where the Security Council meets should not be covered over.[30]

We need to bring something to an image to make sense of its symbolism. The painting is neither 'in here' (point to your head) nor out there (point away from you). If someone smiles at you and you feel pleased, 'the feeling … is not separable from (and cannot be understood separately from) the smile of the other person'.[31] Our thoughts about *Guernica* are never really ours alone, it is a social experience that takes place in the world about us.

Picasso used physical paint, canvas, brushes and other paraphernalia; but no examination of these in isolation would ever explain *Guernica*.[32] How war is depicted – what is shown and what isn't – says much about our conception of war. The idea of war is conceptual. Descriptions of what is happening depend upon how we conceive of the war that is being described. Descriptions must be made from standpoints. Bombs dropped on a Spanish town cause physical death and destruction, but they also bring about a psychological devastation for those living through it, which may in turn come to have cultural significance.

We could get a museum catalogue or read a book about the painting and these might help us to understand something of what the artist was doing when he was putting together the painting.

Perspective painting also had to be invented and was also 'conceptual art' when first devised. It was another way of seeing or constructing the world and not simply a copy of the way things really are. It departed from other accepted creative techniques. There were, and are, different painting traditions around the world. What counts as a depiction of landscape differs markedly when seen through different painting traditions.[33] Similarly, we need to consider that psychology is about how persons are *figuratively* composed and not how they are *literally* represented.

Guernica is an artist's response to war, a person's *act of consciousness* freely made. Once the status of the painting is known – once we know what the painting is about – it has an impact in its own right. A painting may survive both the artist that produced it and those that knew the artist. It can make an impact on the lives of others that could be said to be continuous with the late artist and those that knew them.

The novel

Writing conventions

Have we learned to have a certain kind of interior life because of the way this is portrayed in books and on film? David Lodge suggested that our way of understanding the interior life could have originated with the widening availability of the novel.[34] Lodge argued that the individual as we know it today probably only came into existence since the inception of the novel; the wide availability of printed books meant that stories 'could be experienced privately, silently by discrete individuals', and added that 'The silence and privacy of the reading experience afforded by books mimicked the silent privacy of individual consciousness.'[35] We may view privacy much like the private space of the secluded room because silent reading resembles our subjective solitude. The novel with its first-person narrator came to epitomise the reader's experience, or was it the other way around? Lodge asks us to consider that we may have derived our conception of the familiar first-person voice in our head commentary from how it is to read a book silently and in solitude. Did we take this standpoint from the novel and see our own as analogous to it? Did the convention come to stand in for how things are? Over time, did we come to think that art had imitated life rather than the other way around? The upshot here is that how things seem to us to be in their most familiar, taken-as-read form might say more about our schooling in certain conventions than it says of any universal truth.

The omniscient, often unreliable, narrator in novels and the voiceover in films are examples of the way an interior life is characterised. Did we come to think, privately, like a narrator, because novelists had devised a way of telling about the inner lives of their characters? We can add a commentary track in our head or out loud as if writing a journalist's running commentary of our life and living.[36] The ways we have of telling stories are perhaps themselves ways we have come to tell ourselves *as* stories, to relate ourselves to others. And we become persons in the telling. We could say that biography and autobiography create the life we lead, its trajectory, how we recollect it, how we bundle it up to each other. Literally the story of our lives: the story *is* our life and living. We expect to lead a storied and story-able life. We assume life produces the story of our life, but could it be the other way around: that 'the autobiographical project itself may produce and determine life?'[37]

The use of points of view in novels is one example where we entertain a variety of standpoints established in the different characters. Clearly there is no actual point of view or subjectivity to inhabit; this highlights the way we can simulate or represent to ourselves alternative standpoints. If we approach our own conscious experience from another point of view, we experience problems understanding it. What makes something subjective is that it is embodied in a particular standpoint and that this cannot, by definition, be had by someone else. A point of view may be held that is much like that held by another, but it is still not theirs, it is yours.

Novels may help us to develop reflexive skills for understanding other people, and, in turn, ourselves. They allow us to read about the points of view that others may have. By so doing, they seem to help us to be minded about our life and living and leading this life of ours. We can carry a set of points of view – for example, those of the main characters in a novel – such that each, if well drawn by the writer, has a different feel for us when we read. We can take the standpoint of characters unfamiliar to us and perhaps come to better understand other people because of it. It's not an all or nothing situation where imagining what it is like to be someone else is concerned. The attempt to understand one another is what counts. Those who have read from an early age may take this for granted.

In the novel, the making of a point of view allows the reader to enter into the fiction. The writer affords the reader sufficient information to garner a point of view (or series of points of view) in order to follow the action. The greatest novelists supply only just enough and no more so that each individual reader can make up the rest and have a stake in the book. Each reading will be different and when we compare characters, it may be surprising to find how someone sees the main protagonist in ways that we have either never entertained, or that are very different from our own. Similarly in film, the director leaves room for the viewer to bring something to the feast. By analogy, the same is true for any situation where a situation is any place we can put ourselves. From this we may also not be the fullness we think we are. We only need to carry the gist of our set of standpoints as we can refashion them from a kernel of truth. We put ourselves in the picture because we are granted the scope to have a point of view of our own. In Cubism, we are granted even more scope because some of the conventions in art are shown to be such, freeing us in the process from the business of being positioned by the artwork. The artwork was always a construction; now at least the viewer had a stake in its making. The artwork is made by viewer and artist together and what is constructed now depends upon what the viewer can bring to the party. We are not and never were the passive receivers of a ready-made world that is 'out there'.

We have a problem with point of view. We assume that the narrative form that is usually used to represent it, in film for example, accurately represents what it is really like. I have to say that I don't think it does. My own thoughts are opaque to me quite often simply because they aren't in a neatly set-out narrative form like this writing. Indeed, I don't think they're set out at all. It's only when we speak or write our points of view that they get set out. There's a famous question:

How can I tell what I think until I see what I say?[38]

When we recollect our thinking, it is likely that we populate our ideas, fill out the gist of things, and organise the polyphony into an orchestrated work. It seems as if we are all there when we are required by others to parcel it up.

Subjectivity in written works: writerly[39] consciousness

Nevertheless, because there isn't actually an agent figure in your head on these grounds doesn't make the commonplace *sense of self* an illusion. In a sense, by acting as if there were an agent figure, we enact our ethical world. Arguably, our relations with others work only on the basis of treating each other as if it were so, be it fact, fiction or otherwise. As David Lodge acknowledges, 'If the self is a fiction, it may perhaps be the supreme fiction, the greatest achievement of human consciousness, the one that makes us human.'[40] He does not want to get rid of the idea of the individual as we might also lose our respect for another person, but we should be wary of believing too much in any universally agreed character that is true for all times and all places. The fact that the person is not a physical thing or a natural kind does not mean that it doesn't exist; its character is not physical, it is psychological, social, cultural and historical, and this makes it a human or social kind requiring a different form of enquiry and different forms of evidence.

Just because we can see how we might have taken the readerly experience as how to characterise thinking does not mean that thinking was acquired recently. The way we think today will say much more about today than it does about thinking itself. Thinking could never be divorced from the situation in which the thinking occurs. Thinking is always set somewhere. Novels, films and plays establish location as a way of understanding what is going on, how people are thinking and how it is for them. We seem comfortable about treating earlier periods or types of fiction as having this about them, but much less so when it comes to treating our own time and world as making us how we are. To me, this is another piece of support for the idea that we take as read our familiar world as if it were how things really are.

A scientist takes the standpoint 'I don't know' in relation to experiment, evidence and experience. It is only by virtue of agreement via peer review in a scientific community of which the scientist is part that they would state a particular view. But this is my point: it is the principles of the community that determine the standpoint and therefore that govern interpretation. As ideas change, alternative interpretations *of the same material* become legitimate. Once more the scientist says, 'I don't know.' We need to say 'I don't know' often in order to ensure we do not fall entirely under the enchanted spell of our own standpoint.

Standpoints are situated and this means that all subject positions are social, including third-person standpoints. As Brian Keenan put it, his validation is in the encounter with another: without that contact, there is no him. In solitary confinement, the captive is the only person who is there to deal with it, so the captive simply makes someone up, and this is partly the person themselves in the guise of the observer; the imagined from the position of imagining. This 'third party', which was 'just yourself as the observer', becomes a vital counterpoint when there is no other and allows a person their subjectivity, which otherwise would be dissipated or dissolved in the welter of the remembered lives of others.[41]

And for Bukovsky, he cannot hear the polyphony for the cacophony once he is released. The third-person objective character is one of many subjectivities that are going on. Our ability to observe others as if from outside is a skill. It is likely that this skill is derived from the way we understand others to be observing us. We turn this on us and thus treat ourselves as another would treat us. We develop the skill for self-observing subjectivity as a way of observing ourselves.[42] We use this particularly when we are badly treated, under pressure or in a high-tension environment, but not only under such circumstances. We bring off the trick of treating ourselves as another person and imagining how it is from that standpoint; this way we can observe ourselves, introspect, empathise, turn inwards as Bukovsky did when incarcerated in a psychiatric hospital. This is not simply hyper-vigilance; it speaks of who we are ordinarily and what normally goes unnoticed. In the same way that reflexivity can be problematic when it becomes hyper-reflexivity, so vigilance – the idea of an imagined observer – also could be problematic if it merits the prefix 'hyper', meaning excessive.

Writers may characterise this as voice and hear the different voices of different characters going on alongside each other that contribute to a plotline or story. Philip Pullman's chapter in a book about *Human Nature* attests strikingly to this. He discusses how it is for him when he is writing one of his books:

> You have to learn to be in several contradictory states of mind at the same time, not *this one for a while and then that one*, and not *this one a lot and that one just a bit*, but all of them, and many more, simultaneously, to the full, without judging between them.[43]

And this to me chimes with the idea of polyphony. Pullman's comment is reminiscent of Bukovsky's comments on the many channels of conscious activity and Keenan's different persons writing all the written notes. The musician or composer might hear this as the different instruments played separately but together, with the potential to contribute to an orchestrated piece.

I cannot *have* your experience, although I can have a similar experience. This is what makes it a point of view, a unique viewpoint positioned in your unique brain and body. Nobody can have quite that experience. Does this matter? Yes, because by allowing there to be a person, we have something upon which to anchor acts (and their consequences); someone to shoulder responsibility and someone to make a contribution.[44]

Why is the private subjective experience so important to us? If we were to experience solitary confinement, I believe we would learn this very quickly.

It is because you cannot know what I'm thinking or feeling that I can survive what you do to me. My private sense of self is what I survive with: it is me: it is what it is to live – to live is to *be* a person in the human condition. The extreme situation of solitary confinement serves to amplify what is real for all of us. In the end we are not alone and simply never can be. As Ray Tallis put it: 'Once we are explicitly located in a world, we are not alone. We *begin* living in relation to others.'[45] Your life really is other people's. Your consciousness and your sense of self can be felt as what happens between each of us as 'members of the human family' in the human condition. You do not disappear with this thought; this thinking merely takes away the awful egregious loneliness that is the hallmark of our self-made modern world. Once you recognise yourself in others, you can also see the consequences of your actions played out in front of you. An act of consciousness then becomes an act of conscience. We cannot but see that we are implicated in the lives of others and take a responsibility, a joint responsibility for ensuring that we act with conscience. I can do nothing in isolation or alone, but with you all possible actions are possible. In the end, solitary confinement is the extreme situation that paradoxically highlights that there is no such thing as isolation, that we are not separate one from another, that we are not alone, and that we make a contribution. What is extreme in solitary confinement is the intensity, but what is intensified are all those features of ordinary life that are amplified in solitary confinement.

Similarly in film, we glean a great deal of the main characters from a small range of cues. Of course, we bring a great deal of reading and viewing skill to novels and films and we watch and read in the context of our history of reading books and seeing films. This means books and films can use a variety of shorthands that allow us to get the general idea of subjective lives while allowing the reader or viewer to bring the necessary wherewithal to create the 'what it is like' for each character.

Rather than argue for an objective view of subjective experience, I want to argue for a subjective view of an objective standpoint. Objectivity can be seen as another subjective standpoint if we see the positions we can hold as a set of subjectivities, a sum of all our standpoints. We can learn to take a variety of standpoints and become versatile with them. This must partly be drawn from social experience of play, conversation and other interactions, but also from practices in the arts and culture such as the use of first-, second- and third-person grammars.

Chapter conclusions

Treatments in the arts highlight the way, for example, we may be bundled together by the way we are treated by others. In Part I we asked, 'what collects us together?' One way this collecting up is carried out is by the way others treat us. The treatment of the impostor Martin Guerre brings about a person who is, for all intents and purposes, the selfsame person.

The concept of treatment is useful because it conveys more than one thing at the same time. Treatment is related to the particular ways artists and writers act towards their subject matter.

Artists may treat what appears to be the same subject matter in very different ways and styles. So, for example, a Chinese painting of the Lake District in England may be very different from one painted in a British landscape tradition. Painters see what they paint; they do not paint what they see.[46] The concept of treatment highlights how it is that we cannot simply observe and then say what we see.[47] We are always looking *with* a conceptual framework. This framework may go unnoticed until we are presented with an alternative way of looking that highlights what we may have overlooked. The way we look at things may make us pick out or select certain features and fail to notice others.

There is also the conceptual sense of how we treat one another. If I think of you as someone with whom I share contours, I am likely to treat you differently from someone who thinks of you as existing separately. I can treat you as one of my kind or as other.

Writers may give their characters a certain treatment. They may, for example, give them an interior life. A writer may treat this interior life as if it were literally the private world of someone's thinking and feeling and existing separately from other characters.[48]

We may fail to see that the character and the point of view is particular, partial and partisan and thus renders only a selective account of what's happening in the book. The narrator may be in one way or another unreliable. If the writer offers us another point of view on the same events, alternative versions of events may be revealed.

I believe we can turn ideas from the arts towards our understanding of consciousness and seriously examine how it is to be a minded person in the world about us. Artists and writers engage in just the sort of conceptual problem-solving work we need if we are to investigate our psychological life and living. By examining conventions in the arts, we may be able see our situation differently, entertain alternative standpoints from the conventions we've grown up with and bring about new ways of seeing how it is to be one and other.

So what's important? What can we get from the arts? The arts – all of them – are very good for alternative standpoints, for making the familiar and taken-as-read stand out by breaking conventions, and for opening up new ways of knowing our every-day world about us.

Having turned over some stories and ideas from the arts and culture, I want to turn once more to stories about captivity and start to reflect on the captive's mind as a way also of turning over how it is to be minded.

6   A captive mind

Although many of the texts referred to in this chapter would be categorised as biography, accounts of captivity deserve the term 'genre' to indicate a body of work in their own right. As is the way, I thought that I'd conceived this idea when I came across the following in an edition of prison writings:

> Since so many first-rate writers of the twentieth century have found themselves behind bars, it is hardly surprising that the body of work they have produced about their experiences rates the term 'genre'.[1]

Siobhan Dowd's edition of prison writings is on my further reading list at the end of this book. This chapter draws on parts of her edited volume. The accounts of captivity given by former hostages and political prisoners seem to me to attest strikingly to how it is for a person to be minded. With the volume of sound from the general hubbub of life turned down, the commonality of our human condition is amplified. I believe that we hear about how it is to be a person most clearly through how it is to be captive.

We are not really alone in solitary confinement. Paradoxically, as mentioned earlier, we are probably less alone when we are alone.[2] People still exist for us. Other people may not be present physically, but in captivity, we can think *with* them. We can continue to make acts of consciousness and conscience. Once peopled, we are never alone. We take our kind of consciousness into the cell with us, thank goodness, and others who have helped bring about us as persons, help us survive captivity. There is a kind of fellowship in solitary confinement and if so confined, we have virtual support. Any attempt to isolate us, to destroy us psychologically, can be met with resistance.[3] We can bring our peopled mind to bear on our situation and act towards guards and captivity in ways that turn the tables, as Bukovsky did.[4] We bring a mind to bear on our situation and sustain ourselves through continuing the virtual world *with* our imagination. The sense here is consciousness as knowing *with* others and conscience too; this is very similar to the southern African idea of *Ubuntu*, which is usually taken to mean, 'I am what I am because of who we all are.' We do not exist in isolation.

When I was researching captivity, I was also researching how it is to be free. That a person is conceivably free when held captive highlights what it is to be psychologically free and how any explanation of our physical situation will never exhaustively explain how it is for someone to *be* in captivity. I can imagine what it might be like to be held captive, but if I were to be part of an exchange for someone who really was held captive, I would *know* how it would feel to *be* captive. The captive *has* the experience of being captive. If I am held captive I know captivity from my point of view. I know *that* I am held captive, *that* I am a prisoner. Anyone offering to make such an exchange knows that there is a reality to the subjective experience of being held captive. There is a difference between being the one held captive and being a person who is not. If I am held prisoner, I know that I am not free, that I might never be released. It is the provisional character of being held hostage that makes a particular subjective experience.[5] If *I* am held, *I* do not know whether or when *I* shall be released. If I knew I had a sentence – as might be the case were I to be a political prisoner (though this might not be reliably the case) – and that I was likely to be released, that is one thing to endure. But not to know whether or when or how I will be released gives captivity a very different character. It is the provisional character that changes how it is to be captive. No examination of physical appearances could help us to understand that distinction;

it is psychological and subjective and entirely the point of view of the person held captive: it is their experience and theirs alone. It is because these experiences have been had by others that the world now has these characteristics; they need not have been my experiences to be part of the world in which I live. Nonetheless, if I am ignorant of such practices of holding people captive in hostage situations, my worldview is blinkered. My experience of the world includes others' experiences even when I am ignorant of them.

We can say, 'I wouldn't want to be held prisoner.' We have insight into the kind of hell it would be. If I am held, there really is something it is like to be captive *for* me *from* my point of view. What would be left of my experience of captivity, if you removed my point of view? It is because subjectivity matters that I know that I wouldn't easily change places even for my son. I would worry that he might not endure it, but I would be scared that I could not endure it either.

When we discussed being a hostage in solitary confinement, we looked (in Chapter 3) at how we can be polyphonic: how we can know ourselves to be such, but without assuming the different persons that we are, are really separate entities. In order to live after captivity it was vital that Brian Keenan recognised that the different persons that made him up were all Brian Keenan and that, as he and Vladimir Bukovsky both separately acknowledged, these persons that make us up need to get on with one another even if in counterpoint. The elements need to work in the same musical score so that we ourselves are a polyphonic ensemble and thus able to perform acts of consciousness.

'Turning the tables'

Being free is as much about what a person does *not do*. Captives may have fewer ways in which to act, but this only serves to amplify how their acts are free. The ways that prisoners turn the tables, through acts that unsettle the guards, are examples of acting freely in captivity.

There are acts of rebellion or strategies of independence such as not doing as the guard commands, even to the point of being assaulted by a guard. There are many kinds of resistance that are hugely consequential for the prisoner. The guard is likely to be ignorant of the sustaining feelings that can stem from a short encounter in which the prisoner feels they have gained a small victory of some kind. Anthony Grey was held hostage in his own house in Peking (now Beijing). He was forced to occupy just one room, but when exercising would use the adjoining room. Grey told me:

GREY: And I suppose I did enjoy provoking the guard in small ways. And they would tell me to stop my walk at a certain time. And they would motion with their chin to go in. And I thought that was demeaning and so when they did that I would just pretend I didn't see. And then they would have to make a bigger gesture. And I would pretend not to see that. And I would continue walking. And they would have to come and stand right in my way. And I'd walk round them, you know, till they would virtually get frothing at the mouth and almost calling headquarters to say: 'He won't come in', or whatever. And then I'd go in without them doing anything. You know, it would be some way, very small ways of asserting one's independence of, of some small choice that you're given, of activity or behaviour, which made you feel you're not totally subservient. Which of course you are in the larger sense. You can't get out of there. So you've got to find some small victory. Then I was accused towards the end of being arrogant towards one of these very young guards. And I thought, 'Well, that's a great victory'. I've been arrogant after

195

nearly two years, or two years or whatever. If I can be arrogant, then [I'm] doing all right.[6]

There are consequences, but these always entail those that guard prisoners acknowledging that the captive exists, and this means the captive always wins 'a small victory'; these may be enough to prevent the devastating, incremental effects of being held, particularly, if held in solitary confinement.

Acting freely

Clearly we are not, and never were, absolutely free. Given all that's already been discussed, nothing and no one is wholly free. It makes little sense to talk of free will, but acts that are consciously free and used to protest are real acts with consequences in our human world. When we become a person, we develop a standpoint from which we may consciously act. Freedom to act is a social acquisition. If you disregard me, I no longer exist; this is why shunning is so devastating.[7] And this is also why some prisoners provoke a reaction even to the point of being struck. If you hit me you have to acknowledge I exist, and therefore whatever I did that made you do this forced you to stop in your tracks and confront me, and this is an act I've freely made. If you hit me in these circumstances, then the very fact of hitting me makes me exist for me and for you. To deny you acted thus would be to deny your own existence. I know that you know that I know I am part of your conscious experience at that moment. You have had to acknowledge me and to do so fuels me as a person in a way that offsets the soul-destroying effects of solitary confinement. One of the greatest wrongs we can do is isolating a person to the point of personal annihilation.

But many dissidents, political prisoners and other captives survive captivity; not all of them write accounts testifying to their ordeal. Many that do see it as part of what it is to be a writer/witness.[8] Survivors of concentration camps have asked liberators to say their names because it means they must acknowledge *that* they have survived.

World, as with nature and other similar terms, cannot be defined without reference to ourselves because we are always implicated in any sense in which world or nature is intended. The world about us has about it the character of captivity.

This is the beginning of a discussion on acting freely, agency, control; on how sometimes giving up control unexpectedly gives us the freedom we are looking for; and how surrender is commitment that may open up other possibilities. How letting go is a conscious act of surrender that is both an act of control and an act that is both free from fear and freeing from fear. And I'll develop this further in Part III.

In accounts of prison life there are many signs of the choices prisoners make under appalling conditions. It is not for anyone else to judge them, not even those who endured a similar experience. Each knows their own breaking point or thinks they do. Where some prisoners have been treated like animals, and come to behave as such having been conditioned, others may keep their sense of themselves and their humanity. Some may betray their fellow prisoners by taking roles in support of the oppressors, or betray secrets about the resistance or opposition movement, and some did this because they were at breaking point. These were still choices, but we need to understand why they are made. We hold these persons responsible for their actions, but we also accept mitigating circumstances. We have to judge how we would have acted under such conditions and realise that we might have made the same choice. Bukovksy recounted to me how some political prisoners could not stand 'the box'– the punishment cell where prisoners had to endure at least fifteen days in solitary confinement – and would, having endured one period in 'the box', tell the interrogators what they wanted to know including names of opposition movement members. We may too easily condemn those when we have not been faced with the worst excesses of torture, deprivation and solitary confinement. These prisoners are persons like us and we might have told our interrogators under such conditions. They would then be returned to the same cell as other politicals. But prisoners knew that some could not cope with solitary confinement and this was accepted. How would you cope? Would you give your friends up under such conditions? I believe that we witness freedom when it is most under threat. I believe the genre of captivity is an extraordinary testimony to personal freedom. I want to set out some of this here.

What can you freely do when you cannot choose what you will do, where you will go, who you'll associate with, or what you'll read or watch or listen to? When almost everything is controlled by those guarding you, how could you possibly be free?

As said earlier, I started this academic adventure exploring consciousness when I came across a piece titled 'Freedom through mental activity' written by a Russian dissident named, I believe, Joseph Kovach; however, I have been unable to trace this source. It was the title and the mode of freedom that caught me. I had wanted to research what it is to be free and the use of imagination. I had one of those rare moments of clarity when you can see how to do something, which a moment ago seemed impossible. Now I could see how to do it and how to set about it and it was remarkable how this happened. Having read the piece by Kovach, my direction was clear. Freedom is usually described and illustrated in physical terms, but if you were entirely physically constrained, how could you be free? The idea was classically paradoxical: in order to research freedom, research its opposite: captivity.

Mentally or psychologically a person can be free through using their mind; for example, through imagining something in an unconstrained way. If I imagine what it is like to walk a route familiar to me, I escape at least for a while the fact that I cannot physically do it. Is this real? Yes, because the psychological is real and I am as much psychological in status as I am physical. So I can paradoxically be free whilst being held captive.

So many captives have reported this over historical periods and often without access to other records of captivity (so without the aid of being able to take into the cell this important knowledge) that this pattern of understanding deserves to be acknowledged as a real feature of persons and of the human condition. We are psychologically free across all situations until the person is broken. But what a person can stand should make us very optimistic about our fortitude and resilience.

To survive captivity requires both discipline and the ability to let go. Freedom lies in the abilities involved with *both* setting a direction – a discipline that prevents psychological disintegration – *and* letting go – a surrender that allows a person to see things differently and thus sustain their life and living through the impact what they do in captivity has upon them. That these are both reflexive is necessary – the captive is the only one there to do it. That the captive person is not alone is sufficient – the captive carries their peopled world into the cell with them.

Where discipline is concerned, Dr Edith Bone's account of seven years' solitary confinement is exemplary.[9]

> Dr Bone invented various techniques for keeping herself sane. She recited and translated poetry, and herself composed verses. She completed a mental inventory of her vocabulary in the six languages in which she was fluent, and went for imaginary walks through the streets of the many cities which she knew well. Throughout these and other ordeals, Dr Bone treated her captors with contempt, and never ceased to protest her innocence. She is not only a shining example of courage which few could match, but also illustrates the point that a well-stocked, disciplined mind can prevent its own disruption.[10]

The idea that you give limits to your *captive flight* is in various accounts. The idea of 'letting go' is most clear in the interviews I carried out with Brian Keenan, and in his book *An Evil Cradling*.

In interviews, he told me about how he would relate the situation of solitary confinement to being a writer in the throes – or struggles – of writing. He could use his circumstances to rewrite books that he had read in a carefully crafted disciplined use of himself. But the seemingly endless days make it exhausting to hold the reins too firmly. Some letting go of the reins – having set a scope or trajectory – becomes necessary. There may be fear, but fear diminishes when a person willingly lets go and commits themselves to what it takes to come out of the other end of captivity intact. Paradoxically, after he was freed and he came to write about his experience, he told me about the difficulties he had trying to write about the time when he was a hostage; how he was at the point of giving up on the project.

> KEENAN: I was really at the end of my tether. And I made a conscious decision, look you're not going to get this thing back. It's just not going to happen. And then when I stopped looking for it, it just came.[11]

Brian Keenan's period in solitary was probably three or four months. Perhaps it is because he had always been a writer that the first part of his book about his captivity is the example that I would say takes you into a cell with the captive. I urge you to read it. This is not sad and bad stuff – though there are passages that are difficult to read – this is truly moving. This book and others of its kind are stories of survival and psychological transformation. Prisoners change the psychological landscaping of their physical situation. They make a standpoint to survive with by what for me are the most extraordinary facts about persons and their acts of consciousness. Read more than one account.

Memory and imagination transformed

Many prisoners express how memory is transformed in captivity. Evgenia Ginzburg spent much of her life in Russian prisons, much of it in solitary confinement, and often without anything to read. She wrote:

> Later on, over the months and years I spent in various prisons, I noticed the virtuosity which the human memory develops, sharpened by solitude and cut off from all impressions from outside. One remembers with astonishing accuracy everything one has ever read, and can repeat whole pages of long-forgotten books. There is something almost unaccountable about it.[12]

Indeed, later in her book she recounts an incident which occurred while being transported to another prison by train. She was reciting some poetry at length when the door of the truck was suddenly opened and a guard demanded to be given the book that she was reading from. He was incredulous that she could recite at such length from memory.

In the new prison they were allowed to walk up and down for fifteen minutes in what were euphemistically called 'exercise yards'; in effect they were roofless cells about fifteen paces long.

> To my dying day I shall remember the high clear sky of Yaroslavl. No other town has anything to compare with it. And there were always gulls flashing in from the Volga. And there were the ships' sirens – no words can convey what they meant to a solitary prisoner especially to one who like me had lived by the Volga. I heard them as the living voices of friends, for I knew those ships, every one of them: the proud white swans of the old Samolyot company and the busy, fussy tugs trailing their barges, and the shrill-voiced excursion steamers... It could never have occurred to any warder how many new impressions, dreams, memories a prisoner brought back from a fifteen minutes' walk in a grey roofless cell.[13]

The transformative aspect of imagination affords the leap beyond the prison walls to a life that still exists but from which the prisoner has been separated. The symbolic sense of this is akin to Wittgenstein's 'seeing aspects' that makes for the possibility of seeing something differently and in a way that lifts morale. Ginzburg wrote that to be deprived of exercise was a horrible misfortune.

When Ginzburg and her fellow prisoners arrived at Yaroslavl the prison library was closed, which meant they had to fill sixteen hours a day. She wrote: 'The important thing was not to forget how to talk', so she gave herself a lecture about Pushkin.[14]

> [And] then repeated all I could remember of his poems. My memory, cut off from all impressions from outside, unfolded like a chrysalis transformed into a butterfly. Wonderful![15]

When the library opens Ginzburg looks forward to the company of books. The wonderful irony of Russian prison libraries was that banned books were freely available. The experience of reading is transformed by isolation.

> At home, I had always been regarded as a passionate and indefatigable bookworm. But it was only here, in my stone sepulchre, that I really learned to explore the inner meaning of what I read. I saw that always until then I had skimmed the surface, developing my mind in breadth but not in depth. And when I came out of prison, I once again became incapable of reading as I had read in my cell in Yaroslavl, where I really discovered Dostoevsky, Tyutchev, Pasternak and many others.[16]

I feel something of this as I write this book. I was like this in my early life when drawing or making art. I had what Keenan called 'a filled timelessness', which he experienced when he was in the underground rooms in which he was held and whenever he had been in the throes of 'writing imaginatively'. We think freely when we act freely in whatever circumstance we find ourselves. The captive is in an extreme situation – and this intensifies their experience – but our everyday and commonplace circumstances will do. Other people may not know what it is we do when we think freely.

Private experience

As mentioned in Part 1, Albie Sachs was jailed in South Africa for his anti-apartheid activity. The following extract is from *The Jail Diary of Albie Sachs* (1966). From this diary we learn that he was given pencil and paper and a legal guarantee of more to follow. But he did not feel free to write. He was mindful of who would read what he wrote. He wrote because it helped him endure his prison conditions, but he felt that he could jot down only neutral things such as word games. He knew that using the pencil and paper would help him get through his imprisonment, but he was held back from writing 'by fear that what I write will be seized'. As he said: 'It is difficult to write without directing my thoughts to someone who will read the script.' But in jail he knew what he wrote would be read by those that held him captive. So he kept his thoughts to himself.

> There are no deep thoughts, no descriptions of my new world, no commentaries on my life as a prisoner ... My special thoughts, the insights I have gained, the new emotional depths I have sounded within myself, all these must remain secret until I come out. The police must never be allowed to see into my mind. They must never be allowed to get hold of and to crush my thoughts, for the police are book-burners, destroyers of things delicate. There is only one safe place for my thoughts: in myself.[17]

Most writers write with a reader in mind and any writer imagines how what they are writing will be received and by whom. A writer can tailor what they write according to the reader the writer imagines, or decide not to write because of how a likely reader will interpret, use or turn what is written to their advantage or against the writer.

In jail, Albie Sachs acts privately because his guards, the police, the regime that holds him will use his private world against him given half the chance. But he can turn the tables if those that hold him think he is doing fine. As many captives have done before, turning the tables often causes those holding the captives to have the kind of reflections they would have imagined the captive to have. He chooses not to write in jail on the paper provided. He reflects that what he writes may be used against him by the police and concludes that he will keep his thoughts to himself. But he will still *think freely*. Where Sachs is concerned, the acts of consciousness and conscience incorporate both the reflective thinking and the not writing it down. It's not always what you do but what you don't do that has the greatest impact. Not doing things does matter and does have an impact. Albie Sachs went on to become a judge appointed to the constitutional court by Nelson Mandela, a position he retired from in October 2009.

Why is this important? Because it highlights in a real world situation what we have been discussing in theory. We really do not know what is going on in other minds. We do not know what another's experience is, if anything. We can see that experience is private and subjective in character, that there really is something called private subjective experience. Private because we do not know what is going on in someone else *at any particular time in any particular situation*, not because we, for example, would be unable to imagine it. It is because experience is a shared feature of the world that we can talk about it at all. Were it to be completely private it would be impossible to communicate to others. If we live with another person, we share much of what living together entails, but we never share our unique point of view *about* that experience. We act as we do because of our situation and what we bring to it in terms of previous experience; this makes our experience of any situation unique to us: only we could bring just such a set of experiences to a situation and only we could then turn these into the situation we make of it. We are uniquely minded about our shared lived experiences. We live through and witness what happens in the world about us.

Nonetheless, what is experienced is a matter of shared human experience of the human condition. The testimonies of political prisoners and hostages from all over the world attest to this. The written accounts, the books and other articles were not universally available, so the fact that accounts bear such extraordinary resemblances and justify the idea of a pattern of evidence is testimony itself to our common humanity. We fit the world about us in which we live because the world is: 'The lives of the men and women who live on earth.'[18]

Genre of captivity and the human condition

We can read all of our workings in these books: the human condition writ large. I read accounts from everywhere and everyone I could get hold of. At one stage I was lucky enough to hold a British Library reading ticket and this allowed me to easily access some rare and out-of-print books. I started to see certain similarities in the accounts given and those features that prisoners commented upon that helped them endure solitary confinement.

There seem to be two kinds of life and living from the way I'm using these common terms: the kind that apprehends and stops and fixes and establishes and holds and grasps; this seems more akin to *having*. There's also the kind that moves and is moving, that goes along, and this kind seems akin to *being*. For example: if you try to *have* the experience, you try to fix it in some form, express it in a form of words perhaps, to capture it – this is where it links with the accounts of hostages. We put bars or walls round consciousness to fix it, hold it, grasp it: some features of life are probably like this; others may just appear to be so because they change infinitesimally slowly (and so appear fixed when they are in fact moving). We also engage with living and experience so that we can be the very movement that moves us, feel it moving us without any attempt to capture it.

What the genre of captivity remarkably attests to is the way that we are minded. There are similarities to the writer's experience of voice and writers are perhaps best equipped to survive solitary confinement, particularly if they can turn captive solitude into something akin to what would have been their daily experience of voluntary isolation in the writer's room. Memory and imagination are transformed by isolation into a virtuoso performance by being forced to feed from one's own resources and resourcefulness. And none of this need be visible to the guards.[19] And it may be difficult to describe. As Keenan asked, 'how can I set my book about a time in which nothing happened, but everything happened? And I couldn't. I just couldn't face it. Because I didn't know how to do it.'[20] He described writing about his time as a hostage on his own as like 'steaming up the window' where it is up to the reader to engage with what can be said and to 'wipe it clean'.

We are so used to writing the story of our lives as a series of events, the occasions and the circumstances and what we did and what others did. But what of a time when none of this is taking place, how then do we account for our lives? Keenan found a way in a testimony that I would urge everyone to read.

Our sense of being free is one of the features of the human condition amplified by captivity. It is because we can switch channels that we are conscious at all. I could not be conscious of change unless I could both know how things were and how things are now at the same time. We can only act freely to the extent that we can consciously know anything. The possibility of choosing to act in a particular way presupposes that an alternative existed – one or more that was not chosen. If only one possibility existed, we could not have freely chosen nor consciously known anything. It makes little sense to talk of free will, rather there are free actions.

We may be consciously free and act freely to protest; these are real acts with impacts in the world about us.

Chapter conclusions

So, what is private experience? There is what we can conceal and what we choose not to reveal. But what we call 'experience' is common between us. My captive experience would be unique to me, but how it is to experience captivity is part of the world about us and therefore common ground.

CONCLUSIONS FOR PART II

In Part II we have been dealing with what it is like to have conscious subjective experience and point of view. Drawing on Thomas Nagel's wonderful question 'What is it like to be a bat?' makes us think about something so familiar by making what normally goes unnoticed strange and distinctive. I think the accounts of captivity given by former hostages and political prisoners attest strikingly to how it is for us to have conscious experience. Where Nagel's story and thought experiment looks at the familiar through the unfamiliar, the stories of captivity amplify the familiar by turning down the volume on normal life and living, leaving us with how it is for us writ large. The private subjective experience of the captive relates to us what it is to be human. And yet the genre of captivity – the numerous accounts given by former captives – highlights also our common humanity. The shared patterns of experience say much about the human condition. We are all there and a vast resource for all of us.

I would urge you to read something from the genre of captivity. Our landscaping unfolds in a prison cell and reveals to us what is commonly drowned out by the deluge of everyday life and living. Accounts of solitary confinement are, from my point of view, person–mind–world writ large. We all get glimpses of this. Rather than focus on the potential devastation from such circumstances, we might read between the lines and find our common humanity and be all the better for it.

The arts have much to offer us in our investigation of how it is for us to experience the world about us from our points of view. The same willingness to suspend belief is necessary to let the artist's treatment be ours, just for a while. The ways of seeing offered by artists, writers, filmmakers and others give us alternative viewpoints of the familiar and taken for granted. We may see things differently and this perturbation in the still water of our point of view may alter forever the landscaping of our lives such that we can truly say we were never the same since. There is always a risk in this and fear of what may come of taking risks, but for the captive there's simply nothing else to do.

In order to suspend *belief*, we need to try to put on hold our usual way of thinking, just for a while: we may come to see things differently. It is by entertaining an alternative reality that we are able to do this, much as we do when we suspend *disbelief* and enter the alternative reality of novels, plays and films. Having disengaged in this fashion, we can re-engage and re-evaluate our beliefs.

In Part III, I will turn to what it is for us to know what we know, how it is for us to be minded persons in the world about us. I'll look at the idea of landscaping and how the shaping of gardens works as an analogy for how we come to see *with* a worldview. I'll develop further some of the themes from Parts I and II in a discussion of Frank Jackson's knowledge argument. And I will try to pull it all together with a commentary on the soul classic 'I wish I knew how it would feel to be free'.

Part III

To know consciously

INTRODUCTION

We could say that every creature 'knows' in the sense that it knows the ways of its world. But what makes it different for us, for humans, is that we do not simply know our world, we *know* that we know. And this is what is meant by the phrase 'to know consciously'. This part of the book is about the everyday and commonplace kind of knowing that has its basis in the shared knowledge of our human condition. In the spirit of this book, we need to suspend belief in what we think we know and try out and test out alternative standpoints. Whatever it is to know anything is to have a standpoint and know *with* that standpoint.

Part III differs from Parts I and II in the way that conscious experience is examined. In Part I, we took the verb 'to be' as the main focus. In Part II, we took the verb 'to have'. Here in Part III we will take the verb 'to know' and use this to explore what it means 'to know consciously'.

I believe that knowing is a way of seeing things. It is only because we can see things differently that we can know anything consciously. We look with a way of looking: it's a bit topsy-turvy. Rather than knowing what's 'out there' (point away from your body) using what's 'in here' (point to your own head) we need to start with what we share, with what is common between us. We look with a way of looking and not in some kind of unassuming innocent way. We know *from* a standpoint.

To *know* that you know

To know that you know what you know and that you
do not know what you do not know; that is true knowledge.

This saying, attributed to Confucius, has a variety of trans-
lations and versions. But what was he getting at? There are two
features that seem to combine in this saying: first, to hold true
knowledge of anything, we should know *consciously* what we know;
second, we should know the extent of our ignorance. Wisdom may
be thought of as knowing the limits of what we know.[1] Knowing
that you know what you know is often described as *reflexive self-
awareness*. We do not seem to have a plain-speaking expression for
this, so I will adopt the term 'minded' so that I can talk plainly
through what it is to *know* that I know.

To be minded

To be minded consists in two interrelated reflexive abilities:

- First, to be reflexive is to be able to 'turn towards' as, for
  example, when a person turns towards their life so far, or
  directs themselves towards their imagined future.[2] The
  directing or turning towards is just a manner of speaking.
  Persons, as psychological beings, 'turn' or 'direct' in a
  figurative or conceptual sense. We *turn inwards*, but, as
  mentioned earlier, this doesn't mean there's a self inside
  that is actually being turned to.[3]
- Second, to be reflexive is to act towards others as if they too
  are reflexive. This is normally called *Theory of Mind*. The
  theory in Theory of Mind is the *assumption* that others have
  independent minds of their own. There are competing
  explanations for the development of Theory of Mind.[4]

I cannot know that you have a mind like mine, but I'm
minded to act as if it were so. It seems that the timing of when this

development occurs moves ever earlier.[5] We seem to be proto-minded. Those we owe most to, and who we should thank, are those who first engage us in play, conversation and the vast array of social practices that constitute us.

So, to be clear, I'm replacing both 'reflexive self-awareness' and 'Theory of Mind' with the term 'minded'. I'll say some more about Theory of Mind before using 'minded' exclusively.

Can a person remember their early life?

Infants know but don't know that they know. When we cry, others come. We are cared for in acts of social engagement that also seem to do so much more than help us to develop organically. Sometimes we cry and others don't come. It is through the way others engage with us as infants that we come to be minded people in our own right. Not all at once or overnight, but knowing consciously is irreversible: we cannot know consciously about our life before we become minded beings. Being minded is the very means of *knowing* that we know. Before we become minded, however early we started, we do not *know* that we know anything.

Infants occupy common ground or we could not engage with them and, more importantly, they could not engage with us. Adults may be more versatile and sophisticated, and may have acquired other capabilities, but this is not the same as saying we are very different from infants.[6] The changes have as much to do with upbringing – how our carers bring us up and engage us socially – as they do with physically growing up. We will need to look for some explanations of these changes in the social practices of the world about us.

We could not know what we were developing towards because we did not *know* what we didn't know. To know consciously demands that we can be reflexive, even when this knowing reveals what we do not know. Before reflexivity develops we cannot turn towards anything, let alone ourselves, simply because we have no means of doing so until its development.

Sense of self and proto-minds

Do we know that an infant is not minded? How could we know for sure? Judging on the basis of observable behaviour is never as good as hearing it from the horse's mouth, but we cannot have a conversation with infants. Nonetheless, we could have a proto-conversation – proto meaning an early or first form of something – and the 'biscuit' case given shortly under the heading 'Examples' might be one that we use as evidence. We could think of infants as proto-minded. Proto here is used to suggest a first or an early form of mind that grants the infant the scope to become minded in a fully fledged sense. An infant has the wherewithal to become minded provided minded persons engage the infant in social experience and activity. This wherewithal is a kind of sentience that is not the same as being minded; it is non-reflexive.

How do we know this? We can test children using Gordon Gallup's mark test.[7] Without the child's knowledge, we place a mark on the child's face, and provide them with an opportunity to look at their reflection in the mirror. If they recognise themselves in the reflection and touch the mark, or perhaps try to rub it off, they pass the test. They know that what they see in the mirror is them. All living creatures have some bodily sense of 'this' and 'not this', even if it is the simple boundary of their own skin. It is likely that we understand boundaries from a very early age. It is probable that we develop early boundaries behaviourally through our physical movement about the world and how this affects our place in it. We can also respond to our own movements. This sentience is a naturally realised development that is similar to that of other animals. Nonetheless, this does not mean that other animals have the sense of self that hominids and some others have. All sentient creatures have a bodily basis of identity, with some having more sophisticated responses than others.[8]

The sense of self may be present in other hominids and in feral children, but I do not think this necessarily means they are minded as we are. They may have a proto-mind gained from social play, but without symbolic interaction, they do not acquire fully fledged minds.[9] The mark test highlights a 'this' / 'not this' boundary necessary for a bodily basis of being in the world; but it is not sufficient for a reflexive concept of self. Recognition is not conception. Other species may get as far as 'this body' and the *recognition* of *this* behaviour in a mirror, but not '*my* body' and the *conception* that goes with it. To see what we see in the mirror *as* me is to have some conception or idea of me and is different from recognising that the behaviour we see in the mirror *is* my behaviour. Knowing that *this* in the mirror is *this body* does not make a sense of self; there's a world of difference between *this body* and *me*. Other species may develop into adults much more quickly, but a non-reflexive mind – one that cannot turn back upon itself – need not consciously *know* that it knows.

As we grow up and are brought up, we get the benefit of those around us.

Becoming minded and what is known as 'Theory of Mind'

Theory of Mind is controversial and has been challenged ever since the idea was first coined. It has been used as an idea that might separate us from other hominids, such as chimpanzees. But what is it that's at stake here and what are the challenges? The belief that we somehow attributed mind to others of our kind was put as a question about other hominids: do chimpanzees have a theory of mind?[10]

Do persons get the idea of being minded from social action?[11] It may be that children become minded persons because mind is made in the acts of social experience. We reached out beyond our grasp towards our caregivers who in turn reached towards us. It may be that our minds are constituted in the acts of social exchange that took place between us as proto-minded children and minded persons in our world.[12]

We can test Theory of Mind with what is known as the *false belief* test. A child that passes the test knows that others have an independent point of view.

False belief test

Imagine an adult showing two children – let's call them Jack and Rose – where a sweet is going to be hidden on a table. On the table there is the sweet, a red cloth and a blue cloth. The sweet is to be hidden under a piece of red cloth. The adult lifts the red cloth and places the sweet underneath. Both children watch the adult do this. Then Jack is asked to go out of the room. Rose stays in the room and sees the adult take the sweet from under the red cloth and hide it under the blue cloth. Rose sees this and is then asked by the adult: 'If we ask Jack to come back into the room and find the sweet, where will he look for it?' If Rose says 'under the red cloth', she has Theory of Mind; if she says 'under the blue cloth' she doesn't. If she says 'under the red cloth' she knows that Jack will still believe that the sweet was there because *from his point of view* that is where he last saw it. Rose will have got the idea that her mind and Jack's mind are independent. She knows that Jack doesn't know what she knows. If she says 'under the blue cloth', she does not see Jack as independent of what happened in the room. She thinks that Jack knows what she knows.

It is likely that, if Rose has Theory of Mind and Jack has not, Rose will have no special insight into Jack's consciousness. She may have only recently become minded (and only recently been proto-minded herself in much the same way as Jack is), but this does not mean she can still report on what that consciousness is like. By the same token, Jack may have no idea about the kind of minded consciousness that Rose has. There may be nothing in Jack's proto-mind that allows him to conceive what may also happen to him.

If Rose is minded, she can pretend to take another's point of view. She can imagine what Jack's point of view may be like. She can see herself *as if* from Jack's point of view. She can play *being* Jack. Rose can deceive Jack, but she can also co-operate with him.

I knew nothing consciously when I was an infant and did not know that I would become a person at some point. I was not minded. When I became a person I became something that knows things but would never know again what it was like to be an infant. How could something that had been brought about by development be used to look back at a time before that development had taken place? We would be absurdly trying to use the very nature of our development to look at how we developed. How could any reflexive ability reflect past the origin of its reflexivity? We come to *know* that we don't know. The development that took place brought about the very thing that I didn't have in infancy: the ability to know consciously. The infant knows but doesn't *know* that they know.

The consequences of knowing that we know

We come to the idea that we are one of us; that we are a member of a group, a member with its own separate life and identity. Although it is likely that this is achieved through social engagement, experience, play and all the many and varied ways we interact, nobody knows exactly how it is done. It is probable that others of our kind make us into persons like them and we in turn draw out of them what will make us persons. A feral child may try to do this with other animals.

There are consequences for knowing that we know. I know that I am this body. I know that I am this and you are that. I know that I am a member of a group. I know that I am of this place and time. I see other members of my group die and I come to know that in time I will die too.

Knowing that I will die is a socially realised condition brought about by recognising that I am one of a kind. I do not see someone die, I see *someone like me* die. And I can turn this around. Someone like me dies, so because I am like them, I will die. We share the same kind of life and living, therefore we will share the same kind of death and dying.[13]

We become conscious of our own mortality. 'We know that we will die, but not usually how or when. To know we are mortal is our unique position among species.'[14] We know that we are one of a kind. We learn that others of our kind die and because we are minded, we can turn this back upon ourselves.

Others of my kind die, therefore so will I.

Do other animals have minds like ours?

The ability of infants and some animals to deceive one another is also evidence of a developing Theory of Mind; it suggests they are learning that the other only has its viewpoint and only knows what is in plain view for it. This does not mean that infants or certain animals are minded, although it is hard to try or test how it is for them. Evidence for a creature knowing that others of its kind have independent points of view is harder to come by, though research continues to throw up examples that are difficult to interpret – some of these are discussed below.[15]

What we know of our human development is limited, but we may be able to infer some things from the developmental changes in some other animals, e.g. other primates. They do not acquire language as we do, but some still get something akin to Theory of Mind. They seem to deceive others in their group and would seem to need the capability of taking another's point of view in order to know what the other animal does not know and to know that they do not know it. They appear to be at the very least proto-minded; in other words, show all the signs an infant shows, but without the 'knowing that it knows' part. Work in the field of primatology allows for at least two explanations:

- That all hominids (humans, chimpanzees, bonobos, gorillas and orang-utans) are on a continuum of development, such that a great deal of what we might think of as exclusively human is shared across the hominid group (although it may differ in the form that it takes). Each has their own ways of their world.
- That aside from humans, only acculturated hominids display certain kinds of development. Other species are not minded. Acculturated means to convert to the dominant group or to adapt to a dominant group in order to better fit in with it or meet expectations. Thus, some of a chimpanzee's behaviour may come about as a consequence of mixing with humans.

Examples

First, a few years ago I saw a natural history documentary that showed a female hamadryas baboon moving to groom a young male behind a rock. She took about twenty minutes to shuffle across about two metres, while maintaining a seated position, to a place behind a rock. She made sure – she seemed to be checking – that the alpha male could not see what she was doing. The fieldwork report suggests that, had the alpha male spotted her, he would have punished her for such an act.[16] Evidence from DNA studies of offspring suggests that young males do indeed mate with females supposedly only available to the alpha male. Nonetheless, it is not necessary to suppose that the hamadryas baboon knows that it knows what it is doing; it could have a proto-mind gained from social play that makes it act as if it were minded. It does not seem to reflexively turn the matter back upon itself. It does not go away thinking about what it has just done and saying to itself 'Look what

I just did'; it just does it. We, the human observers trying to make sense of what the baboon is doing, are overinterpreting perhaps. We may be imagining what we would be doing were we to have been in the female baboon's place.

Second, there is the example of Santino, the stone-throwing chimpanzee at Furivik zoo in Sweden. Santino seemed to prepare piles of rocks when the zoo was closed that he used as ammunition to throw at visitors when the zoo was open. Trying to make sense of this, some at the zoo have suggested that this is evidence of planning and anticipation. Santino seemed to anticipate a future event and made the piles of stones, in advance, for throwing later on. Others have argued that the stone-throwing behaviour is associative learning, often called conditioning.[17] Piling of stones was only documented following stone-throwing, so we do not know whether or not Santino engaged in this kind of activity before this. Each element may be conditioned, but the whole thing may appear as if it demonstrates planning. Without knowing the history of this chimpanzee – beyond the facts that he had been born in Munich zoo in 1978, hand-reared and transferred to Furivik zoo in Sweden aged five – it is very difficult to know what he is doing. Observations were made over about a ten-year period.[18] It may be that having been among humans for so long, he has acquired different characteristics. It's not as if being in a zoo is anything like a chimpanzee's normal life or habitat. Nonetheless, chimpanzees throw sticks and stones in the wild.[19]

The third example is of a human infant who seems to set up her father by playing with his expectation using a biscuit:

> She stretches out her arm once again to her father holding out the little biscuit, her eyes on his face, watchful, a slight smile on her face. He obediently (but perhaps now wanting to get on with his dessert) stretches his arm out for it again. As his hand starts to approach she pulls back, smiling more and wrinkling her nose. He is surprised and laughs, saying

'Give me, gimme, gimme!' and stretches further forward for it. She pulls it back further, smiling. He withdraws his arm, turns away. Her eyes have never left his face. She stretches her arm towards him again, offering the biscuit, watching his face with a half-smile; as he reaches out in response she quickly whips it back.[20]

This infant seems to play with her father's expectations. There is common ground between the infant and father. They turn towards each other and bring about the act of consciousness that is offering a biscuit and then withdrawing the offer. We work with others where engagement is concerned: it is a mutually constituted performance; much as an ensemble cast in a play bring off a theatrical performance by acting together.

The young child certainly seems to be reflexive in a minded way, so we may need to think again about our social development. The young child, when it tricks or deceives us in some way, seems to know that it knows. It seems not simply to get pleasure from doing it – which could be a learned or conditioned response – but to engage the one tricked in ways that say 'I want you to know that I know what I'm doing here.'

Gesture / symbol

Natural communication is of a one-for-one correspondence kind, such that gestures come to be used to mean one thing. Arms raised by an infant may start as a co-operative gesture when being picked up. Infants initially use gestures and only later understand that, in the adult world, one gesture can have more than one symbolic meaning. *Knowing* that you know is the entry point into symbolic activity. We come to be able to treat any particular meaningful action in more than one way.

We can have something in our hand and know when it is not in our hand. What starts out as action develops into the use of skills that can stand in for action, such as gesture and later symbol use, for example, in play and imagination. We develop co-operative signs and symbols that make it possible for us to play with adults and have them respond to us. There is evidence of this in the way an infant engages an adult in getting itself picked up.[21] Arms can be raised at will as a gesture that can also mean, 'I want to be picked up.'[22]

Vasu Reddy also refers to how infants raise their arms to be picked up or how they may arch their backs in preparation. Is the infant trying to help the adult? Is the infant engaging with the adult's intention? The performance of picking up an infant can be seen as one that is brought off by both parties acting together in some kind of shared engagement in the adult's intention. In much the same way, adult conversation is successfully carried off by two active engagements towards the same end: *both* speaking *and* listening.

It may be that some other hominids – and perhaps other mammals that share in human social worlds – also acquire something of this, if for no other reason than human contact. A dog's lead may be symbolic for us. For example, we can signal to others some distance away that we're taking the dog for a walk. If the dog picks up its lead, this may be a gesture that it learned as a gesture from us. We might think that the dog is doing what we would do and using the lead as a symbol for 'going for a walk', but the behaviour can be learned and rewarded by us *when* we take the dog for a walk *after* the dog has brought us its lead. Much of what we do may be behaviourally conditioned. Acts of consciousness and conscience are necessarily conceptual: to be minded or act mindfully means to *know* that I know what I do. To be minded is to know consciously.

Over a long enough period of time non-conceptual behaviour may appear as if it were conceptual, particularly if we do not know its history. The problem with deciding what Santino is doing lies in just such a problem. Our own action can be similarly ambiguous when we do not know why we do what we do.

Example: A novelist writes up a journal before beginning again to write the novel on which they are working. We might conceive of this as a minded act. But it could be that on those occasions when writing the novel went well, the author wrote up the journal before starting. The writer's act of writing the journal may have become conditioned and its continuance may be attributed to the writer's belief that writing the journal is a way of 'warming up' before starting on the novel.[23] Of course, this will only help to get the writer started. Writing a novel is not simply achieved by getting warmed up to start writing the work in hand.

Mind-minded conversation

As we develop, we come to refer to ourselves as if in the third person: 'Guy, bad boy!' I might refer to myself as I have learned others do. Adults respond to me as if I have certain skills and this in itself is helpful to their acquisition. If a caregiver engages a child in 'mind-minded' conversation, the child crosses the threshold and acquires Theory of Mind earlier. There is evidence that the earlier we engage children with an early form of conversation, the sooner they develop, the earlier they become minded.[24]

Hearing as a sense is truly reflexive because we have both mouth (larynx) for sound production and ears for sound reception. It may be this that gives spoken language – and the early use of it with children – its extraordinary power to build us as persons. Hearing is a reflexive act because we can produce the sound we hear. When we speak we are both speaker and listener. If, when alone, I talk to myself, I act reflexively. Sign language can do this across different sensory modes of action by combining my kinaesthetic sense of movement with my visual sense: I can see what I am saying as I move my hands. Making visual art is a reflexive social practice because I am both artist and viewer.

I can see *what* I draw and see *that* I draw. I am both the producer of the artwork and the artwork's first viewer.

We support children through what Vygotsky called the 'zone of proximal development'.[25] We can do more when with others who can do more than us. Those that are more developed, but close enough to be 'proximal', help us to stretch towards their capability. All education relies on the idea that there is scope or room for improvement. We can all benefit from time with those more developed than ourselves. The idea that animals are accultur-ated stems from the very idea that other animals may acquire abilities from living in proximity with humans.

Those that are developed 'scaffold' us in ways that allow us to achieve beyond our known level of skill by reaching beyond their grasp into the skill level exhibited by those that are further developed.[26] We are able to do a number of things that we were nearly ready for. Children draw things out from those around them, a process which in turn draws those children to greater achievement; this is a kind of education. As mentioned earlier, we cause our caregivers to act towards us in ways that will draw us out and help us develop. Most infants are open to dialogue – to play – and it is openness that draws an engagement. If we are open to others, we *feel* them.

Conclusions for the introduction to Part III

For any creature whose participation in the world takes the form of non-consciously knowing, there is no reflection. This can be likened to absorption or enchantment. We all do this some of the time. If I am only conscious of one thing it would be as if I were not conscious at all. All minded activity for any person must therefore involve more than one thing going on at the same time. A minded person is polyphonic.

There's a world of difference between knowing and know-ing consciously. To know consciously is to be minded, capable of turning what we know this way and that. Only persons can do this. Minded consciousness is brought about by people around and about us who engage us in various forms of social experience such as play and conversation. Ideas such as the self-concept and Theory of Mind are relevant here, but I argue that knowing I am the one in the mirror with a mark on my face is not the same as, or as developed as, passing the false belief test. I think we become *minded* and in this chapter I've called this *minded consciousness* to distinguish it from the non-reflexive consciousness of infancy. Once we are transformed, the development is irreversible and we no longer know what it is like to be an infant. The infant doesn't know the person or vice versa.

Our knowing is manifold: to know consciously means knowing more than one thing simultaneously. Minded consciousness could be likened to a musical piece where the instruments are the many kinds of thing played out and the unity is the experience of the music as one piece of music. It is like hearing the ensemble – all instruments played together in a polyphonic composition. Importantly, the music is played *with* others and we listen not to ourselves but to the counterpoint reflected back from other people and from other things.

Conceptual conclusions

To know is not simply behavioural recognition or rather to *know* that you know isn't. Behavioural recognition is a non-reflexive way of knowing, a 'do it in one's sleep' kind of knowing. I want to try and to test the '*knowing* that I know' conceptual kind of knowing that sets us apart from the natural world. If I have an experience, it is conceptually unique to me: only I can have that experience and what comes from that particular experience. But I know also that we can all come to know this. What is not unique is experience itself. Experiential learning is particular to one member or part of the group. But we can pass it on. And living longer means that we are able to pass on all that the world about us has to offer. If I come to know something about the human condition, I can tell you about it because we have various means of cultural exchange that can hold conceptual knowledge for a person.

We need to 'catch ourselves on' or 'wise up'.[27] But wise up to what? We need to catch ourselves on to those who know and to the rich and diverse culture in which we find ourselves. To know is to catch ourselves on to someone who knows and to know what we know *with* them. Only persons *know* in the sense described here. Conceptual knowledge is knowledge that people have. It cannot be stored in books or in a retrieval system, or rather, it can be retrieved from a storage system only by someone who can read the code. Knowledge isn't *in* the book; it's afforded to those who have the wherewithal to turn it into something we know.[28] And you need a person for this kind of act of consciousness.

Artists know this. There's more than one piece of art about mortality because there are many experiences and ways of saying something about it *through* art. Any particular artist can give you theirs. Conceptual knowledge is not one-for-one. When we understand something, we have many ways we can talk about it and it is this that demonstrates that we understand it. When we understand something we can turn it this way and that, turn it towards our own life and times, or our life so far, or inwards, or towards an imagined future, or all manner of ways.

World about us

I've used the phrase 'the world about us'[29] because in English it has more than one meaning. I'm using world as shorthand for 'human social, cultural and historical world' – the kind of world at least partly envisaged in Hobsbawm's definition: world as

The lives of the men and women who live on earth[30]

This conception of 'world' conveys much of what I want to say about *knowing* that we know.

First, the 'world about us' conveys the idea that world is all around us, the world of time and place and periods of human existence. World shapes us; it is the negative shapes, spaces and contours.

Second, the 'world about us' conveys that what I mean by world is to do with people; it's *about* people and how life and living are *for* people.

We needn't have books. We can, after all, talk to each other and share ideas about our world. Talking to each other is the basis for talking to ourselves, which, in turn, is the basis of – though not the same as – thinking. I can write down my thoughts because they can, in part, be put into text. But my thoughts are also not text but some kind of symbolic shenanigans that could come out as conceptual art, for example. Rachel Whiteread's *House* is a good example.

She wanted to make volume, such as the volume of air in a room, stand out in some form. 'As a young artist she had the thought of "mummifying the air" in a room.'[31] Casting the negative spaces is a sculptural way to do that. Whiteread 'used the technique that has become her signature form in her "nameless library" Holocaust memorial in Vienna, an impression of a room of books with their blank pages facing outwards'.[32] It's also conceptual as it is an idea about space and a way for a person – an artist in this case – to say something about it. There are many languages in which we can become well-versed.

We need all the diverse ways of knowing if we are to know anything. We need others to know because to know anything is to know *with* others. We do not know anything until it is shared even if it is only shared in the polyphonic community that is us. We sound it out in ourselves and see whether it sounds right and to hear what comes back: to see how *well* we know what we know.

How do I know you?

I know you as a person. What does that mean? I know you through conversation, through all the ways we can act together, play together, do anything together. I know you through the acts of consciousness and conscience that characterise you as a person. This kind of knowing is knowing *consciously*. Even when you're not around, I still know you. I can imagine what you're like and what you might do. If I were held captive, I'd still know you. I could imagine what you would say if I were to ask you certain questions. This is why we are devastated if we are isolated, shunned or 'dissed' – disrespected, discredited or disparaged. If we are persona non grata, we are not a person.

To be a person is to be understood. We want to be understood because this affirms us as the person we think we are. We are what others think we are. We are if we are recognised and acknowledged. We are what our thoughts make us. We come to know ourselves through those that know us. There is no other route. We see ourselves as others see us. We know ourselves through the negative contours we share. Our knowing is the making of us.

The impact a person has that is known about by others in the world about us continues to exist because it is carried by others in a variety of social practices. All social practices involve other people. Our upbringing, for example, is a social practice. Gatherings and ceremonies are social practices, as are meetings and rituals, games or sporting encounters (including online variations). Any activity that is shared by a membership, and shapes the lives of those living them, is a social practice (even if the social part of the activity is delayed as, for example, when reading a book). Reading a book is a social activity because it had to have been written. As the reader relates to the writer in reading, so the writer relates to a reader in writing. A book is a virtual conversation. As I write this, I have to think of a reader. I wonder what you'll make of it. I think about how to convey an idea that both sustains your interest in it and how to put it into a form that plainly puts the idea so that you can follow it. Those that know me hear my voice in the way I write.

In Chapter 7 we will look at the *world about us* through the idea of *landscape*: how the way we treat the land ends up as our point of view on it; and how our ways of seeing establish what we see. This will be followed in Chapter 8 by the third and last thought experiment, *Mary the colour scientist*. I will offer a new variation on this that will allow us to open up a discussion on captivity and freedom. Chapter 9 will address freedom more directly and ask 'How does it feel to be free?' Conclusions for the whole book will follow these.

7 Landscape and the world about us

We tend to believe that we look out upon an existing landscape from a viewing point. The general idea is that the landscape is out there waiting to be looked *at*. I'm going to draw on ideas from the *landscape garden movement* – and the picturesque in particular – to turn some of our basic beliefs on their head. In this chapter we will discuss landscape as something we look at the world *with*. I'm going to liken our situation to landscape. I believe that we make the landscape that landscapes our view of it.

We will examine conventional views through an analysis of our conception of landscaping. In particular, we will explore the example of how landscape gardeners composed our conception of what a landscape *is*.

The landscape garden movement

The word 'landscape' was first used as a noun and referred to natural inland scenery or, more obscurely, to the background of scenery in figure (portrait) painting. Landscape was later used as a verb meaning 'to lay out a garden *as* a landscape'. As a verb, it was used by those in the *landscape garden movement* to refer to the way a landscape gardener would compose a garden. For a garden to be 'landscaped' (adjective) the garden would be 'laid out *as* a landscape'. A landscapist could be either a landscape painter or a landscape gardener – one skilled in landscape work.

To 'landscape' an area referred to the human intervention of taming and controlling the wilderness. The meaning of the word came from the task of actively transforming the natural world. It was only much later that the word 'landscape' came to refer to the view seen from a vantage point. In the landscape garden movement, gardeners would make the vantage points in a garden, and this may have included building rocky crags from which the effects of the worked landscape could be best viewed. The garden would look *as pretty as a picture* because the landscape architect had a picture in mind when reworking the garden.

Originally, the view was as contrived as what it was you were looking at. In much the same way as landscape painting positions the viewer in relation to a supposed landscape that the painter has actually painted, so landscape gardeners composed what was to be seen, and thus where it was to be seen from, as part of the same landscape work. A view was produced by laying out paths so that a viewer would arrive at a point where what was to be seen would be framed, much as it would be in a Romantic landscape painting. So, a landscaped path arrives at a landscaped viewpoint where a view of part of a lake or a cascade and perhaps a temple building – all of which were built as part of the landscaping – would form the idyllic 'view'. Importantly, the view was a conception of the idyllic. When a person goes to the viewpoint and says what a beautiful view they see, they are seeing it *with* an idyllic conception and not with an innocent eye. If you go to one of these landscape gardens, it is important to find out about the history of its making and what it would have looked like had it been left in its natural state.[1]

In a landscape garden, there could be many viewing points produced as part of the laying out and landscaping of the garden. Viewing points were arrived at by working backwards *from* the landscaping work *to* a point where a viewer would get the full effect of what the landscaping had produced. Thus, those visiting a garden would see *with* a landscaped view.

As it is with gardens, so it is with minds. I believe that the landscape of the mind is our conception of it. We do not so much see the landscape; rather, we see *with* a landscaped view. We see with our conception, with our beliefs. We see what we think of as a garden because we see with a convention. We do not copy a world that is out there to a form in here that represents it; we actively make our world because of the way we look at it, the beliefs we have about it, and the stance we take towards it.[2]

We can suspend beliefs. We can sabotage the familiar and entertain alternative standpoints and come to know things differently because we come to see things differently. We may break existing conventions. And this is why I believe that the arts will be helpful in any psychological investigation. Artists and writers have a long history of breaking conventions and showing our conceptions up for being just that. But let's get into some details by unpicking the landscape example.

We make the landscape that landscapes us

There is no such thing as 'background' where landscape is concerned. It's true to say that some things in the landscape can appear to be nearer to you than others in a physical sense; they may stand out simply because they are closer to you. And you could divide up the appearance of things into foreground and background. But then if you move through the landscape, what's in the foreground changes – what stands out changes. Something that was once in the foreground could now be in the background – it doesn't stand out any more – and vice versa.

If we talk about the psychology of figure and ground, we've changed the subject subtly. A figure may be a person and the ground may be the landscape they are standing in, for example, a garden. A figure may stand out from the ground because, as people, we tend to be more interested in what the image is about or what it is an image of; often this means what is in the centre of the image or what takes up most picture space. Figure need not mean person, though it often does, but it will normally mean central image. It could be a building such as an old ruined castle in a rural setting. What decides which is figure and which is ground usually comes down to what's *important* to us as the viewer. The important bit need not be in the centre of the image (if part of a painting) but it may be central *for us*. What follows from this is that background is often viewed as unimportant – because it seems only to pick out the interesting part, and not to contribute anything to the image. So, background is passive, neutral, simply *there*.

We can come to see the world *as* background. I want to turn this around: first, by suggesting that the so-called background is doing a lot more work than is credited; and second, by setting out a case for the importance of how we conceive of the world about us. I believe that it is our conceptions – and the conventions derived from them – that is making the world seem to us as it does. I believe that both aspects of the above have much to do with upbringing, convention and schooling so there'll be further links here to earlier discussions on Cubism and Cubist Psychology, polyphony and negative contours. As promised, this is a further opportunity to go round the key ideas this book is about. How we look at things makes us see (and fail to see) what we think is 'out there'. So, this chapter will help develop the idea of worldview introduced very much earlier in the book. We do not simply view the world, we see *with* a worldview.[3] I will tie this in both with captivity – the virtual world and worldview of the political prisoner or hostage – and also look ahead to the next chapter in which there will be a discussion of how it feels to be free. The paradoxes evident in being free whilst held in captivity say a great deal about how we are minded and the landscaping effects of the standpoint we take.

I believe that the landscape example is useful because it gets at a problem in our conceptual thinking. We're going to be talking about 'world' in this chapter, but we need to be clear at the outset that no such world 'out there' exists. It's not 'in here' – point to your own head – either. The landscape is *neither* out there in the world *nor* in our heads, it is brought about by the way we engage and this includes our conception, our upbringing, our contemporaries and our conventions, among other things. It's as difficult to say how landscape gets started as it is to say how anything we take for granted today gets going. And this is why the distinction to be made here between natural world and the landscape of our human world is so important.

Landscapes wild and tamed

Designed landscapes of the seventeenth and eighteenth centuries bore no relationship to the natural world. Where landscapes were concerned, there was no such thing as 'the natural world' during that period. The wild exposed places were not visited by many. What people wanted to look at was the order and perfection of a tamed and trained landscaped garden.

> Tamed landscapes ... were attractive: landscapes which had had a human order imposed upon them by the plough, the hedgerow and the ditch.[4]

It was not until the nineteenth century that 'mountains began to exert a considerable and often fatal power of attraction on the human mind'. Robert Macfarlane suggests that it was not until this time that the experience of being in the mountains was sought after.[5] In the seventeenth and eighteenth centuries, most 'found wilderness dislikeable'.[6] Mountains were desolate places and, therefore, to be avoided. This new way of appreciating 'natural' landscapes was revolutionary. Macfarlane proposes 'that our responses to them are for the most part culturally devised'.[7] He writes:

> When we look at a landscape, we do not see what is there, but largely what we think is there. We attribute qualities to a landscape which it does not intrinsically possess ... We

read landscapes, in other words, we interpret their forms in the light of our own experience and memory, and that of our shared cultural memory.[8]

A mountain is our conception of it, truly a 'mountain of the mind'.[9] A landscape is our view of it – a landscape of the mind – just as when the word 'landscape' was first used. It was first used to convey the view of natural scenery in a painting. There is only our conception of natural landscaping and, what is more, if the conception is widely shared, it becomes a taken-for-granted convention. We have our ways of seeing and these ways make things cohere or hold together as they do. Our conceptions of landscape put certain things together as if they always belonged together. A convention can seem like a natural intuition until we discover first, how widespread the conception is and, second, how our conception isn't held universally and eternally.[10]

> The idea of the beautiful view, which now seems to us as instinctive a reaction to a landscape as is possible, does not seem to have had currency in the common consciousness, or at least not to have been triggered by mountains.[11]

Travellers often chose to be blindfolded to prevent them being terrified.[12] We go from conventions of fear to those of excitement. A different orthodoxy takes over. Some may have felt this in earlier times, but this now moves to the foreground.[13]

> In Britain, during the second half of the [eighteenth] century, under the influence of the picturesque movement, a chic raggedness of design came to supplant the carefully proportioned ground-plan of the Enlightenment garden ... Many of the more modish landowners chose to turn their manicured estate lands into symbolic wildernesses ... And ... they usually asked for a miniature crag or some similar vantage point from the top of which the extent of their gorgeously unkempt demesne [estate] could be viewed.[14]

Critics offer similar evaluations today. An article on the variety of traditions that make up British art included a short paragraph about the gardens at Chatsworth House. Jonathan Jones wrote that the gardens can be seen as 'one vast art installation'; that Capability Brown's landscaping work was a 'great gift to the world of art' and full of international influences.[15] The work of landscaping was taken to be – and is taken to be – making art. This is perhaps most easily seen in the picturesque movement.

Example: the picturesque

Picturesque means 'like a picture' and was once used as a verb meaning 'to make a place picturesque'.[16] It was first used in 1795 and thus would coincide with the *landscape garden movement* of the same period. As an adjective, it was more commonly used to mean 'Having the elements or qualities of a picture; suitable for a picture; *specifically* (of a view, landscape, etc.) pleasing or striking in appearance; scenic'.[17] Originally it was used of a certain style of French painting, where what was painted deserved to be turned into a picture.

Well before the picturesque, gardeners had composed a landscape garden. Landscapers were thought of as contributors 'to the world's visual arts'.[18] In the same way that houses could be composed as architecture, so gardens were to be composed as *landscaped* architecture. There were many influences and movements, but I'm taking the picturesque because it highlights the way the land was made to look like a picture; the way a garden became a framework of composition, something framed and a framing for the viewer. And this relates to earlier discussion about treatments in the arts.[19]

The picturesque influenced English landscape architecture in the late eighteenth and early nineteenth centuries.[20] The idea was to create for the viewer the same effects painters produced in Arcadian scenes.[21] Arcadian scenes were idealised landscapes devised by painters who put certain kinds of features together for a pleasing effect (and not to mimic any natural scenery in any real place in the world). Landscape painting provided the blueprint of the picturesque. The landscaping was the set of elements included by painters: the woody foreground; the ruined stonework or similar in the middle ground; and the mountains lit by sunlight in the background setting off the rural idyll. Gardens became works of art in their own right rather than the works of nature of wild places.[22]

When we turn to the so-called natural landscape, we bring the sense of landscape to bear on how we see it. Viewing points or vistas were established and act in much the same way as they do with a painted landscape hung in a gallery or museum. They position us as viewers. We are given a vista to see *with*. We tend to take pictures at picturesque viewing points and some research I heard about a few years ago reported how photographs people took of places they had expected to visit tended to be taken from the same spot as the picture on postcards or in the guidebook they had used when planning their trip. The photo in situ actualised the expectation brought about by the postcard or guidebook. It was as if the viewpoint with which we had learned to conceive of, for example, Machu Picchu *was* the landscape of Machu Picchu.[23]

Standpoints in the arts

What is remarkable is the fact of viewpoint and what this amounts to. In social psychological literature, many people talk about 'standpoints'. And this is, in part, to get away from the use of visual metaphors that a phrase such as 'point of view' perpetuates. Point of view may distance us as if we were not part of what it was that engaged us. We are in the landscape. We are of the landscape. Our standing means we stand somewhere. We are part of the landscape with which we view the world. We're in the picture. We are our standing in the world and we need a standpoint for that.

In the arts, as discussed earlier,[24] it would be impossible to tell a tale in a film, play or novel without standpoints; we always have a *take* or stance on things and we have to make a *take* or standpoint in order to tell a story.[25] Having a standpoint seems just obvious in any reading of our lives and in our reading of the lives of others. We ask: from whose standpoint is the novel written? Who is the central character? What approach is taken to an historical moment in order to characterise it on screen, in the theatre or in the novel? When we start to write anything, we have to manu-facture the standpoint from which the written account or story takes place. The action must be from a position. We have to put the camera somewhere. We have to set up the easel at a location. We have to set the scene and decide what should go into the frame or shot.

Treatments and landscape

So, does landscaping show us another misconception? The standpoint does not comprise a set of things *in* the individual, rather it comprises the consequences of the set of positions that a person has taken up with others in social, cultural and historical times and places. The standpoint is a set of negative contours made from the engagements we have with the world about us. The individual is the end of all this activity, not its creator; nonetheless, by being the end the individual can act as an agent of change by altering the standpoint to be taken now and consequently the ways by which a person engages with other people in the world about them.

And this is why the accounts of solitary confinement are so important: they are exemplary illustrations of what it is for a person to know consciously and thereby to act freely. We slip the bonds of place and time. We shift standpoint and are therefore free.

I can try and test (and thus treat) your standpoint as if it were mine. I can treat the standpoint offered in a novel as if it were my own. I could rewrite *Robinson Crusoe* from the standpoint of Friday.[26] I can treat an academic position as if it were my own and try it out – see where it fits and where it snags. I can treat it as if from my own standpoint and test my ideas.

When we read, we bring our landscaping to the text. We may test out what we read, ask questions of the text that we are minded to ask. We may be a critical reader raising objections, but we may switch and try out the landscaped viewpoint available in the text. We may try it out. We may try to suspend our beliefs and try to wear what we read like a new set of lenses with which we can look around us and engage afresh. We may switch between these different positions we take to the text and know that such a switching is always possible. And in this way we know freedom of thought. We may commit to certain kinds of enquiry. There is a certain kind of fatality about all enquiry: having spent time engaging in certain ways it may be very difficult to change our ways of seeing. Paradoxically, freely acting in this way may lead to a situation where we know for certain how we will act and know we cannot do otherwise. But our freedom lies in commitments made earlier and not simply in subsequent situations.

To be free in captivity is a matter of standpoint. If I keep to my virtual world that sustains me, I can have freedom through mental activity. I commit to the fellowship of those that know me and trust in those that sustain me. There are many ways of acting freely.

Freedom and commitment

The landscape of infancy is another country: a developing world. We come to treat others as having a mind of their own. We come to treat ourselves as if witnessed by another's viewpoint. We come to adopt a singular viewpoint. How does this work? I don't know. Nobody knows. But I believe that we are social or second-person people first.[27] We get the idea that others are independent and thus gain mastery of the third-person view. We come to treat ourselves as if witnessed by other minds – a third-person view of *this* body. You treat me as independent (as well as dependent). We come to see ourselves as singular minds of our own – a first-person standpoint. I treat this as you treat it. But I believe that it all stems from the social and highlights how the independent individual is *another way of looking* at the same subject, as Cooley argued many years ago (and we discussed in Part I).[28] I act as if I'm independent as an individual member of a social group on which I am dependent. We get the idea that we are both: the two forms are two standpoints on the same subject – individual social person and group social people. Second person is implicitly third person and first person. Persons are made of people and people make us as persons. There isn't a chicken and egg situation because the first people were the first persons. We came to treat each other *as* persons.

When an orchestra plays, we can listen to the ensemble – the impact of all the musicians playing together. But we can also focus on one or two musicians in a particular part of the orchestra, such as the woodwind. We hear the contribution made by individual members of the orchestral group. We can hear the same piece of music over and over as many different pieces in which different features of the composition are heard as foremost.

Freedom lies in commitment even though freely acting in this way lands us in situations where we cannot act otherwise than in keeping with our commitments. To understand freedom requires that we look at a person's history. And this means seeing a person as sustained over time.[29]

Ways of viewing

We are educated in the ways of viewing. When we read a novel (or are read to as a child) we take in *how* viewpoint is put together with the viewpoint presented. In film studies, we learn early on that we view films in the light of other films of a similar genre that we have seen.[30] We are practised in the art of watching a film. Films have their own language and we can pick this up just as we pick up other languages. As we learn the language, so we also learn what the conventions mean, although much of the time this is tacit knowing and, unless studied, not something we know consciously. We become practised in the art of knowing.

How it *seems* is not a guide to the natural world, rather it is more usefully a guide to local conventions; however, there are many conventions such that in any particular setting various kinds may be available. The prominent fashionable prevailing convention is likely to be the one most in synch with how it seems to be the case for us. If we feel in synch with today, it seems likely that today has 'synched' us.[31] There is much talk today of having gadgets synchronised or synched so that each updates another every time changes are made.

If I am a person of today, it is because today made me this way. This doesn't mean that I am made only by the times in which I live. I may also forge standpoints of my own making, uniquely, freely, consciously. We are the landscape of our minds because we are both the consequence of what we look at our world *with* but also a consequence of our landscape activity – the impact we have on the world about us. We view with the twenty-first-century zeitgeist, with the eyes of those around and about us, and with what is important for us.[32] More than this, we may turn what we see back upon itself and ask, 'what does it show?' We ask, 'how does the world seem to others to be?' We may try to assume another way of seeing to try out and to test how things seem from an alternative standpoint.

The ways of seeing I use are given not by some personal achievement of mine, but because I am a member of a community stretching back through recorded history. The influences on any particular painter are legion such that, for example, Rothko is part of the same visual art community as Turner, even if Rothko never saw a Turner.[33]

The writer Jonathan Franzen has often been asked 'who are your influences?' He said:

> When I write, I don't feel like a craftsman influenced
> by earlier craftsmen who were themselves influenced by
> earlier craftsmen. I feel like a member of a single, large
> virtual community in which I have dynamic relationships
> with other members of the community, most of whom
> are no longer living.[34]

This is the sense of world about us partly given in my earlier definition, and I want to take Franzen's comments above as a way to extend this. We discussed world as 'world about us' with the idea that world was taken to be 'the lives of the men and women who live on earth'.[35] I want to extend this to include the lives of those who have lived and a virtual world of others. I want to draw on the ideas of virtual reality – the way that we easily think of entering virtual worlds created by games designers, novelists, filmmakers, among others – to give world about us the full sense of our shared and common humanity. We share our history of humanity even when we do not always know what that history comprises. We inhabit a world about us that includes all those that have lived. And we could call this our shared and common humanity. This is the shared world of Simon Armitage, where he suggests that we live as long as we do to allow us to pass on our culture.[36]

Social practice is what has become established practice, what it is normal or traditional for people to do in society. They may be easily understood through the idea of conventions. Conventions are those things that we do as people that have become customary practice for us; the things we do almost without thinking because they seem natural. The reason why they are so important is that they go unnoticed and may seem to be as natural as sunrise and sunset. It is only when we take on established traditional viewpoints that we may come to realise that what is normal and customary for us may not be so for all people in all times and in all places. For example, I've used the example of sunrise and sunset in the sentence before last, yet we know that it is the Earth turning away from the sun that is what is actually taking place. The idea of a sunset is a conventional way of seeing an event as if it were true that the sun was going down.[37]

We hold ourselves together as people through the ways we use ourselves in life and living. If we were to be taken captive and held in solitary confinement, it is likely that we would need a different set of practices to hold ourselves together in captivity from the ones with which we had become familiar. Using ourselves differently would mean we would also be likely to look at things differently. We might have found an alternative way of seeing from the changes we were forced to make in our social practices. The difference would only make a difference for us when we were released. We might find the old ways so unfamiliar as to make it difficult to resume normal life in the same way as before.

For example, the idea that we are separated out and separable from the world about us is a conventional treatment. This is the positive space that is like an outline drawn around an object with the object supposedly enclosed by the line. This is *a* way of seeing.

Conventions are treatments, customary ways to view persons, minds and worlds. Negative contours offer alternative treatments, unconventional ways of engaging with the world about us. By seeing in this fashion, we will make out an alternative way of engaging with the world about us. Our very presence in the world is marked by those who sustain us.

We share contours. We could conceive of ourselves as that with which we share contours. The world about us is a set of shared contours. We inhabit spaces derived from our relationships with others. For example, our workplaces can be conceived of as composed of networks of relationships. I work in a university and, if asked: what is a university? I would reply that it is the working relationships I have with other staff and with students and, from my standpoint, it is these that could be said to compose my workplace.

Artists, writers, directors and others have to work with social conventions in order to make artworks, tell stories, direct films. And I think this is why they are both very good at seeing the familiar and very good at sabotaging it when they break the rules of their art form. 'There are always people dreaming of changing the configuration.'[38] Artists and writers are always trying out and testing out new ways of seeing the seemingly familiar. Perhaps it is the writer or artist who best exemplifies the trying out and the testing out of life and living. Their projects, whether or not deliberately or serendipitously, are often personal explorations of identity, mortality and how it is to live this life of ours. A book (or work of art) is the coalescent remnant of all the struggles collapsed into a single negotiated form. As they illustrate the world about us, they also serve to illuminate it.

What something means depends on how ideas are used in our community. We learn the meaning of things as we learn to use them. So we use images and words in a set of relations that make it seem just obvious that an individual is a positive shape; but using images and words differently would convey a whole different set of meanings about how it is to be a person. Landscapes in British and Chinese art may be very different, and both be called landscape by the different communities.[39] Each is familiar to each and the other is seen as strange and, which is worse, may even be thought of as wrong. So there is no such thing as landscape as such, but there are accepted uses of the term within any community of artists. And this is why Magritte's work is very important to me. He showed us our conventional uses of words and images by sabotaging them. He shows us what we have learned is just a convention. An explanation for something that has become conventionally the case does not make for a universal, eternal truth. Conventions are contested.

The landscaping of the mind is its composing, where composing is both composers and compositions.

Chapter conclusions

As we discussed earlier in this book, impact might be continued after a person's death through the lives of others who have known the person or through artefacts that to some extent have a life of their own. So Picasso is part of the world about us because people like John Richardson continue to write from a standpoint of having known Picasso and also because paintings like *Guernica* continue to engage us long after Picasso died. So Picasso continues to have an impact and is still a person *for us* and continues to form part of the world about us.

A standpoint is brought about by being physically located *and* by being set socially. Imagine walking up to a known viewing point on a hillside – somewhere marked on a map as a place to see a wonderful view. We may walk up and round a corner and find a vista opens up. We are bringing all kinds of viewing capability to the viewing point that will have an impact on what we make of the view. No such thing as '*the* view' exists. A view we find on rounding a corner is always a particular view known by a worldly minded person in an act of consciousness.

We are *both* the location – the bodily basis for viewing anything, *and also* the landscaped mind that has the view. We do not see the landscape, we see *with* a landscaped view. To view a landscape at all requires that we bring a landscaped mind to a viewpoint and engage with what we see. If we express our notice of a change of aspect, we express something of both the new way of seeing and the old unchanged way of seeing at the same time.[40] We have to have the physical capability to see the world, but we need to have the social capability to view the world with. We stand in the world with a standpoint on the world. Our standpoint is a disjunction. We learn to slip the bonds of period and place when we come to treat ourselves as both one and another.

Were we not able to change standpoints we would not have conscious experience at all. If we were not conscious, we could not know that something had changed. It may be that when we learn that others have independent minds and come to see ourselves as others see us, we may also develop a disjunction with our world. Our separation and sense of being alone is also a breach with the world about us as well as with each other. But I think this form of landscaping is a conventional view from an individualist standpoint and not expressive of a universal or eternal truth about existence.[41]

The knowing that we know is further examined in the next chapter in which we will work through the third and final thought experiment, plus a variation of my devising. We will look first at Frank Jackson's original 'Mary the colour scientist' also sometimes known as 'the black and white room' before turning to my variation 'Mary the captive scientist' or 'the black and white cell'.

8   'Mary the colour scientist' (Jackson)

Frank Jackson has given us a rich thought experiment in what is known variously as 'Mary the colour scientist' or 'the black and white room' or simply 'the knowledge argument'.[1] The following is only part of Jackson's original text, but it is a part that has been much discussed.[2] First, let me outline a plain English version of this part that I hope still carries all the required elements from the original. As with the thought experiments in Parts I and II, I want to use it as a launching platform for a discussion about persons. I'll outline briefly the original idea, ask a question about it and move to a variation of my devising.

> **Mary the colour scientist**
>
> Mary is a neuroscientist who is, for whatever reason, forced to investigate the world from a black and white room via *black and white* technology. She specialises in the neuroscience of visual systems and has acquired, let us suppose, all the information that there is to acquire on the material, physical bases of colour vision. She knows what happens when a person sees ripe tomatoes or the sky and she can use terms like 'red' and 'blue' to describe accurately what a person sees when she is looking at a ripe tomato or at the sky. She discovers, for example, just which wave-length combinations from the sky stimulate the retina and exactly how this produces, via the central nervous system, the contraction of the vocal cords and expulsion of air from the lungs that results in the uttering of the sentence

'The sky is blue.' She has discovered just what happens when light hits the retina and how the visual system is activated and how a particular area of the visual brain is responsible for colour vision. So, Mary is an expert colour scientist. From her black and white room she has come to know everything there is to know about the physical bases of colour visual consciousness.

Two questions: 'What happens if Mary leaves the black and white room and sees colour for the first time? Will she learn anything new about colour that she did not already know?'

Stop! Write down what you think before reading on. When we hear the story, most of us probably answer 'Yes, of course Mary learns something new. She learns what it is like to experience colour.' We may think such a conclusion is self-evident or even that it is inevitable given the set-up. It may seem simply obvious that someone who had never seen colour before would learn something new about colour. Surely, we think, Mary would now know for the first time how it *feels* to see the colour red. Mary would have experienced colour qualia.[3] Nothing in her experience in the black and white room could have prepared her for the raw feel of seeing colour for the first time herself. But is this right? It may seem obvious that she must learn something about the world and her visual experience of it, but then this must mean that she did not know everything there was to know about colour vision when she was in the black and white room.

If we take the first part of the story seriously and imagine Mary really does know everything there is to know about colour, it is conceivable she could have used this knowledge in her laboratory to construct a system whereby she would have had the experience of colour that she already knew others had. There are ongoing arguments about this and many of them hinge on what we are asked to believe that Mary knows and, therefore, what she would be capable of doing because of what she knows.[4]

Nonetheless, even Jackson, the creator of the story, has acknowledged that what Mary comes to know need not be new knowledge as such, but a new form of something she already knows. What Mary learns is how to recognise colour for herself rather than via others. She knows about colour in a new way, but she does not acquire new knowledge that she hadn't already acquired in her black and white room. The conclusion from Jackson's story is supposed to be that qualia – or the qualities an experience may have – are left out of the materialist account of how things work.[5] The claim made here is that it is possible to 'have all the physical information without having all the information there is to have'.[6] But Jackson has himself stepped back from the strongest claims.[7]

What Mary learns when she leaves the room is know-how – the wherewithal or capability *for* doing something – and not a new quality of the world. She develops her capabilities in a new way, but this does not mean that she now knows something about the world for which her previous knowledge was insufficient. All that she comes to know comes under the heading of knowing how to do; there are no new facts about colour that she did not already know. She now knows them in a new way, but she does not have new knowledge. Nonetheless, Jackson would still answer 'yes' to the basic question 'What will happen when Mary leaves her black and white room, will she *learn* anything or not?' Even if what she learns is know-how, she still learns something. Much that we know about colour is know-how and means that we can use colour vision to help us make sense of the world about us. This kind of knowing is a one-for-one correspondence such that when Mary sees colour for the first time, she cannot, initially, do any more than correlate her black and white room knowledge with her new personal experience of colour.

And this is true for the way things feel: it may seem as if the phenomenal property or raw feel of something ought to be a separately existing quality, but this is not sufficient to make it so.

The argument turns on what it means to know something and, in keeping with this chapter, what it is to know *consciously*, and that is, to *know* that you know something.

We discussed very early in this book how we talk easily of two kinds of things as if these were two truly separate and separable things.[8] We discussed dualism and, for example, how some have thought that mind and body are separate things. We might think it obvious that we can separate how it feels to look at a red sunset from an actual red sunset. We might suppose that an alien, such as a replicant in the film *Blade Runner*, could know all there is to know about red sunsets and yet not have a subjective feeling in reaction to seeing one. But could we be wrong about the distinction? If we look at sunsets *with* our conception of them, there is only one act taking place. We do not derive feelings of sunsets *from* the sunset; rather, we bring our conception of sunsets *to* a sunset and the event or experience is brought about dynamically. The feel of an experience is brought about by a person. Persons are psychological in character such that knowing cannot be reduced to our physicality, even though this for sure is also part of our make-up. Only persons can be said to *know* about consciousness. Persons have both physical and psychological characteristics (among the many kinds that make us up).

Drawing on earlier workings out in this book, I wish to take an alternative approach to Jackson's thought experiment that takes Dave Chalmers's comments about properties of persons rather than properties of mental states as its starting point. He said:

> Phenomenal properties can also be taken to be properties of individuals (e.g., people) rather than of mental states, characterizing aspects of what it is like to be them at a given time; the difference will not matter much for present purposes.[9]

It matters here when discussing phenomenal properties as social in character.

So, what is Chalmers getting at here? Why does it make a difference if phenomenal properties are properties of people? It matters because we will look for a different kind of explanation: a *social* kind.

Let's recap. The psychological is a form of a different kind from the physical, such that if we take the psychological as a starting point, we will look at what is important to us as people and work from there. What has *feel* for us is what is important to us; this is the subjective dimension and it relates to what persons do and how they do it. What characterises us as persons is what is important to us. As quoted earlier, Ray Tallis said:

> Self equals what I am conscious of, which is, roughly
> speaking, what is or what has become important to me.[10]

Although I would use 'person' rather than 'self' here, I believe the point is the same. The qualitative feel is a quality of what it is to be a person; it's how people are. I mentioned the idea of qualia as properties of people in the introduction to Part II. What follows will address this subject more fully.

What's important for people is where we seem most wanting to make distinctions: everything is graduated when it matters most. To find examples of what's important in *how* a person does something, we need to look at adverbs.[11] Adverbs such as 'freely' in the phrase 'acting freely' say something about *how* a person is acting. We may, at times, find it difficult to talk about or write about how it feels, but how it feels has always been a concern in culture such that there is an abundance of work in art, literature and music filled with just such important matters. I cited Theo Sarbin's comments on this at the beginning of Chapter 5. It is because it is significant to us that artists, writers and composers have always returned to certain subject matter. There are perennial questions, such as 'what does it mean to be free?'

Let's work through a variation devised by me and derived from Jackson's original 'Mary' story.

Variation: 'Mary the captive scientist' or 'the black and white cell'

Rather than work on Mary's experience of seeing red when she leaves the black and white room, I want to suppose that Mary has been held captive in a black and white cell; that she has learned everything it is possible to know about human freedom, but she herself has always been held captive. I want to ask the question, if she is released from the black and white cell, will she learn something new about freedom? I think she will learn how it feels to *be* free.

Acting freely is something we put into practice and it is through this act of consciousness that Mary will learn something new about freedom: She will learn how it feels to *be* free. For sure, she has always in a limited fashion acted freely in her cell – on the basis of the kind of *freedom through mental activity* I've discussed before – but what would be new for her would be how it is to *be* free. She will not know this immediately, as she is likely to be disoriented by being released after such a lengthy captivity. She may well believe that it is a trick and that she will be put back into the room or that she is in a larger space, but still under house arrest for example.

She would test herself and her life against the idea of freedom by exercising her right to speak freely, to move about freely, to mix with people freely, to have freedom of thought, conscience and religion, to have freedom of opinion and expression, to be free from fear, to know that she is free, to be recognised as a person before the law, among other rights and freedoms.[12] To be free is to live life freely. It is to lead one's life. To live and act freely has consequences in a real world. In short, Mary would try out and test out her worldview by her continuing engagement with the world. She would judge her situation by the way others responded to her actions, by the consequences her actions had for her. How else could we make judgements about our social world? How else can we know what we know?

This takes time. Nonetheless, by degrees and with the help of others, I think she could know how it feels to be free and that this 'how it feels to be free' was something that she could never have known from her captivity. She could imagine it. She could recognise what others experienced when they were free. She could know it intellectually by reading about it in books. This is the knowledge argument writ large. It would not be possible for the chained Mary to know, but she might wish that she did. To know in this form is to *know* that you know what you know. And this to me is the form of the knowledge argument that wants our attention. It is because Mary can reflect on her situation and *knows* what her situation was that she can now know that she had not been free; that now, having left her cell, she *is* free.

Let's work through some further examples from world history and, with these, develop our conception of what it is to *know* that you know.

Example 1: Rosa Parks

Rosa Parks was a civil rights activist who sparked the Montgomery, Alabama, bus boycott in 1955.[13] She knew that she would be supported in her protest, but she was also very conscious of the consequences of staying in her seat on the bus when asked to give up her seat to a white person. She wasn't the first black person to refuse to give up her seat in Montgomery, but hers was the act that was taken up as a test case against segregation and brought about the bus boycott.

> She was an activist who knew she'd have backing for her stance; but she was also very brave.[14]

If we ask 'what did Rosa Parks do?' we find that she did not move down the bus when asked to give up her seat for a white person still standing after some whites had just boarded. On the day that she didn't, she hadn't planned to refuse to give up her seat.

She knew others had refused to move earlier that same year. On the day she refused to move, three others seated near her moved. She said:

> People always say that I didn't give up my seat because I was tired, but that isn't true. I was not tired physically, or no more tired than I usually was at the end of a working day. I was not old, although some people have an image of me as being old then. I was forty-two. No, the only tired I was, was tired of giving in.[15]

Rosa Parks might not have stayed in her seat. There were very many bus journeys on which she would have moved to the back of the bus. Any explanation needs to take this into account. Many could have acted as she did, and in similar circumstances, but the fact that someone does and others do not highlights the committed freely chosen act.

Example 2: Aung San Suu Kyi

Aung San Suu Kyi advocated non-violent protest in her opposition to Burma's illegitimate rulers.[16] She has said that people having freedom from fear was more important than power by any means.[17] Her stand highlights the extent to which most on the world's stage act fearfully. At the time of writing, her party has won 43 of 45 vacant seats in the lower house of Burma's parliament. But the party she leads will need continuing support for reforms aimed at re-establishing Burma's democracy.

We can think of freedom in distinct forms: freedom *to* act in certain ways and freedom *from* restrictions. Restrictions can be psychological in kind and include the use of fear such that freedom from fear is a basic human right.[18] This is not all of what it is to be free, but it is a useful starting point for our discussion on freedom.

Aung San Suu Kyi wrote about freedom from fear in an essay with the same name. In the essay she describes people with a 'fear of the scourge of power' and how those subject to a government, even a democratic one, respond in this way. And how fear stifles freedom. She refers to the *Universal Declaration of Human Rights* in her essay in support of people defending rights that are inalienable, which are rights that are not transferable and that should not be taken away from a person. People commit small daily acts of courage in the face of oppression even though these may be ridiculed. She talks of 'grace under pressure' as emblematic of the courage needed when refusing 'to let fear dictate one's action'. The quintessential revolution she calls for is 'that of the spirit' because it is the courage of a united people that can struggle against the 'corrupting influences of ... fear'.

> Among the basic freedoms to which men aspire that
> their lives might be full and uncramped, freedom from
> fear stands out as both a means and an end. A people
> who would build a nation in which strong, democratic
> institutions are firmly established as a guarantee against
> state-induced power must first learn to liberate their own
> minds from apathy and fear.[19]

Aung San Suu Kyi draws a great deal on Burmese history, among other histories. She cites Gandhi, for example, partly because of his own non-violent struggle, but also because of the way he drew on ancient Indian philosophy. She quotes him: 'The greatest gift for an individual or a nation ... was *abhaya*, fearlessness, not merely bodily courage but absence of fear from the mind.'[20]

Unless we remind ourselves of these kinds of struggle, we may fail to recognise how we are acting fearfully because we have become fear minded when dignity requires us to have the courage to act fearlessly. With matters of importance for us as persons, it is more obviously meaningful to talk about such things as experience, point of view and what it is to know what we know. Sometimes we need to start from the other end. We should discuss what's important to us, the non-trivial, by way of an example of how it is for us to know consciously; this is why I've discussed a variation on Jackson's theme at length.

Simply because a person is free to act, that they are free from constraints, does not mean that a person will act. Freedom has to be exercised. Conversely, simply because a person is held in captivity does not mean that they are not free. This is where I came in. A person can be psychologically free because they exercise 'freedom through mental activity'.[21]

The first liberation in any struggle mounted by an oppressed people is that of a psychological kind: the liberation of minds. As discussed earlier, a person may be their own jailer. Fear constrains us even when fear is of one's own making. All of us can be turned into docile bodies policing ourselves for fear of what may happen to us if we act.[22]

The first move in a struggle is often asserting the basic right to be treated as a person.

What makes Aung San Suu Kyi's struggle so remarkable is her pursuit of rightful power under the principle of people being free from fear. The principle of governing without fear is one the rest of the world should embrace.

Acts of conscience are those that stem from a principled stand. A prisoner of conscience – as Aung San Suu Kyi was – could not have done otherwise than they did. But this does not mean they did not act freely. Acting freely sustained over time will lead a person to situations where they could not have done otherwise, but each step along the way was freely made. When Rosa Parks refuses to move down the bus, this speaks to a lifetime of activism and cannot be interpreted as a single event. Where persons are concerned, actions are sustained, spread over often quite long periods of time, spread across different places and situations.[23] Actions are recollected from earlier events and may be envisaged as future events; therefore, a snapshot view of any event will not do justice to what a person is doing. To know what a person is doing and why means knowing about the character of a person, how they have acted in the past, knowing where they stand on things, among many other properties that a person brings to bear on the conditions of their life. We would need to know about Aung San Suu Kyi's standing. For example, we would need to know about her father.[24]

Example 3: Nina Simone

Nina Simone was a civil rights activist. In an interview she was asked: 'What's freedom mean to you?' And quick as you like she came back: 'Same thing as you: you tell me!' Then she turns serious and says:

> Just a feeling; it's just a feeling. It's like how do you tell somebody how it feels to be in love. How are you going to tell anybody who has not been in love how it feels to be in love? You cannot do it to save your life. You can describe things, but you can't tell them. But you *know* when it happens. That's what I mean by free.[25]

It has to be your first-person experience because to know consciously *anything* demands that you reflexively know what something means. Unless and until it is *your* experience, you cannot know consciously anything. Mary the captive scientist would say 'I wish *I* knew how it would feel to *be* free', much as Nina Simone sang in the jazz standard. We'll turn to a reflection on this song in the next chapter.

Nina Simone continued: 'I've had a couple of times on stage when I really felt free ... I'll tell you what freedom is to me: no fear ... That's the only way I can describe it. That's not all of it, but it is something to really feel.' She tails off in thought and then restarts somewhere else: 'Like a new way of seeing, a new way of seeing something.'[26]

And that's the nub of it for me: a new way of seeing means being able to see how you have been seeing – for example, from the standpoint of being held captive – and a new way of seeing – from the standpoint of being free – and know consciously what it means because you have the two together at the same time. It's only possible to know consciously anything because we can do this.

We can act fearfully or fearlessly. When we act fearlessly, we know how differently this feels from acting fearfully. And we want the fearless feeling to be sustained because we know the alternative. We recognise the way things feel as properties of people, of how it is to be them, and we may come to see that it is in what is important to us as people – the significant things in our life and living – where these properties can be found.

In Chapter 9, I will treat the song 'I wish I knew how it would feel to *be* free' as an example of how qualia are properties of people. I will build a commentary around the words. By adding a commentary for this song I hope to show more clearly how being minded – being reflexive and turning what's important to us this way and that – is part and parcel of our life and living in what I have come to call acts of consciousness and conscience. The song provides me a means to more clearly say things about how it is to be conscious, to have conscious experience, and to know consciously. In this way I will offer an alternative way of arriving at an explanation of what it is *to know that I know what I know*.

9   Knowing how it feels to be free

Song: 'I wish I knew how it would feel to be free'[1]

> I wish I knew how
> It would feel to be free
> I wish I could break
> All the chains holding me
> I wish I could say
> All the things that I should say
> Say 'em loud say 'em clear
> For the whole round world to hear
>
> I wish I could share
> All the love that's in my heart
> Remove all the bars
> That keep us apart
> I wish you could know
> What it means to be me
> Then you'd see and agree
> That every man should be free
>   . . .

As we reach the concluding part of this book, I want to try to gather up the main conceptual work of what's gone before this point. And I wish to use the song lyrics above as a way to do it. If I had to sum up the conceptual work of this book in one sentence, it would be 'I wish I knew how it would feel to be free.' What follows offers a commentary that shows my workings out. Once we understand acting freely as a new way of seeing, I believe that we have a way into this song and of understanding our shared humanity.

Commentary

The song starts with how the singer knows what they don't know; how the want of this is the wish to have this standpoint. We start with: 'I wish I knew...' and I'll treat this song as if it were my standpoint.

If only *I* had the wherewithal to see things as you do, I'd know consciously how it is to be free. If I could only see the world as you do, this new way of seeing would give me a way to know for myself how it is. You can describe to me how it is for you to see the way you do, but this will only give me your take on things. For me to know is for me to *have* that take on things. Unless freedom is *my* experience, I cannot know freedom consciously. I know that you have freedom and that I don't. I wish that I knew it too and know at the same time that I don't know freedom.

There is a taken-for-granted sense of how it is to be free for many whose status has never been in doubt. When someone says there is not how it is to be free there is just how it is, I would say that is because the 'how it is' is taken for granted, transparent to the person because never in doubt, never disputed, never denied. If we were to have this shaken even by imagining how it is not to be free, we might 'get it'. We might understand what the song is getting at. If, just for a moment, just a glimmer of what not being free means could be our experience, we would understand what it means to be someone who is not free. And that could be me.

I know that you know how it feels to be free. If you were in my shoes, you would know how it feels to be chained. You would know both how it is to be free and how it is to be chained and know also that, while I am not free, you are not truly free. I would know that things could be different from the way they are. I would know that my life could have been different from the way it is. I know that I do not know how it feels to be free. I know that you know this to be true of me. I want to be in a position where I also know that I know how it feels to be free. To gain this knowledge I need to be free, to live as a free person. I need to be set free. As it says in the song, 'I wish I could break all the chains holding me.' I know that I am captive. I know that I am not free. I know this because I know what it would mean to be free and this being held captive is not it.

Then there's the extraordinary move that asks, in turn, for someone whose way of seeing is to feel free to try to see what it means not to be free. The song asks, how about trying to see things from another's standpoint? Will you imagine how it is for me to be chained? The singer petitions: 'I wish you could know what it means to be me.' I want you to see things differently. I want you to try out, to test out and to imagine how it is to be me and, therefore, how it is to be not free. If you were in my shoes, you would *know* what it means not to be free. If you did this, 'You'd see and agree that every man should be free.' You would be able to *see* as in you'd see what I mean. You would understand. You would 'get it'. You would 'catch yourself on'. You would wise up to how it is for someone holding a different standpoint from your own. And 'you'd agree'. You would have to understand and by understanding commit yourself to the principle that everyone should be free. You would recognise that 'Nobody's free until everybody's free.'[2] Knowing consciously like this is itself a commitment. Now that you have both ways of seeing, there's only one conclusion: everyone should be free. It would be a principled matter of conscience.

Conclusions

And this is why I think this way of telling the story of Mary as 'Mary the captive scientist' comes out differently. Once we change to an idea about the way things feel and what they mean to us as properties of people, we are no longer looking for something that can exist separately from the person. It is a person who acts freely where 'freely' tells us *how* the person acted, in what manner they acted. In a similar vein, acting fearlessly has a feel to it too: there is something it is like *for a person* to act fearlessly.[3] Much of the difference can be picked out in the consequences of acting fearlessly and the impact fear has on people and how they live.

Qualia or phenomenal features can be taken as properties of persons and therefore acting freely and being free are *both* only possible from a point of view, whether this be mine, yours or someone else's. For a person to know certain experiences they have to have them. With some phenomena, it may be that the only way to validate such an experience is to have the experience. There may be no other verification for a given phenomenon than the experience itself. No amount of simulation or reading other people's accounts can really prepare a person for their experience of, say, being and acting freely. We would be patronising in the extreme to assume that we could voice their experience for them just because it might be said to be like theirs. We are ignorant in the extreme if we do not recognise the plight of others because of what we do not know. Even though we cannot know directly how the other person is feeling, this does not mean we should ignore it. It is one thing to acknowledge that we would be patronising to say that we know how you feel, but it is another to be oblivious to the plight of others on these grounds. The fact that we try to understand another person's situation is what makes us human; it gives us our humanity. We need to take seriously the voices of those in particular situations if we are to understand what a person is doing.

Subjunctive mood

In the song, there is much use of what is often called the subjunctive mood. This is expressed through words such as 'would', 'could', 'should', 'might' and these are often prefaced with the conjunction 'if'.[4] The subjunctive mood often highlights what is *supposed* or what we *suppose* to be the case. This mood asks us for our consideration and some effort to engage with what it is someone means by what they say. These words may express distinctions in time: how things 'might have been' – the idea that things could have turned out differently – or how we express things in the future 'might be' – that the future has possibility, that what happens next is not inevitable.

We entertain possibility and slip the bonds of place and time: '... that we can be in one place and thinking of another';[5] that we can think of what might have been and through seeing the past differently turn this around to imagine how things might be different tomorrow. Doing things differently today will have an impact. We are part of the world about us and the lives of others that have constituted it, but we make a contribution to the whole such that small, unique, individual efforts can make a difference in the long term.

Richard Sennett commented that in civic society the use of the subjunctive opens space to somebody else. He says the subjunctive is the mood that voices 'I would have thought ...' rather than 'I think' and thus 'invites response from others'.[6] It invites other people to engage. We open space for others to engage. This means floating ideas for people to engage with equally rather than advocating a stance.

There are two things that need to happen for a conversation to take place: I want to know how it feels to be free and I want you to want to know what it means to be me, what it means not to be free. If we both entertain alternative standpoints from the ones with which we are familiar, we can start a conversation. We will no longer be closed to each other. We will have willingly suspended belief in our current standpoint.

Rather than try to gather up particular conclusions here, the next chapter will encompass conclusions from the whole book; these will include conclusions from Part III.

Conclusions

In these concluding pages I will set out the bigger picture as I see it. I will leave behind the details of earlier chapters. If you have read from page 1, you should be able to follow the conclusions from here on without the need to look up the endnotes. If you have started the book from here, you may need both the endnotes and the index to help you find the detailed workings out for any particular conclusion, and to find detailed descriptions of terms.

These conclusions are contemplations on freedom and captivity. The conclusions are set out with headings that highlight the key ideas discussed in this book: 'Captivity', 'Acts of consciousness and conscience', 'Minded', 'Persons', 'World about us' and 'Cubist Psychology'. The idea is to pull together my contribution in a few concluding comments, leading up to a manifesto advocating a Cubist Psychology.

Captivity

We don't all get taken prisoner – thank goodness – but we can gain insights into everyday life and living from the stories of captivity. Captivity amplifies the familiar features of life and living by turning down the volume on everyday events and thus allowing how it is for us to be heard loud and clear.

If you were to find yourself held in solitary confinement, you would know that the main problem you face is the absence of other people; this may seem obvious but it doesn't go without saying. Without other people in our lives, we are likely to fall apart. We are sustained as people by other people.

When I read about feral children, I thought that this was evidence for the importance of social and cultural experience. Infants do not unfold into children by themselves. If we were to have survived growing up on a deserted island without other humans, we would have needed a different kind of caregiver and they would have made us like them.

When I read of how Victor, the Wild Boy of Aveyron, is said to have responded to the housekeeper, Mme Guérin, I thought of the importance of loving kindness in how we are brought up. She treated Victor as one of her own and Victor responded to her. I came to see the concept of treatment as a way of thinking through the implications of this both in other stories of wild children and also in what happens to neglected children.[1] When I read about Jean-Dominique Bauby I thought of how, being a person with locked-in syndrome, he experiences similar problems with life and living.

We may get the idea of the social experience of isolation much more easily today because of the widespread use of virtual social worlds; nonetheless, artists and writers have always done this. A captive is like the writer in a writer's room or the artist in a studio, but without the usual paraphernalia. For the lack of pencil and paper, a captive is forced to write in their head. In their head is not to be taken literally. The idea of inner is a manner of speaking.[2] It is *as if* we were in a writer's room inside our own heads, even though no such actual location exists. A captive plays out their acts of consciousness in a virtual world of their own making. They see *with* an imagined. A captive uses the skills they bring with them, such as those borne of their engagement with others.

Captives engage with a life of captivity. We might be put in solitary confinement, but we would take our social world into the cell with us. We could populate our isolation with a virtual world of people. We could occupy ourselves. We might continue to have an impact on our life and living and thus would be capable of sustaining ourselves as persons. Solitary confinement seems to pare down the person to the psychological nitty-gritty of what makes us up. Without the distracting excess of events, we witness clearly how persons in captivity hold fast to what matters most to them.

A captive may be fearful of engaging with this kind of imagined world, but the greater fear may be what may happen due to the sheer boredom of the endless days of captive isolation. And so the captive engages with a virtual world about them because there is simply nothing else to do. The captive flight of imagination becomes a new form of occupation and a captive learns how to live from an imagined world and not to be over-whelmed by it. A virtual world offers what Bukovsky called a 'sideways escape'. The provisional character of some captivity – when a captive doesn't know if or when they will be released – means they don't really have a future and the past is a reminder of all they are separated from. A captive occupies their burgeoning virtual world and is occupied by it. They inhabit their own landscaping.

Captives often have a virtual sense of fellowship. There may be a movement that continues beyond the prison cell. There may be a clamour for a person to be freed, as happened with the Chinese artist Ai Weiwei.[3] Simply the thought of such a fellow-ship may be personally sustaining. Acts of consciousness are sustainable because a person making a stand is not alone. As long as there are others that share similar principles, a person can endure solitary confinement.

Here in these and the many other stories I found evidence of what it took to be a person, what it took to sustain oneself as a person, what it might mean to cease to be a person and how they might regain that status. There is a basic principle of fellow feeling that encourages most of us to act in a spirit of fellowship. It is by acting towards others in a spirit of mutual respect that we carry out an act of conscience.

Acts of consciousness and conscience

What is an act of consciousness? In one word: commitment. We choose a particular direction and we know that we have done this; this is what gives leading a life a sense of responsibility: we know that the consequences are ours. Freedom stems from commitment. When we knowingly choose to commit ourselves to a course of action and see it through, when we accept the consequences and take responsibility for the impact our actions have in the world about us, we act freely; this is what a person can do; these are the acts of consciousness and conscience. The contemplative knows this. But it isn't necessary to retreat from the world to carry out minded contemplation.

I believe that there is a fatality about life and living: having made certain decisions and committed oneself to certain actions, there comes a point where it is difficult to do anything else. We are committed by the commitment of repeated acts of the same kind. Commitment is a kind of fatality. Once having chosen, acted and brought about change it cannot be easily undone. Having acted in particular ways, certain things follow and change irrevocably the person we are. Having taken a particular direction, there may be such an impact that makes it impossible to take another direction. There may have been alternative directions we could have taken but these may no longer be alternatives for us. Commitment constrains what we can now do; but commitment also opens up other possibilities unavailable unless we made a commitment in the first place.

Acts of consciousness and conscience can be witnessed when a person acts freely. I think that we are constrained in our freedom to act but that acting freely is not ruled out. I think acting freely relates to other acts of consciousness such as the commitments we make. It is because we are constrained by our commitments that acting freely is possible. Rosa Parks acted freely when she stayed in her seat on the bus. She was an activist and part of a supportive community but 'she was also very brave'.[4] Some ask, could she have done otherwise than she did? On previous bus journeys to and from work, she did move back down the bus when asked to do so. On the day that she stayed in her seat, others moved back down the bus. She was the only one who stayed where she was. She knew there would be unpleasant consequences; by acting with that knowledge, her action is a minded act of consciousness and conscience. She knows what will happen and yet remains in her seat. Rosa Parks said that she was not tired, as many suggested; rather, she was 'tired of giving in'.[5]

Without an understanding of Rosa Parks's activist history, we could not understand what she was doing when she stayed in her seat on the bus. Having been an activist for many years, when she stays in her seat on the bus it is freely done. She knows what some of the consequences of her actions will be, and she still acts *with* that knowledge. Acts of consciousness cannot be isolated in snapshots. Without the historical traces, we cannot understand an act of consciousness. Acts of consciousness do not exist in isolation, nor are they registered in a single moment. We need a different kind of enquiry to investigate the ongoing affairs of life and living. We need to take psychological time – the idea of sustained time or duration – as part of our circumstances. Psychological time includes events that haven't happened yet, such as the deadline for this manuscript (at the time of writing). Prospective events may constitute the reason for action even though they have yet to happen. I can think about the deadline for this manuscript and thinking about *that* can act as a spur to get this manuscript completed.

Turning the tables on the guards holding captives is another example of acting freely under highly constrained conditions. When I spoke to Vladimir Bukovsky, he told me how he could transform a situation where he was being bullied. By acting fearlessly, by laughing in the face of a bully, he confounded the guard. The guard didn't understand what was happening. He was forced to turn back upon himself and was stopped in his tracks, caused to doubt what he was doing.

Similarly, when Anthony Grey ignores the instructions from those holding him and then, later, suddenly does what is asked of him without being asked, he gets accused of being arrogant. He realises that if his guards think this of him after being held for nearly two years, he must be holding himself together very well.

Making art is an act of consciousness. When I make a visual artwork, I am both artist and viewer. I can see *that* I draw and that the marks I make each go towards the art I am making. But I am also always the first viewer. I see the marks that I make and I may be minded towards them. I may evaluate the marks and how well they work in the production of my artwork. When I draw, I may move backward and forward in a way that physically illustrates my reflexive character. I move forward and make marks on the paper: I move back and view what I have done. I move forward again and alter or add to the marks already there. And then once more I move back. I may spend an extended time making marks. I may spend an extended time viewing what I have done and trying to see my way forward. Necessarily, I turn towards the art not only as something I am in the process of making but now also as something that is a work in its own right. A finished piece is both my art making and an artwork that may continue to exist independently of me.

Minded

It is because of the way we experience having a past we remember that we come to realise things change over time. This remembrance of our past grants us the scope of having a future, because we can imagine how the present time would have been for us in our past. Therefore we can treat this time now as like time past and imagine our future. This is what it is to be minded. We reflexively turn one thing back upon itself and come to see things differently by so acting.

The most striking thing about consciousness is the skill of doing more than one thing at the same time. If I am to imagine something being different from how it is now, I must also consciously know *at the same time* how it is now. I must necessarily know my situation and know how it might be different.

To be minded can be expressed as 'a person acts in such and such a way'. To be minded means to be capable of switching standpoints and can be expressed as 'a person switches standpoints and comes to see things differently'. Mind is an important word to use because it reminds us that what we are investigating are psychological phenomena.

A minded person can act freely because of the ability to switch between different standpoints on what matters to them. A minded person is capable of conceiving more than one thing at the same time. To know consciously means knowing both how I currently see things and also seeing things differently at the same time. 'Minded' is an established word that is perhaps much less used today. It is a means of conveying what it is that a person can do and how it is that a person makes acts of consciousness and conscience.

There are a number of things going on at the same time and the phrase 'minded person' is designed to convey them. To be minded consists of two reflexive abilities:

- First, to be reflexive is to be able to 'turn towards' as, for example, when a person turns towards their life so far, or directs themselves towards their imagined future. The directing or turning towards is just a manner of speaking. Persons, as psychological beings, direct themselves.
- Second, to be reflexive is to act towards others as if they too are reflexive. We assume that others are also minded as we are.

I act towards you as a person minded in the same way as I am. I do not want this set of conclusions to constrain you. I want you to have room to think about things for yourself.

To give an example of how it is for a person to be minded in the world about us, let's take what happens when we go to an art gallery. Let's say we go to the Reina Sofía in Madrid and look at Picasso's *Guernica*. We go to the room in which it is hung. We look at it. As it's very large, we may scan across the surface of it looking at various parts of the painting. We may disengage from this activity and turn towards information about it and engage with that. But when we do so, we are simply carrying out a different form of engagement from the one we professed to be carrying out before. We are engaging differently with the painting. We may turn towards others who have come with us and they may give us other ways to engage with the painting. We may turn towards the commentary given in our headphones; this may give us another kind of engagement with the painting. Now we look with an idea of looking at particular parts of the painting. Perhaps we are educated about Picasso's use of the bull in his work and what it may symbolise in *this* painting. If we reflect on looking at this painting later, we turn towards it with a reflective engagement.

Psychology is the study of people, minded persons acting in the world about us. I believe that it is as Vygotsky supposed. He concluded that what was once a social action – one carried out with the help of other people – was an action that we became capable of carrying out privately. Our physical acts of turning this way and that may become psychological turnings, the reflexive acts of consciousness. Once we are capable of such acts, I believe we are minded persons. Before this transformation, we can be thought of as proto-persons. We develop another way of acting in the world. We become psychological kinds of being. And this is simultaneous with our physical life and living, granting us more scope, but not simply adding something separate. There are differences between the psychological and the physical, but there is neither a division between them, nor are they mutually exclusive. Both are acting at the same time just as the sound we hear of an orchestra is the sound of all the musicians playing together. Consciousness is an ensemble performance.

We turn towards others and imagine that they are doing likewise; this is what it is to be minded. We become able to do psychologically what once we could only do socially. We turn towards others in all kinds of social activity and experience: play, conversation, work, study, among many others. We learn how to do the same thing privately, personally, psychologically when we turn social action into private thinking, remembering and imagining. In my thinking, I may turn towards writing this book and trying to write a new draft for the conclusions. In my remembering, I may turn towards the different ways that I've talked about the ideas in my conclusions. In my imagining, I may turn towards how I believe a reader will understand what's written in the conclusions. Although this directing may be privately undertaken, thinking, remembering and imagining can be revealed. What I can carry out privately has been carried over from acts carried out socially.

I believe that we can slip the bonds of place and time. We can think about how our life has been, how it is today and how it might be tomorrow. We are like the subjunctive mood in grammar. We are moved by what *could* be the case. We suppose how things *might* be different, how we *could* see things differently and what the impact of this *would* be *were* it to be brought about by us. We can be moved by something that has not happened. I believe that it is because we are psychological in character that something which is *not* the case can move us.

There are many psychological moves we make when we slip the bonds of place and time. We can be in one place and thinking of another. For example, when Evgenia Ginzburg was given exercise in a roofless prison cell, she heard the sounds of ships' sirens as 'the living voices of friends for [she] knew those ships, every one of them'.[6] She's supposedly exercising in a prison and yet she's replenishing herself with memories of home. Her guards cannot know what she is doing when she walks. She wrote: 'It could never have occurred to any warder how many new impressions, dreams, memories a prisoner brought back from a fifteen minutes' walk in a grey roofless cell.'[7] She exercises her freedom to act because she can be in one place and yet thinking of another.

It is a person who is minded. There aren't two things – minds and persons; there's one whole that can be expressed as 'minded persons' in the world about us.

Persons

The way we treat life and living is a matter *of* and *for* psychology. Consciousness has to do with our conception of the world about us. What matters is the way we treat each other as persons. A person is someone so treated. We are made persons by those already persons who treat us as one of their kind.

Treatment is a word that conveys several meanings. I believe that our psychological life rests on the way we treat each other. What makes this a psychology book is that all the conceptual analysis concerns how we treat each other – in other words, how we act towards each other. Treatment is what makes a psychological life: how others act towards us and how we in turn act towards others. Treatment is used here to convey also the idea of how we consider what it is like for someone else. We think about them and may play out, *as a presentation*, how we imagine their experience would be if it were to be ours.[8]

Persons are socially constituted facts of life and living: persons are simply what we treat them to be. Psychology is the study of minded persons acting in the world about us. I think that it is because others who are already persons act towards us in particular ways that we become persons like them. Others treat us as persons, so that, over time, we come to see ourselves as others see us. By using the word 'person' rather than 'individual', we can see easily how a change from singular to collective does not change the subject. We have person, singular form, and persons (or people) plural form. I think Cooley was right to point out that the singular and collective forms aren't two different subjects; rather, they are two different standpoints on the same subject.[9] We can easily shift between these standpoints. We can entertain alternatives and this means we can hold more than one standpoint at the same time.

A person has standing in the world. A person *is* their standing in the world and the crediting and respecting of another that acknowledges that. And this is why practices that take away a person's standing arbitrarily, or deny that a person has standing, are violations of a person's rights and are, if allowed, personally devastating.

- A person is a set of standpoints that make up their standing in the world.
- A person is their acts of consciousness and conscience and what these amount to as a set.
- A person is the shared contours that compose them.[10]
- A person is a socially constituted fact of life. Persons are real and the support for this assertion is human history, the arts, law, custom, convention and belief. Persons are fundamentally psychological in character.

What it is to know persons is to acknowledge and recognise them. I acknowledge consciousness in others. I recognise them as persons as they do me. This recognition is itself an act of consciousness and conscience.

Psychology is the study of people first and foremost.[11] We need to draw from people in the arts and their experience of examining life and living in order to do likewise in psychology. We need to study conventions as these may form what is most familiar to us. We need to study what matters to people, what's important to people in any particular time and place. We need to study the conditions of normal living: being brought up, going to work or school, family life, community living and how any particular community treats people. Much of this is taken for granted, familiar and perhaps this is why the 'goes without saying' needs to be said. I believe it is the very familiar facts of life and living that constitute us as the people we are. Any investigation needs to deal with the conceptual framing of what we think needs explaining. And this is why I believe the arts offers such an exemplary psychological investigation. By framing ideas, by always taking standpoints, and by putting together different treatments, I believe that artists, writers and directors examine how it is to be one of us.

Psychology can only apply to persons as wholes irrespective of how much is derived from researching what makes up a person. When we say something about someone's mind, we are saying something about them as a person. What we're talking about is what characterises our life and living as a human. A person exercises certain psychological powers that are characteristic of them as persons, such as thinking about how things might have been and how things might yet be.

What can a person do? A minded person carries out acts of consciousness by entertaining alternative standpoints. As persons, we collect ourselves together. If we lose the ability to collect up what makes us persons, because, as an example, we suffer memory loss, we may come to rely on others to collect us up. As long as there are others to treat us as persons in our own right, we are sustained. We cease to be persons only when no one does this for us. We cease to be persons when we are treated as less than human or, what is worse, acted towards as if we no longer existed. Under these conditions, we may personally disintegrate or fall apart.

We may be collected together as a person by other people. If those that know us deny our existence, it will be as if we no longer existed. When I read the accounts of solitary confinement written by former hostages and political prisoners, I came to see how each built a virtual social world through acts of imagination. They imagined doing things with other people, occupied themselves and populated their solitary cells. When I read of the consolation derived by Terry Waite from receiving a postcard on which was written 'You are not forgotten' when he was held hostage, I could see a pattern of evidence emerging. Anthony Grey told me that the importance of knowing others had campaigned for him even after he had been released was of enormous importance. Paradoxically, it is a person in isolation, when held captive in solitary confinement, who highlights the social character of us as persons. Here is the human condition writ large. Being a person is based on being with others. When there are no others present, the captive simply makes them up.

Persons do not die. Persons are not born and persons do not die. Bodies may be said to be born and to die, although the timing of these events has often been disputed. With persons, it's different. We may start to think about a child before it is born. For the family, the child may already exist for them. After the body dies, the person we knew may have a continued existence in the lives of others who knew them. Our acts of remembrance continue to collect up the person in ways that mark them as psychologically present even if physically absent. I'm not saying that they continue to make an original contribution; nonetheless, this way of thinking makes the person a psychological character in our life and living.

If a person produces something, such as an artwork, this may continue to be shown after the artist dies. We could say the person continues through this act of consciousness and in our continued interest in it. Picasso's *Guernica* still moves us today and therefore I think that Picasso still exists as a person for us. He is part of the world about us.

As it is possible to compose a person in the first place, it is possible for a person to cease to be. It seems likely that it may also be possible for someone to regain their status as a person. When I read about locked-in syndrome, I thought that here was an example that says much about us as persons. Jean-Dominique Bauby continued to be a person after the stroke. Those around and about him knew nothing of this. They assumed that Bauby's life as a person had ended when he had the stroke. During this time, he remained minded but could not act in the world about us. He could not make an original contribution. He existed for himself alone. For Bauby, it was as if he had died and was living in some kind of afterlife like a ghost. He was treated as if he were absent. For those that knew Bauby, it was as if he had died after the stroke and that the person they knew had died too. He existed for himself reflexively because, as with those held in isolation, he could continue in private as part of a virtual social world. From outer appearances alone, it was not possible at that time to tell whether Bauby *the person* still existed.

When it became known that Bauby could make small voluntary movements, his status changed for all concerned. Once it was recognised that Bauby the person was still present and that there was a means of communication available, others engaged him and he became a person, once again, for them too. Once more he had an impact on the world about him. He regained the status of being a person in the world capable of making an original contribution by blinking one eye. By this means, Bauby wrote the book that is testimony to that person and his life with locked-in syndrome. He became once more part of the world about us. He figured in the world and contributed to its landscape. He died not long after finishing his book, but he remains a person for me because his story still moves me to write these sentences about him.

A person's point of view is particular to each of us. If we want to understand how it is to be someone else, we need to know it from someone else's standpoint. A minded person carries out an act of consciousness and conscience by entertaining alternative standpoints. We are capable of trying out and testing out other standpoints. We can hold many different standpoints simultaneously. We are Cubist people.

Reflexively we get the idea of who we are from how others see us and we act similarly towards others. We turn things over. We are who we are in acts of engagement with others. And we need to engage with others to achieve this. The clearest markers of our character are found in the presentations we make that are respected and credited by others. We are recognised and acknowledged. We become the person we are acknowledged to be through the encounters with others that forge us as persons.

We are our contemporary presentation. Presentation is the end of the line, the product of all our peopled activity. As with any presentation, our presenting needs to be accepted, respected, credited by others. Who we are – our presentation – is an act of consciousness. Having acted a certain way – and thus having been engaged with by others who know us – we become the way that others treat us to be.

We make ourselves up as we go along. There isn't a script or a future. Acting isn't false or pretence, it's an act of composition. Making ourselves up has a fatality about it. Our repeated presentations over time lead us to a condition where we cannot do otherwise than act as we do. This is one of the insights we can derive from the film The Return of Martin Guerre.[12] I believe that we become the person our commitments bring about and having done so we cannot easily change. Flexibility comes from a willingness to always entertain alternative standpoints, to sabotage the familiar, to test ourselves against others, to try something different even if only for a while.

Much as any painting if X-rayed may show a history of reworking, so it is with us. Who we are is the latest reworking. We are more like a palimpsest.[13] A palimpsest was a manuscript that was reused such that what had been written previously, even though rubbed out, would often show through any contemporary writing.[14] By analogy, we are similarly written and written over in a way that means the traces of earlier editions still show through.

We are like this book, like the current version of this book. All the many earlier versions have traces in this, the current version. The current version may be the end of a long line of revision, but it still bears the traces of all the earlier versions that have gone into the making of this one. I believe that we are all of us like this. We could think of the final version as a Cubist combination of all the revisions.

Reflexively, we get the idea of who we are from *both* how others see us – how they hold up a mirror to us – *and* how we, in turn, become able to use others as mirrors. Becoming minded is developing the ability to do for ourselves what we once did solely in practice with others. Our reflexively minded contemplation is a social act of consciousness carried out privately by a particular person.

We can act thoughtfully, fearlessly, freely and it is these ways of acting that characterise us as persons. It is the person who is conscious. The psychological properties of people are knowable, describable, performable in ways that we recognise in the world about us.

We acknowledge *that* a performance tells us something of how it is to be free. For example, we listen to Nina Simone sing 'I wish I knew how it would feel to be free'. We hear the words and how she sings them. We can get an idea of how it is to be free *from* how she sings the song. What's important to us is what has a phenomenal property.[15] It is because it matters to us that there is how it feels, for example, to be free. Acts of consciousness, such as acting freely, cannot be independent of the minded person carrying them out.

World about us

Acts of consciousness and conscience are the myriad ways we create the world about us. I've used the phrase 'the world about us' because in English it has more than one meaning. I'm using world as shorthand for 'human social, cultural and historical world' – the kind of world at least partly envisaged in Hobsbawm's definition: 'The lives of the men and women who live on earth'.[16] The phrase 'world about us' conveys more than one thing at the same time: the idea that world is all around us, such that the lives of people make up the fabric of our world *and* that world is concerned with us as people, the idea that persons are the subject matter of world.

In this book, I've set out the way in which seeing people as positive shapes is a convention derived from social practice. We tend to look at people as individuals and to see the skin as an envelope housing the person who lives inside. But we could conceive of an alternative way of seeing people as negative contours made out of the relationships they have with other people and where the practices of conversation, play, work, among others, make up the social action.

What does it mean to say that we are held together by social practices? What is familiar to me – often so familiar as to go unnoticed – are the ways we think about our lives. When we see persons as positive shapes, in isolation, on their own, we may come to believe that persons truly are separate entities. We may believe that we can draw a line around the outside of an individual person and that we need to look inside the positive shape line to find out what is going on. We believe that persons have insides just as their bodies do.

But usage differs. René Magritte took the familiar and sabotaged it by making the familiar seem strange. In this book, I have wanted to try out and test out the taken for granted and see what happens when we don't take certain things for granted. In painting, there were traditions in place before the advent of the use of perspective to create the illusion of depth. The use of perspective was a new tradition, one which seemed strange at first. When we entertain alternative ways of looking, the world will seem strange and we may feel uncomfortable with this feeling. Just because it feels uncomfortable does not mean that something is wrong. When we try out and test out something different, it's likely to feel strange at first. If we live in another country, this may be our experience at first. Given time, we may come to feel so much at home that when we return to our native country, we may feel like an outsider.

I was asked about what I would like by way of cover illustration by my publisher, Cambridge University Press. I wanted one in particular of Cézanne's Mont Sainte-Victoire series of paintings. Why did I want this for the cover illustration? Many have said that Cézanne was probably the first Cubist painter.[17] Of course, it wasn't called Cubism then, but art historians often refer to this series of paintings as an early beginning. He was trying out and testing out what painting was about. He built the composition by juxtaposing painted daubs of light and dark colours. He did not paint the entire canvas. He left white canvas showing through to show that it was a canvas. The painting was important in its own right and not because of what it referred to.

We can still view it as a painting of a mountain, one that captivated Cézanne for many years, but it can also be seen as a composition, an early Cubist kind of composition. Here is a conceptual painting that shows signs of its composition.

Our psychological world is conceptual in much the same way as the art world is conceptual; it is about how we think about it. Modern art was said to be conceptual art, but all art has a conceptual basis.[18] How we conceive our world landscapes our world. The world about us *is* a conceptual world.

Our seeing has already been shaped such that we could never simply observe anything. It would be more accurate to say we conceive the world about us when we look, because how we look brings about the world we see. Our conceptual frameworks make a human situation what it is, just as landscaping makes the natural world seem the way it does, such as wild, or Arcadian.[19]

Cubist Psychology

A Cubist Psychology takes many different conceptions of the same psychological subject at the same time. The 'Cubist' part of the title derives from Cubism in the visual arts (and painting in particular). Painting under 'Cubism' came to be an act of composition and not a supposed attempt to faithfully copy the world as it is.

I think of consciousness as like a Cubist form; that is, as a simultaneous composition of many things going on at the same time. I think that consciousness is a simultaneous composition just as the many different perspectives on a guitar are shown simultaneously on one of Picasso's Cubist canvases. Rather than additive sequences of this feature and that – as if these are separate and separable features, I believe consciousness is simultaneous.

When I read about Jonathan Franzen's and Philip Pullman's views of their work, I thought that these two exemplify what I mean by a Cubist Psychology of persons.[20] Franzen said that he felt like a member of a single large virtual community in which he had 'dynamic relationships' with other writers 'most of whom are no longer living'. I think this is exactly the sense that I want to convey in the phrase 'world about us'. I think it's a Cubist composition because the world is composed of all the people who have ever lived. This way of thinking is akin to a visual art sensibility in which everything is always present at the same time simultaneously. We are part of the same composition; nonetheless, each person, each part of the composition is Cubist because each part is also a composition, another collection. Building a person is a collective achievement.

Similarly, Philip Pullman's comments on 'how it is' for him when he was writing a book testify to this conception. He wrote that it was necessary 'to be in several contradictory states of mind at the same time'. He says explicitly that they are not one state after another; but rather, that they occurred 'simultaneously'.[21] Brian Keenan told me that he thought the nearest experience to 'how it is' to be held in captivity was to be writing imaginatively about something.

It is because we are psychologically Cubist that we are both conscious and capable of acts of consciousness and conscience. We can hold more than one standpoint simultaneously because, as Wittgenstein explained, we can have both a current idea of something and a new idea at the same time.[22] The only way we could know that it was a new idea is to know both simultaneously. If we could not do this, we would not know our ideas were different from before. We would have different ideas but no reflection upon them. Having more than one idea at the same time gives us the capability to switch to alternative standpoints, to see things differently – the very definition of imagining. And this is where I came in. Joseph Kovach had freedom through mental activity because he knew that he was seeing things differently. Thus he used this practice of imagining as a way to act freely while held in captivity. In captivity, it was the only freedom to act he had left open to him.

In painting, it is possible to juxtapose many things by placing them next to one another. We can have many views simultaneously placed next to one another on the same canvas. Nonetheless, there is still a legible painting that can be read for meaning. Perhaps because it's unconventional, we are forced to examine how the effect is brought off, how elements within the work combine. Our effort to find meaning highlights the way that meaning is not a given, but always has to be made.

I believe there are problems with the conventional linear way of thinking that is conventional in much of the modern developed world. I think this stems from a particular conception of time that comes about because of the importance of the written word. I drew on the German words *nacheinander* and *nebeneinander* as a way of making a distinction. *Nacheinander* translates as one *after* another and *nebeneinander* as one *next to* another. I think the one next to another conception offers a different standpoint on the world and our place in it. The one next to another conception is more typical of the visual arts and particularly of painting. We read one word after another when we read written texts and books; necessarily they follow this conception. When we look at a painting, we can see many things going on simultaneously. In Cubist painting in particular, there is the possibility of having many views juxtaposed – put next to one another – on the same canvas, such as found in Picasso's Cubist guitar paintings.

A Cubist Psychology can contribute to our understanding. We can take many standpoints on the same subject at the same time and collect them up in a series, much like Cézanne's paintings of Mont Sainte-Victoire. Also, we can approach the same issue from many different conceptions at the same time. Gormley did this in his body-cast sculptures, which he called a 'psychological Cubism'.[23] I've tried out and tested out both in this book. I've looked both at the different ways captives write about how they used their time in captivity, and also at the many different kinds of isolation. Both of these were used to address the same issue of how it is for us to be conscious, to have conscious experience and to know consciously.

The idea with this contribution is to turn certain ways of working into what I'm calling a Cubist Psychology.

- First, a Cubist Psychology gives the freedom to move around subject matter and to approach it from many standpoints simultaneously. For any particular subject, such as consciousness, these standpoints can be put together to compose our psychological conception. The idea is to resist the temptation to tidy up the miscellaneous character of such a composition. The idea is to stick with contradictions, ambiguities, absurdities and paradoxes. We can conceive of ourselves as more than one thing at the same time.

As artists and writers often attest, we should stick with the apparent contradictions, paradoxes, absurdities and ambiguities because these are ways that lead us to examine our conceptions. We are who we conceive we are. Persons are brought about: they are not a given. The world about us is conceived not given.

- Second, there isn't one fixed view of anything that will somehow encompass all there is. We need to keep the gaps obvious just as early proto-Cubist work had plain white painted canvas showing through in places. The cover illustration for this book shows a work by Paul Cézanne that is a very good example.[24]
- Third, Cubist Psychology still has a realist standpoint, but one that accepts that our conceptions are a very real part of what exists for us.[25]
- Fourth, the Cubist composition is an object in its own right and neither a window on the world nor simply a symbolic representation of something that does exist. Cubist artists implored us to look at the painting as an object in its own right deserving of our investigation. We need to examine our conceptions, our everyday conventions, and to look at what we take for granted. There are many ways to 'sabotage the familiar'.[26] A Cubist Psychology would stand in its own right.

I'm putting forward a Cubist Psychology as a way of drawing attention to an alternative conception of psychological matters.

We misconceive if we think our conceptions point to what is real. We may misconceive when we fall for the idea that our psychological conceptions *represent* what is real for us when, in psychological terms, our psychological conceptions *are* what is real for us. Just as the painting exists in its own right and not merely as a representation of a supposedly greater reality, so would a Cubist Psychology. I believe that psychology is a discipline in its own right and does not point to some other more basic reality that lies in other fields of investigation. Our psychological reality is what is real for us as persons because we are psychological compositions. That is what persons are. Persons are quintessentially psychological.

Last words

For me, this book brings together four main features of my life and living: my background in the arts, my interest in consciousness, my research into captivity of all kinds and my work in social psychology. These conclusions are not simply assertions but are based on research in its broadest sense. There is conventional research cited throughout this book, including some of mine. But there is also research carried out in the arts and literature, which is also cited. And then there is the tried and tested research that we all of us carry out simply by engaging in this life of ours. I believe that all of these are valid forms of research. All the accounts attest to the human condition: how it is for us to experience the world about us and to carry out acts of consciousness and conscience. The conclusions I draw out are a genuine attempt to conceive our human condition and an invitation to readers to do likewise. This is how it is for me, how about you?

Notes

Preface

1 Gablik 1970, p. 9.

Introduction

1 If you recognise the name or the title, please get in touch. I would very much like to read this piece again (and properly reference it).
2 Siobhan Dowd used such a term in her edition of prison writings (1996).
3 Derek Parfit is a philosopher who has written extensively on the problem of identity. The teleporter thought experiment is discussed in his book *Reasons and Persons*; see Parfit 1984.
4 See Nagel 1974.
5 Cubism and Cubist Psychology are both described in the introduction to Part II or see, for example, Golding 1959.
6 See also comments in the opening pages of Carter 2002, pp. 8–9.
7 A brief discussion of dualism and the mind–body problem is given in the introduction to Part II.

Introduction to Part I

1 See the *Universal Declaration of Human Rights*, 1948.
2 See Descartes [1637/1641] 1968 and the introduction to Part II.
3 Waite 1993, p. 263.

Chapter 1 To teleport or not to teleport? (Parfit)

1 Adapted with due respect from Parfit (1984, 1987).
2 Reported first in the journal *Nature* in 2004 and, over a greater distance, in *Nature Physics*; see Ursin *et al.* (2007).

3 I recommend reading Ray Tallis's work on this. His latest book is likely to be the best place to start. I have read and would recommend both *Michelangelo's Finger* and *The Kingdom of Infinite Space*. Also read anything by David Chalmers on the 'Hard Problem'. From an entirely different standpoint, read one of Dan Dennett's books. He would argue for information being sufficient and reading *Consciousness Explained* or *Sweet Dreams* is likely to give you a way in.

4 See Birbaumer *et al.*'s (1999) work on Brain Computer Interfaces (BCIs) and people who have locked-in syndrome, access to some of which is available online.

5 Read Richard Powers, *Galatea 2.2*.

6 Read Jean-Dominique Bauby's (1997) book *The Diving Bell and the Butterfly*. There is more commentary on Bauby in Chapter 5.

7 See the film *The Diving Bell and the Butterfly* (2007); this is discussed briefly in Chapter 5.

8 Damasio (2000) uses the terms 'polyphonic' and 'symphonic' in a similar way in his book *The Feeling of What Happens*. See pp. 43 and 88–9.

9 Dan Dennett coined the term 'Cartesian Theatre' to refer both to the dualism of Descartes and the idea of the ego sitting in a kind of movie theatre in one's head. See e.g. Dennett (1991).

10 In slow-wave sleep a person rarely dreams and they are unlikely to have a first-person perspective. If awoken from this kind of sleep, they will be unable to report anything about what it was like to be in slow-wave sleep. See e.g. Revonsuo 2010, p. 161.

11 View Magritte's *The Interpretation of Dreams* (1930).

12 Mead 1934, p. 223, note 25.

13 Danziger 1997, p. 190. Also see Maiers *et al.* 1999.

14 Taylor 1985, pp. 190–1.

15 From *Jeremy Hardy Speaks to the Nation*, episode 8.1 'How to grow up', BBC Radio 4, 30 June 2010.

16 Ciarán Benson (2001) uses the term 'place-time' to distinguish the familiarity of places in human situations from the physical space-time normally referred to. I discuss this idea further in other places in the book, as specified in the Index.

17 Benson 2001, p. 6.

18 Hobsbawm 1997, p. 308.

19 See 'branch line' case in e.g. Parfit 1984.

20 See *The Return of Martin Guerre*, 1982. Well worth your while to find and watch the original film.

21 See also the French film, originally titled *L'Homme qui voulait vivre sa vie* [The man who wanted to live his life] (2010), but given the title *The Big Picture* in English. This film examines questions of identity and is 'about a man who recovers his identity by losing it' (quoted from notes put together by the Watershed cinema in Bristol).

22 See Parfit 1987.

23 A Buddhist text reported by Parfit cited in Blakemore and Greenfield, 1987, p. 19.

24 These last comments come from Duncan Gillard as part of his response to reading this part of the book.

25 Cooley 1902, pp. 1 and 2.

26 Gillibrand *et al.* 2011, p. 16.

27 See Hume ([1739] 1969), *Treatise on Human Nature*, particularly p. 306.

28 See Neisser 1981.

29 Bartlett 1932, p. 213.

30 See Ost and Costall (2002).

Chapter 2 To be a person: ego, bundle and social theories

1 For further detail on these arguments, chapter 7 of Julian Baggini's book *The Ego Trick* (2011) is worth reading.

2 Fisher 2004.

3 See Dennett 2003, pp. 173 and 287 in particular, but with surrounding pages to get the general idea of his argument. I think Dennett arrives at a similar idea to the person, but from a different starting point and with a very different justification and consequences. Nonetheless, even if we hold very different worldviews, I think it is interesting that some of the adding up is so similar.

4 See Reddy 2010, chapter 7 and p. 121 in particular, but also throughout the text.

5 Use 'Rubin's vase' as a search item to see the images online. The description I give in the chapter should be sufficient if you cannot view the image.

6 See the series of cut-outs Matisse made in 1952 called *Blue Nudes*, for example.

7 View work by Rachel Whiteread on her website or related websites that show her work. Have a look in particular for *House* and for her bookshelves sculpture *Untitled (Colours)* (2002). These evocatively highlight the idea of negative spaces, shapes and contours.

8 See Reddy 2010, p. 27.

9 Attributed to Peter Michael Dedes.

10 See Gillibrand *et al.* (2011) on continuous and discontinuous development, e.g. p. 16.

11 *Ibid.*, p. 16.

12 See Perry (2002) on the effects of neglect, particularly a lack of interaction with caregivers.

13 See Gillibrand *et al.* 2011.

14 See the *mysterian* position as discussed in, for example, McGinn 1993.

15 Freud's 'infantile amnesia' as well as current neuropsychological evidence.

16 See Reddy 2010.

17 See Richards 1974 and Reddy 2010.

18 See *Mind, Self and Society*, a collection of notes from Mead's lectures (1934).

19 Mead [1938] 1972, p. 189.

20 *Ibid.*, p. 190.

21 *Ibid.*, p. 222.

22 *Ibid.*, pp. 616–17.

23 Vygotsky 1978 cited in Zelazo *et al.* 2007, p. 408.

24 Vygotsky 1990, 1991.

25 See Vygotsky 1990, 1991, discussed later in this book.

26 Vygotsky [1933] 1966.

27 *Ibid.*

28 *Ibid.*

29 See Bruner 1986, 1990.

30 Vygotsky [1933] 1966.

31 Anthony Grey did this by writing his first fictional work, *A Man Alone*, while a hostage.

32 Burr 1995, pp. 29–30.

33 See Tallis 2010, p. 19.

34 Elephants are thought to remember being badly treated.

35 See Newton 2002.

36 See the Introduction to Part III for an explanation of Theory of Mind.

37 The mark test and arguments about what this test shows that a child or young chimpanzee *knows* will be reviewed in Part III.

38 See Russon and Andrews 2011.

39 See Tallis 2010, pp. 19 and 20.

40 Example suggested by Duncan Gillard.

41 See Cooley 1902, particularly chapter 1.

42 See Shapin 1991.

43 See earlier explanation of Benson's term 'place-time' in Chapter 1, p. 28.

44 See Alan Rayner 1997. In biological terms, the skin is a permeable membrane.

45 From Robert Burns's poem 'To a Louse', verse 8.

46 See Cooley 1902.

47 See Parks 1992.

48 See Mead 1934.

49 See Conrad 1998.

50 Various sources have been drawn upon and the following are good starting points on the social identity approach: Tajfel 1981, Hogg and Abrams 1988 and Robinson 1996. More recently, see any of the work of one of Tajfel's students, Stephen Reicher (e.g. 2011) and Alex Haslam (often writing together).

51 See Harré 1993, p. 77.

52 Miłosz 1953, p. 25.

53 See Reicher 2011.

54 See Biko [1978] 2004.

55 See Harré and Gillett 1994, e.g. pp. 20–1.

56 Gombrich 1950, pp. 454–5.

57 See, for example, Richardson 1996 and Golding 1959.

58 See Goffman 1961, 1971.

59 Attributed to the eighteenth-century Romantic philosopher
 Jean-Jacques Rousseau.

60 Itard 1962.

61 See Truffaut's film *L'Enfant Sauvage* based on Jean-Marc-Gaspard
 Itard's book *The Wild Boy of Aveyron*.

62 Some think Kaspar Hauser is the first account of a case of someone
 with autism, e.g. Perry 2002.

63 Genie became well known not only because of the abuse and neglect
 she suffered at the hands of her family, but also because of the
 academic interest in her case and the theories of language acquisition
 academics thought Genie might demonstrate.

64 See Newton 2002.

65 See Itard 1962.

66 See Perry 2002 for a discussion of the effects of neglect as shown in
 brain scans of neglected children.

67 See Ashworth 2000, chapter 6, 'Social being'.

68 Viewing the film *Moon* is recommended.

69 See Pullman in Headlam Wells and McFadden 2006.

70 See Bartlett [1932] 1964 and Middleton and Edwards 1990.

71 For *flashbulb* memories, see Conway 1995.

72 See discussion of John Dean's testimony in Chapter 1.

73 See Harré 1992, p. 154.

74 Gore Vidal used this word for the first part of his autobiography:
 Palimpsest: A Memoir.

75 See, for example, Nowell-Smith 1990.

76 Gymnasts may switch from internal to external perspective during
 performance; it may be a skill we all have to some degree. See White
 and Hardy 1995.

77 See Sacks 2008.

78 See Wearing 2005.

79 *Ibid.*

80 Sacks 2008, p. 215. Oliver Sacks is a physician and professor of
 neurology and psychiatry; he knew of Clive Wearing's case history
 long before he met him.

81 *Ibid.*

82 *Ibid.*

83 Proust 1922, *Swann's Way*, p. 3.

84 Sacks 2008, p. 225.

85 Márquez 1989, pp. 280–1.

86 One-to-one correspondence is discussed further in Chapter 5 in a discussion about images.

87 From John Donne's evergreen phrase 'No man is an island, entire of itself; every man is a piece of the Continent, a part of the main', from *Meditation XVII*.

88 Arnheim 1986, p. 199.

89 Tallis 2008, p. 161.

90 See Shapin 1991.

91 See Mead 1934, p. 223, note 25.

92 William James [1890] 2007, p. 293.

93 Hoare and Nowell-Smith 1971.

Chapter 3 To be captive

1 See Jack Vernon's *Inside the Black Room* (1966).

2 Sachs 1966, p. 244.

3 The reason for his captivity was the imprisonment of the Xinhua (China news agency) employee; he was held until the Chinese detainee was released from (former British territory) Hong Kong.

4 In Saunders 1998, p. 136.

5 He pays warm tributes to many who helped him through the early days of his return (see Keenan 1992, pp. 7–8).

6 In Saunders 1998, p. 134.

7 *Ibid.*, p. 45.

8 Bukovsky 1978, pp. 22–4.

9 See Clark and Holquist 1984, p. 240; and Bakhtin 1981, p. 430.

10 Saunders, 1998, p. 123.

11 *Ibid.*, pp. 123–4.

12 *Ibid.*, p. 124.

13 *Ibid.*, pp. 124–5.

14 *Ibid.*, p. 125.

15 *Ibid.*, p. 126.

16 *Ibid.*, p. 126.

17 Keenan 1992, p. 81.

18 Saunders, 1998, p. 127.

19 Keenan 1992, p. 68.

20 An expression used in Northern Ireland for 'wise up' or 'get wise to'.

21 Saunders 1998, p. 128.

22 *Ibid.*, p. 129.

23 *Ibid.*, p. 129.

24 *Ibid.*, p. 130.

25 *Ibid.*, p. 115.

26 *Ibid.*, p. 96.

27 *Ibid.*, p. 131.

28 Sara Maitland discusses this in her book on solitude (2008).

29 Attributed to Viktor Frankl.

Conclusions for Part I

1 Jeremy Hardy on *Jeremy Hardy Speaks to the Nation*.

2 See Bennett and Hacker 2003

3 This is a paraphrased version of Julie Ford's statement (Ford 1975, pp. 19 and 20).

4 This is a variation on Merleau-Ponty's (1964a) view of imagination. We do not so much see an imagined, we see *with* an imagined.

5 Gombrich 1977, p. 5.

6 See Harré and Gillett 1994, pp. 20 and 21.

7 See Saunders 1998, pp. 34–6 and 153–5.

Introduction to Part II

1 Nagel uses the expression 'how it is for the subject himself' in a footnote, but mostly sticks with the form 'what it is like' even though, as he suggests in the footnote, this tends to lead to a misconception: that of looking for something that experience resembles or is analogous to.

2 David Hume tried to look inside himself and wrote that he only ever found 'a bundle or collection of different perceptions'. But he doesn't question what he was looking inside *with*. See Hume [1739] 1969, p. 306.

3 See section with subheading 'Turning the tables' in Chapter 6.

4 Bukovsky told me about this during one of our conversations.

5 Vernon 1963, p. 29.

6 See Harré and Gillett 1994, pp. 20–1 and Harré 1993, p. 77.

7 The section in Part I on John Dean's testimony is also relevant here and may be an alternative working example to the example of sensory deprivation.

8 See *OED*.

9 Chalmers 2002 or 2003, in a footnote.

10 There are examples of a person not having a subjective experience of their own leg – and this would seem to be an argument against the position in this book. But the counter-argument is that the person still has subjective conscious experience: they subjectively experience their own leg as not their own leg. Subjectivity need not be rational or we could never explain a whole range of issues from Capgras syndrome to anaesthesia.

11 Saunders 1998, pp. 132–3.

12 There is such a thing as non-narrative filmmaking, but still the director has a standpoint. See, for example, *Samsara* (2011), directed by Ron Fricke.

13 Coined by Samuel Taylor Coleridge in his *Biographia Literaria* (1817) in the context of creating and reading poetry.

14 James Joyce [1922] 1993, p. 37 and notes on p. 784.

15 Picasso's painting *Guernica* is further discussed in Chapter 5, where we deal with treatments of subjective experience in the arts. See sections headed '*Guernica*' and 'Denote, connote and signify' in Chapter 5.

16 The term 'Cubist Psychology' was coined by me and first outlined in my doctoral thesis (Saunders 1998).

17 See Gombrich 1950, p. 208.

18 Many artists change parts of the actual scene when they make decisions about the balance of a painting, so a person going to a particular place may see how an artist has made changes. Also, an artist may be trying to convey a scene in ways that are painterly and not actually in the scene. For example, the colour palette chosen by the artist may not accurately reflect the colours of the scene itself.

This furthers the point being made because it highlights how the artist's experience – as painted – is not simply a recording of a viewpoint.

19 Two kinds of Cubism – analytic and synthetic – are covered here under the shorthand single term 'Cubism'. The term *Cubism* may have been first used by Metzinger in 1910 and elaborated a few months later by Allard (see e.g. Golding 1959, p. 33). The term *Cubist* may have stemmed from a comment by another critic, Louis Vauxcelles, after he saw a Braque painting that Matisse had described as 'full of little cubes'. Others say that this was Cézanne's comment that a critic overheard. It may have been Cézanne's simplification of natural forms into cylinders, spheres and cones that influenced Braque and Picasso (see e.g. Becks-Malorny 2006). This text was also referred to in Part I when Cubism was first mentioned.

20 *Antony Gormley*, exhibition catalogue, Malmö Konsthalle, Tate Gallery Liverpool, Irish Museum of Modern Art, Dublin 1993, p. 48.

21 See Turner 1988.

22 Tacit knowledge is what we know without knowing that we know.

23 But see Eccles 1994.

24 See Bennett and Hacker 2003, p. 64.

Chapter 4 'What is it like to be a bat?' (Nagel)

1 Nagel 1974.

2 *Ibid.*, p. 168.

3 *Ibid.*, p. 169.

4 *Ibid.*, p. 172.

5 *Ibid.*, p. 173.

6 *Ibid.*, p. 180.

7 *Ibid.*, p. 166.

8 *Ibid.*, p. 170.

9 *Ibid.*, p. 166.

10 Recent work with brain scanning techniques – see note 12 below.

11 See Bennett and Hacker 2003.

12 See Cyranoski 2012 for discussion of Adrian Owen's neuroscientific work helping to communicate with persons with locked-in syndrome.

By asking them to imagine either a tennis game or walking around a house it is possible to code these as yes and no answers to questions.

13 Ibid., p. 166.

14 Ibid., p. 167.

15 See Strawson 1997 and Harré 1998.

16 Much of this will be taken up in Part III in a discussion of what it is to be minded; this will help us with what's begun here.

17 I would recommend Reddy 2010 as a good starting point.

18 See discussion of Albie Sachs in Chapter 6.

19 See discussion of Vygotsky in Chapter 2, section entitled 'The making of persons'.

20 See Bennett and Hacker 2003, pp. 88ff.

21 Wittgenstein 1953, 196^e.

22 This was Brian Keenan's response at one point of his captivity. 'At one point his captors give him metal cutlery and he chances on his reflection in the spoon. He is struck by the reflection such that his voice cries out, "That's not me"' (Saunders 1998, p. 129).

23 See Vygotsky 1990 and 1991.

24 Saunders 1998, p. 126.

25 In Sutton 2005, p. 604.

26 See the British Psychological Society website and the tagline used there: 'Psychology is the scientific study of people, the mind and behaviour'. Available from www.bps.org.uk/

27 Varela pursued the idea of intersubjectivity, but this does not get round the problem either. It shows how objectivity is achieved intersubjectively by agreement within a community (see Blackmore 2005, p. 224).

28 *Ibid.*

29 See Bennett and Hacker 2003.

30 When, as has happened, a person says they do not experience their arm *as* their arm, this is their subjective experience, i.e. their subjective experience is that their arm is not theirs.

31 No author could offer a comprehensive or complete book on 'consciousness', although some may seem to. A 'complete' picture of anything is probably a misnomer.

32 The discussion of John Dean's testimony (Neisser 1981) is relevant here.

33 See Chapter 1, section entitled 'Persons and place', and Benson (2001).

34 With due respect to John Berger's (1972) book *Ways of Seeing*.

35 Lyrics from the song 'I wish I knew how it would feel to be free' by Billy Taylor and Richard Dallas. Copyright © 1964 Duane Music Inc., USA. All rights reserved. Used by permission.

36 Berger 1972, pp. 7–8.

37 With all due respect to Merleau-Ponty (1964a), who made a similar comment about imagination.

38 See section titled 'John Dean's testimony' in Chapter 1.

39 Lodge 2002a.

40 See Burr 1995.

41 Attributed to Alfred Korzybski, but others have made similar statements in different forms.

42 Attributed to Parmenides of Elea.

43 See Bennett and Hacker 2003.

44 See also Reddy 2010, p. 14 – with reference to Gilbert Ryle.

45 Nagel 1974, p. 171.

46 See Lodge 2002a, p. 42 and McEwan 2001.

47 See e.g. Bennett and Hacker 2003, p. 275.

48 Tallis 2008, p. 161.

49 NB. Co-operation also requires trying to take another's standpoint to bring about whatever it is co-operation is jointly aimed at producing.

Chapter 5 Treatments of subjective conscious experience in the arts

1 Sarbin 1986, p. vii.

2 See Goffman 1971.

3 See Benson 2012.

4 This paraphrases a quotation from Kierkegaard, although I do not have a specific source for it.

5 *Being John Malkovich*, 1999.

6 Directed by Spike Jonze; screenplay by Charlie Kaufman.

7 An alter ego is like a second self inhabiting the same body as, for example, in the case of Dr Jekyll and Mr Hyde; though they need not be good and bad egos.

8 Now usually 'dissociative identity disorder' and very different from beliefs about multiple personality disorder.

9 But see different standpoint on hearing voices in e.g. Miss Beauchamp in Harré 1994, pp. 109–10 and 'Hearing Voices' network – see their website – and the work of the late Terry McLaughlin.

10 Dennett's expression. See Chapter 1, note 9.

11 The film *Inception* (2010) takes the same idea but for dreams rather than waking life. Although this film includes the idea of an 'uninvited guest' or visitor to someone's dream being active and committing acts of 'extraction' and 'inception'.

12 Karl Popper famously asked people to 'observe' and then discussed how it is impossible (see Hergenhahn 2008, p. 9). We cannot simply observe, we would ask, 'observe what?' Immediately, we would have brought theoretical selection to the looking.

13 This is known as breaking the 180° rule. Directors have broken this convention.

14 *The Road* (2009), directed by John Hilcoat.

15 Recommended to view *The Wire* (HBO).

16 Coined by Coleridge; see introduction to Part II, note 13.

17 Directed by Daniel Vigne (1982).

18 From act II, scene vii of *As You Like It* by William Shakespeare.

19 Directed by Ridley Scott, from *Do Androids Dream of Electric Sheep?* by Philip K. Dick. Various versions since the original theatrical edition (1982). The director's cut (1992) is the recommended version.

20 See Descartes 1968. His philosophy of doubting existence led to his assertion that he was a creature who doubted, and to his belief in us as 'thinking beings'. And thus to 'I think, therefore I am'.

21 Including e.g. Rowlands 2005.

22 Whitehead c.2002.

23 Directed by Julian Schnabel and based on the book by Jean-Dominique Bauby of the same name.

24 See also the discussion of Bauby and of the book he wrote in other parts of this book.

25 Television drama. HBO.

26 This is not new: TV programmes such as *Hill Street Blues* (Steven Bochco) garnered many awards and critical acclaim for similarly

avant garde approaches with ensemble casts, multiple characters and ongoing storylines as back and main story.

27 Writers and many others also do what artists do, but the idea here is to keep to a clear line of argument.

28 See Elkins 2003; Morgan and Welton 1992, p. 113.

29 Gombrich 1950, p. 455.

30 See various online references including *The Guardian*. Most report that in February 2003 a curtain was used to cover up the tapestry in front of which Colin Powell, then US Secretary of State, would have made a report to the media following his speech to the UN. At the time of writing, the tapestry copy is on indefinite temporary loan.

31 Reddy 2010, p. 121.

32 See Arnheim 1962 for an account of the painting, its inception, context and history.

33 See Gombrich 1950.

34 Lodge 2002a. Read the chapter with the same title as the book, 'Consciousness and the novel'.

35 *Ibid.* p. 40.

36 Anthony Grey parodied this in a short story 'A man was later detained' – in his book *A Man Alone* (1971).

37 Paul de Man cited in Josselson and Lieblich 1993, p. 193.

38 Often attributed to E. M. Forster, who wrote, 'The little girl had the making of a poet in her who, being told to be sure of her meaning before she spoke, said, *"How can I tell what I think until I see what I say?"*' (as quoted by Wallas 1926).

39 This is coined by me to follow the idea of 'painterly' in painting. Painterly refers to the kinds of visible brushstrokes used in the finished painting by some artists. The corollary in writing would be *writerly*: writing that draws attention to itself because it hasn't been smoothed out and the 'tricks' of composition are apparent.

40 Lodge 2002a, p. 16.

41 Keenan 1992, and Saunders 1998, p. 134.

42 We can even be our own self-policing 'panopticon'. See Foucault [1975] 1977.

43 Philip Pullman in Headlam Wells and McFadden 2006, pp. 189–90.

44 See Dennett 2003, particularly on using the colloquial term 'person'.

45 Tallis, 2008, pp. 147–8.

46 See Gombrich 1977, chapter 7, and pp. 81–2 in particular.

47 Popper in Hergenhahn 2008, as cited above.

48 See Lodge 2002a, chapter 1.

Chapter 6 A captive mind

1 Dowd 1996, p. 9.

2 Shapin 1991.

3 See Cohen and Taylor 1972.

4 See commentary on Bukovsky in Chapter 3.

5 The idea of the 'provisional existence' of a prisoner is attributed to Viktor Frankl.

6 Saunders 1998, pp. 133, 134.

7 See, for example, the William James quote relating to this in Chapter 2

8 Primo Levi's standpoint in his book *If This is a Man* ([1958] 1996).

9 See Bone 1957.

10 Storr 1988, p. 48.

11 In Saunders 1998, p. 113.

12 Ginzburg 1968, p. 62.

13 *Ibid.*, p. 156.

14 *Ibid.*, p. 157.

15 *Ibid.*, p. 157.

16 *Ibid.*, p. 163.

17 Albie Sachs 1966, pp. 244–5; and also quoted in Dowd 1996, p. 66.

18 Hobsbawm 1997, p. 308.

19 See Ginzburg (1968) describing in her own words what remembering is like when imprisoned and how the guards did not believe that she was reciting such lengthy writings from memory.

20 Saunders 1998, p. 92.

Introduction to Part III

1 Often attributed to the Sceptics.

2 See Husserl 1977. Not an easy read, but this is where I first read about the idea of 'directing towards'.

3 See Benson 2012.

4 See 'Theory theory' and 'simulation' in Reddy 2010 and Farley, López and Saunders 2010.

5 See Reddy 2010.

6 See *ibid.*, p. 48.

7 Gallup's self-recognition test using odourless dye marks has been used on most primates, some dolphins and whales, elephants and even magpies. There are debates about how to interpret the findings.

8 See Byrne and Whiten 1988.

9 Symbolic Interaction and the work of one of its principal conceptual developers, George Herbert Mead, is discussed in Part I.

10 See Premack and Woodruff 1978. They coined the term 'theory of mind' and asked whether chimpanzees have it.

11 See Byrne and Whiten 1988.

12 See Reddy 2010.

13 *Ibid.*, p. 20.

14 Tallis 2008, p. 250.

15 See Whiten and Byrne, in Byrne and Whiten 1988, chapter 16, pp. 211–23.

16 Hans Kummer's work is reported and discussed in Byrne and Whiten 1988, chapter 16, p. 215.

17 See Shettleworth 2010.

18 Various, including Mathias Osvath – see 'Spontaneous innovation for future deception in a male chimpanzee' available at plosone.org.

19 See documentary evidence of this in a *YouTube* clip with the naturalist Jane Goodall, available online at time of writing.

20 Reddy 2010, p. 150.

21 The development of being 'picked up' as an infant described by Martin Richards (1974).

22 From conversations with John Pickering and Martin Skinner, who referred to the work of Martin Richards, e.g. Andy Lock (ed.), *Action, Gesture and Symbol*. Personal communication.

23 During one of our interview conversations, Bukovsky told me about how Pasternak went about his work.

24 Meins and Fernyhough 2006.

25 See e.g. Vygostky 1987.

26 The term 'scaffolding' is usually attributed to Jerome Bruner.

27 Brian Keenan introduced this form of words to me; see Chapter 3, note 20.

28 See Bennett and Hacker 2003, pp. 151–3.

29 The uses of the terms 'world' and 'world about us' are more fully developed in Chapter 7.

30 Hobsbawm 1997, p. 308.

31 See Lawson 2012, p. 16.

32 *Ibid.*

Chapter 7 Landscape and the world about us

1 See, for example, Hestercombe gardens in Somerset, UK, which has the tagline: 'paradise restored'. It is worth a visit in its own right, but also it does show a spectacular transformed landscape and how viewpoints are made as part of the landscape work.

2 This refers to comments by Gombrich on Picasso; see Gombrich 1950, pp. 454–5.

3 Merleau-Ponty 1964a.

4 Macfarlane 2004, p. 14.

5 *Ibid.*, p. 16.

6 *Ibid.*, p. 14.

7 *Ibid.*, p. 18.

8 *Ibid.*, p. 18.

9 *Ibid.*, p. 19.

10 In Gombrich's *Art and Illusion* (1977) he discusses the style of landscape painting in both Chinese and English cultural traditions. Each would take their own art tradition to render what a landscape is like. The different styles would seem alien to another tradition. Artists *see* what they paint rather than paint what they see and, thus, end up with very different images.

11 Macfarlane 2004, p. 145.

12 *Ibid.*, p. 145.

13 *Ibid.*, p. 145.

14 *Ibid.*, pp. 150–1.

15 See Jones 2012.

16 See *OED* online.

17 *Ibid.*

18 Hunt 1964, p. 24.

19 See Chapter 5.

20 Hunt 1964, p. 50.

21 The term 'Arcadian' derives from a region of Greece taken to be the ideal region of rural contentment; so, anywhere ideally rural or rustic.

22 Edmund Burke, in Hunt 1964, illustration 'The art of gardening' facing p. 64.

23 See Gillespie 2007, pp. 172–5.

24 See Chapter 5.

25 As noted earlier, there are non-narrative films, although these would still have a standpoint.

26 Brian Keenan told me that he would often rework novels in his head when in solitary confinement and had the idea of reworking *Robinson Crusoe*.

27 See Reddy 2010 and the discussion in the introduction to Part III.

28 Cooley 1902.

29 See Dennett (2003) on persons, p. 242.

30 See, for example, Turner 1988.

31 'Synch' as in *synch*ronisation, which means to occur simultaneously or contemporaneously with something – see *OED*.

32 For an appreciation of our modern world and the culture that makes all of us, I recommend *Modern Times, Modern Places* by Peter Conrad (1998).

33 Howard Hodgkin talking to Melvyn Bragg, discussed in Saunders 2007.

34 Franzen 2012.

35 Reference as before, Hobsbawm 1997, p. 308.

36 I read this in *The Guardian*, but I do not have the reference for it.

37 Berger 1972, pp. 7–8.

38 See Okri 1997, p. 53.

39 See Gombrich 1977, pp. 81–2.

40 To paraphrase Wittgenstein 1953, 196^e.

41 See Saunders 2005.

Chapter 8 'Mary the colour scientist' (Jackson)

1 Jackson 1982.

2 See Ludlow, Nagasawa and Stoljar 2004.

3 Qualia were discussed in the introduction to Part II (and I worked through an example).

4 Beaton 2005.

5 I'm using 'qualia' here only because it is the term used by Jackson.

6 Jackson 1982, p. 130.

7 See Ludlow, Nagasawa and Stoljar 2004.

8 See the section on dualism, and the *mind–body problem* in particular, at the end of the introduction to Part II.

9 Chalmers, 2002 or 2003, in a footnote.

10 Tallis 2008, p. 161.

11 See Reddy 2010, p. 14.

12 See *Universal Declaration of Human Rights*.

13 See Parks [1992] 1999.

14 *Jeremy Hardy Speaks to the Nation*.

15 Parks [1992] 1999, p. 116.

16 Burma is also known as Myanmar.

17 See Suu Kyi [1991] 2010. This is not to say that the PAC in South Africa was wrong to change tactics. It is difficult to see how some regimes would negotiate without such action. Opposition in Burma has not been without bloodshed. At the time of writing, Aung San Suu Kyi has gained access to the lower house of the Burmese parliament, but of course this is a long way from her party governing Burma, as should have been the case following her landslide victory in 1990. She still seeks help from outside Burma for reforms to re-establish democracy; see her speech to both houses of the UK parliament in June 2012.

18 See the *Universal Declaration of Human Rights* available online.

19 Suu Kyi [1991] 2010, p. 183.

20 *Ibid.* pp. 184.

21 As stated by Joseph Kovach, but I do not have a reference for it.

22 See Foucault 1975.

23 See Dennett 2003, in particular p. 173 – about 'mental powers smeared over time' – and p. 242 – about 'persons'.

24 See Suu Kyi [1991] 2010 for an essay about her father.

25 See Simone 1970 (DVD 2008).

26 *Ibid.*

Chapter 9 Knowing how it feels to be free

1 The lyrics given are the first sixteen lines from the song and used here by permission of the copyright holder: © 1964 Duane Music Inc., USA assigned to Westminster Music Ltd, Suite 2.07, Plaza 535 King's Road, London sw10 0sz. International Copyright secured. All rights reserved. Used by permission. The song was written by Billy Taylor and Richard Dallas.

2 Attributed to Fannie Lou Hamer.

3 See Reddy 2010, p. 14, on the use of adverbs.

4 Some call words such as *would* and *could* 'modal' verbs.

5 Gormley in Saunders 1998, p. 38.

6 Sennett 2012, p. 122.

Conclusions

1 See Chapter 2 for further details on feral or wild children.

2 See the introduction to Part II for further details on the uses of terms such as 'inner' and 'outer'.

3 See, for example, *Ai Weiwei – Never Sorry*, a documentary film made by Alison Klayman.

4 From *Jeremy Hardy Speaks to the Nation*, as cited earlier.

5 Parks [1992] 1999, p. 116.

6 Ginzburg 1968, p. 156, cited in Saunders 1998, p. 67.

7 *Ibid.*

8 See Goffman 1971.

9 Cooley 1902, pp. 1 and 2.

10 See section on 'negative contours' in Chapter 2.

11 See BPS website: 'Psychology is the scientific study of people, the mind and behaviour. The British Psychological Society is the representative body for psychology and psychologists in the UK. We are responsible for the development, promotion and application of psychology for the public good.' Available from www.bps.org.uk/

12 See *The Return of Martin Guerre* (1982).

13 Also see my discussion on palimpsests in Chapter 2.

14 See *OED*.

15 See the introduction to Part II for further details about what is meant by 'phenomenal' properties.

16 Hobsbawm 1997, p. 308.

17 See further commentary on Cézanne and Cubism in the introduction to Part II and related endnotes.

18 See Gombrich 1977, chapter 'Truth and the stereotype' and p. 81 in particular.

19 See Chapter 7.

20 See Chapter 7 for details about Franzen, Chapter 5 for Pullman, plus endnotes in these chapters.

21 Pullman 2006, pp. 189–90.

22 See Chapter 4 for further details about Wittgenstein.

23 See the introduction to Part II for further details about Gormley.

24 Paul Cézanne's Mont Sainte-Victoire paintings and the 'Seen from Les Lauves' series in particular. The cover illustration of this book is one of that series.

25 See Saunders 2005.

26 See Gablik 1970, p. 9.

Further reading, viewing and listening

The following is a short list of my recommended further reading, viewing and listening. The list includes just a few of those sources that I think are directly relevant to this book; those which I have drawn on a great deal. (Please see the Bibliography for full reference details.)

Further reading

For following up 'The three stories', try putting the title of one of the stories, e.g. 'What is it like to be a bat?' in your web browser's search window. You may find that authors' homepages also have the original articles to download. I've included some book titles that may also be available via online booksellers. The original articles may be a difficult read for non-philosophers, but worth your efforts in following them up if your interest has been sparked:

> 'Teleportation' by Derek Parfit. Try 'Divided minds and the nature of persons' (also available in Blakemore and Greenfield 1987);
>
> 'What is it like to be a bat?' by Thomas Nagel (1974; also available as a chapter in Nagel's book *Mortal Questions*, 1979);
>
> 'Mary the colour scientist' by Frank Jackson. Try using the title, 'Epiphenomenal Qualia' (also available as a chapter in Ludlow *et al.*, 2004).

For an account of what it's like to be taken hostage, read Brian Keenan's *An Evil Cradling* (1992). The first part of this book, in which he tells how it is to be kept in solitary confinement as a hostage, is the most remarkable account of such an experience I have read.

For prison writing of all kinds, including extracts from accounts given by political prisoners, read Siobhan Dowd's (1996) edited volume *The Prison Where I Live*. This volume includes extracts from Vladimir Bukovsky and Albie Sachs, both of whom are discussed in this book.

Read *Rosa Parks: My Story* ([1992] 1999). A plain-speaking account of her life, civil rights work and the Montgomery (Alabama, USA) bus boycott that she helped start in 1955.

For stories of feral children, Michael Newton's book *Savage Girls and Wild Boys* (2002) is the most engaging I have read and I thoroughly recommend it. It includes discussions of some of those included in this book, for example Victor, the wild boy of Aveyron, among many others.

For something from a standpoint in the arts, read David Lodge's book of essays *Consciousness and the Novel* (2002a). The first essay has the same title as the book and is recommended.

For an introduction to social psychology, the social identity approach and social worlds in general, I would recommend any of the current work by Stephen Reicher (e.g. 2011), who was one of Henri Tajfel's students.

For an introduction to ideas about the self and sense of self, read Julian Baggini's *The Ego Trick* (2011). See chapter 7, in particular.

For an absorbing if academically difficult tour around the conceptual issues covered in this book, try dipping into Bennett and Hacker's *Philosophical Foundations of Neuroscience*. I've drawn on the 2003 edition, but a later edition that includes comments from, and responses to, Dennett and Searle is the one I would recommend. It is possible to look up, for example, Nagel and the 'what it's like' idea of experience; the *mereological fallacy* and its relevance for arguments about 'persons'; among many others. Their italicised index system in the margins is a useful guide to the paragraphs alongside them. I didn't discuss the mereological fallacy directly, nor did I name it, as I didn't want to add another diversion. Nonetheless, Bennett and Hacker's arguments form part of the critical background to my philosophical position.

For an introduction to the broad subject matter of *consciousness*, read Susan Blackmore's *Consciousness: An Introduction* (2010). This book is easily the best entry point for those wishing to read about the field of consciousness studies; it is written in a very engaging style that makes you want to read on.

For an exploration of 'How infants know minds', read the book of the same name by Vasudevi Reddy (2010). I have drawn on this book extensively when discussing how infants become persons. Although controversial in places for some in the field of developmental psychology, the author marshals evidence and argument in support of her 'second-person' approach to understanding minds. To read the whole book is well worth your time. The book won the BPS book award for 2011.

Read the *Universal Declaration of Human Rights* (available online).

Further viewing

Films

Blade Runner. There are various versions of which the director's cut is usually thought the best – although see the 2007 DVD. Watch any of the editions for a futuristic storyline about androids called *replicants*. Viewing this film may help a reader to understand some of the issues, including ethical issues, concerning what it is to be human and what counts as a person.

Being John Malkovich (1999). This film puts the ego view of person on screen in a funny and engaging way.

The Diving Bell and the Butterfly (2007). What it is like to have locked-in syndrome extraordinarily shown on screen. The film is faithful to the book (of the same title) written by Jean-Dominique Bauby. I would recommend the book as well.

L'Enfant sauvage (*Wild Child*) (1970). The story of Victor, the Wild Boy of Aveyron. This is wonderful filmic storytelling that is not unduly spoilt by having a positive ending to the story. The ending is not in keeping with what is known about what happened to Victor, and particularly where it concerns the last years of his life. Nonetheless, Truffaut's film shows what it is like to live a feral life and the kindnesses and cruelties visited upon the boy.

Le Retour de Martin Guerre (*The Return of Martin Guerre*) (1982). Watch this original French version rather than a later remake. This original telling stays close to what is supposedly a true story. This story of identity is compelling both as a film and as a case study in what it means to *be* a particular person.

Art

See *Guernica* (1937). Go to Madrid, go to the Reina Sofia gallery and view Picasso's extraordinary painting (or see a good quality, large-scale reproduction).

See any of Rachel Whiteread's negative space sculptures, e.g. *House* (1993). You should easily find illustrations online, but visit an exhibition if you have the opportunity.

Further listening

Music

Listen to Nina Simone singing 'I wish I knew how it would feel to be free' and, if you can, see the documentary *Nina: A Historical Perspective* available with the collection *To be Free: The Nina Simone Story* (1970 / 2008). Nina Simone was a great singer and songwriter, but she was also active in the civil rights movement in the USA.

Further interest

Social psychology, social theory and social practice

The Centre for the Understanding of Social Practices – CUSP (based at the University of the West of England – UWE – in Bristol) – is one of my research homes and, as such, a place from where I derive a great deal of academic support. It is an active research community with a diverse membership. Have a look on the UWE web pages for latest news and events. The following web address may have changed, so you may need to put CUSP into the search window once on the main UWE website: www.uwe.ac.uk/hls/research/CUSP

Consciousness

The Consciousness and Experiential Psychology group (CEP) is an influential body in the field of consciousness studies and is another one of my research homes; a place from where I derive a great deal of academic support. CEP is an active section of the British Psychological Society (BPS) that holds regular conferences and other kinds of meetings for members, but is also open to the public. CEP is a warm and welcoming group, so if this book has sparked an interest, going to one of the CEP meetings would be a great place to further your interest. The following web address may have changed, so you may need to put 'Consciousness and Experiential Psychology' into your web browser's search window: www.bps.org.uk/CEP

References to films, paintings and other artworks

Ai Weiwei – Never Sorry (2012) Written and directed by Alison Klayman. United Expression Media and MUSE film and television.

Being John Malkovich (1999) Directed by Spike Jonze. Screenplay by Charlie Kaufmann. Gramercy Pictures / Universal.

Blade Runner (1982 and 1992 – director's cut – among later others, including 2007 DVD) Directed by Ridley Scott; based on the short story *Do Androids Dream of Electric Sheep?* by Philip K. Dick. Warner Bros.

Cave of Forgotten Dreams, The (2010) Directed by Werner Herzog. Creative Differences and History Films.

Cézanne, Paul (1904–6) *Mont Sainte-Victoire, Seen from Les Lauves*. Kunsthaus. Zurich.

Diving Bell and the Butterfly, The (2007) Directed by Julian Schnabel. Pathé.

L'Enfant Sauvage (Wild Child) (1970) Directed by François Truffaut. Based on the book *Victor de L'Aveyron* (The Wild Boy of Aveyron) by Jean Itard. Les Artistes Associés.

eXistenZ (1999) Directed by David Cronenberg. Alliance Atlantis.

Gormley, Antony (1993) *Testing a World View*. Turner Prize show, 1994.

Inception (2010) Written and directed by Christopher Nolan. Warner Bros.

Jeremy Hardy Speaks to the Nation, episode 8.1 'How to grow up'. BBC Radio 4, 30 June 2010.

Matrix, The (1999) Directed by the Wachowski brothers. Warner Bros.

Memento (2000) Directed by Christopher Nolan. Newmarket Capital Group.

Moon (2009) Directed by Duncan Jones. Liberty Films UK.

Picasso, Pablo (1937) *Guernica*. Oil on canvas. Museo Reina Sofia. Madrid.

Return of Martin Guerre, The (*Le Retour de Martin Guerre*) (1982) France. Directed by Daniel Vigne. Dussault.

Road, The (2009) Directed by John Hilcoat. From a book by Cormac McCarthy. Dimension Films.

Simone, Nina (1970/2008) *To Be Free: The Nina Simone Story*. Compilation including *NINA: A Historical Perspective* (1970) [DVD] Produced by Peter Rodis. Sony BMG.

South Bank Show, The (1991) Howard Hodgkin interviewed by Melvyn Bragg. LWT.

Taylor, Billy and Dallas, Richard (1964) I wish I knew how it would feel to be free. Lyrics © Duane Music Inc.

Wire, The (2005) The Complete First Season. [DVD] HBO.

Bibliography

Arnheim, Rudolf (1962) *Guernica: The Genesis of a Painting*. London: Faber and Faber.

(1986) *New Essays on the Psychology of Art*. University of California Press.

Ashworth, Derek (2000) *Human Nature*. London: Routledge.

Baggini, Julian (2011) *The Ego Trick*. London: Granta.

Bakhtin, M. ([1981] 1994) *The Dialogic Imagination*, ed. Michael Holquist and trans. Caryl Emerson and Michael Holquist. Austin: University of Texas Press.

Barfield, Owen (1965) *Saving the Appearances*. New York: Harcourt, Brace and World, Inc.

Bartlett, Frederick ([1932] 1964) *Remembering*. Cambridge University Press.

Bauby, Jean-Dominique (1997) *The Diving Bell and the Butterfly*, trans. from the French by Jeremy Legatt. London: Fourth Estate.

Beaton, Mike (2005) What RoboDennett still doesn't know. *Journal of Consciousness Studies*, 12(12), 3–25.

Beckett, Samuel (1965) *Imagination Dead Imagine*, trans. by the author. London: Calder and Boyars.

Becks-Malorny, Ulrike (2006) *Cézanne*. Cologne: Taschen.

Bennett, Max and Hacker, Peter (2003) *Philosophical Foundations of Neuroscience*. Oxford: Blackwell.

Benson, Ciarán (2001) *The Cultural Psychology of Self*. London: Routledge.

(2012) A secular spirituality? In Fran O'Rourke (ed.), *Human Destinies: Philosophical Essays in Memory of Gerald Hanratty*. University of Notre Dame Press, 495–528.

Berger, John (1972) *Ways of Seeing*. London: BBC and Penguin.

Bermúdez, José Luis, Marcel, Anthony, and Eilan, Naomi (eds.) (1995) *The Body and the Self*. A Bradford Book. Cambridge, MA: MIT Press.

Biko, Steve ([1978] 2004) *I Write What I Like*. Johannesburg: Picador, Africa.

Birbaumer, N., Ghanayim, N., Hinterberger, T., Iversen, I., Kotchoubey, B. and Kübler, A. (1999). A spelling device for the paralysed. *Nature*, 398, 297–8.

Blackmore, Susan (2005) *Conversations on Consciousness*. Oxford University Press.

(2010) *Consciousness: An Introduction*, 2nd edition. Hodder Education.

Blakemore, Colin and Greenfield, Susan (eds.) (1987) *Mindwaves*. Oxford: Blackwell.

Bone, Edith (1957) *Seven Years Solitary*. London: Hamish Hamilton.

Bronowski, Jacob (1973) *The Ascent of Man*. London: BBC.

Bruner, Jerome (1986) *Actual Minds, Possible Worlds*. Cambridge, MA, and London: Harvard University Press.

(1990) *Acts of Meaning*. Cambridge, MA, and London: Harvard University Press.

Bukovsky, Vladimir (1978) *To Build a Castle: My Life as a Dissenter*, trans. from the Russian by Michael Scammell. London: André Deutsch.

Burns, Robert (c.1785) Poem: 'To a Louse'.

Burr, Vivien (1995) *An Introduction to Social Constructionism*. London and New York: Routledge.

Byrne Richard W. and Whiten, Andrew (eds.) (1988) *Machiavellian Intelligence: Social Expertise and the Evolution of Intellect in Monkeys, Apes and Humans*. Oxford: Clarendon Press.

Carroll, Lewis (1992) *Alice in Wonderland*. Wordsworth Classics. Ware: Wordsworth Editions.

Carter, Rita (2002) *Consciousness*. London: Weidenfeld and Nicolson.

Chalmers, David (1996) *The Conscious Mind*. Oxford University Press.

(2002, 2003) Consciousness and its place in nature. *Online Papers on Consciousness*. Available from http://consc.net/online but also published elsewhere – see online paper for details.

(2010) *The Character of Consciousness*. Oxford University Press.

Clark, Katerina and Holquist, Michael (1984) *Mikhail Bakhtin*. Cambridge, MA, and London: Harvard University Press.

Cohen, Stanley and Taylor, Laurie ([1972] 1981) *Psychological Survival: The Experience of Long-term Imprisonment*, 2nd edition. Harmondsworth: Penguin.

Conrad, Peter (1998) *Modern Times, Modern Places: Life and Art in the 20th Century*. London: Thames and Hudson.

Conway, Martin (1995) *Flashbulb Memories*. Mahwah, NJ: Lawrence Erlbaum.

Cooley, Charles Horton (1902) *Human Nature and the Social Order*. New York: Scribner.

Cyranoski, David (2012) Neuroscience: the mind reader. *Nature*, 486(7402), 157–286.

Damasio, Antonio (2000) *The Feeling of What Happens*. London: Heinemann.

Danziger, Kurt (1990) *Constructing the Subject*. Cambridge University Press.

(1997) *Naming the Mind*. London: Sage.

(1999) *Natural Kinds, Human Kinds and Historicity*. In Maiers *et al.* 1999.

Dennett, Daniel (1981) *The Mind's I*. London: Penguin.

(1991) *Consciousness Explained*. London: Penguin.

(2003) *Freedom Evolves*. London: Penguin.

(2005) *Sweet Dreams*. A Bradford Book. Cambridge, MA: MIT Press.

Descartes, René (1968) *Discourse on Method and The Meditations*. Harmondsworth: Penguin. (Originals 1637 and 1641 respectively.)

Dick, Philip K. ([1968] 1999). *Do Androids Dream of Electric Sheep?* London: Millennium.

Donaldson, Margaret (1986) *Children's Minds*. London: HarperCollins.

Dostoevsky, Fyodor (1994) *Crime and Punishment*, trans. from the Russian by David McDuff. London: Penguin.

Dowd, Siobhan, ed. (1996) *The Prison Where I Live: The Pen Anthology of Imprisoned Writers*. London, and New York: Cassell Academic.

Eccles, John (1994) *How the Self Controls its Brain*. Berlin: Springer-Verlag.

Eco, Umberto and Sebeok, Thomas A. (eds.) (1988) *The Sign of Three: Dupin, Holmes, Peirce*. Bloomington and Indianapolis: Indiana University Press.

Edwards, Derek and Middleton, David (eds.) (1990) *Collective Remembering*. London: Sage.

Elkins, James (2003) *Visual Studies: A Skeptical Introduction*. London: Routledge.

Farley, Adam, López, Beatriz and Saunders, Guy (2010) Self-conceptualisation in autism: knowing oneself versus knowing self-through-other. *Autism*, 14(5), 519–30.

Fisher, Len (2004) *Weighing the Soul*. London: Weidenfeld and Nicolson.

Ford, Julienne (1975) *Paradigms and Fairy Tales*, vols. 1 and 2. London: Routledge and Kegan Paul.

Foucault, Michel ([1975] 1977) *Discipline and Punish*. London: Allen Lane.
  (1982) *This Is Not a Pipe*, trans. from the French and ed. James Harkness. Berkeley and Los Angeles: University of California Press.

Fowles, John (1969) *The French Lieutenant's Woman*. London: Jonathan Cape.

Franzen, Jonathan (2012) The path to freedom. *The Guardian*. 26 May. Review section, p. 2.

Gablik, Suzi (1970) *Magritte*. London: Thames and Hudson.

Gillespie, Alex (2007) Time, self and the other: the striving tourist. In L. Simao and J. Valsiner (eds.), *Otherness in Question: Development of the Self*. Greenwich, CT: Information Age Publishing.

Gillibrand, Rachel, Lam, Virginia and O'Donnell, Victoria (2011) *Developmental Psychology*. Upper Saddle River, NJ: Prentice Hall.

Ginzburg, Evgenia Semyonovna (1968) *Into the Whirlwind*, trans. from the Russian by Paul Stevenson, and Manya Harari. Harmondsworth: Penguin.

Goffman, Erving ([1961] 1991) *Asylums*. Harmondsworth: Penguin.
  (1971) *The Presentation of Self in Everyday Life*. Harmondsworth: Penguin.

Golding, John ([1959] 1971) *Cubism: A History and an Analysis 1907–1914*, 2nd edition. London: Faber and Faber.

Gombrich, Ernst (1950) *The Story of Art*. London: Phaidon.
  (1977) *Art and Illusion*, 5th edition. London: Phaidon.

Gray, Jeffrey (2004) *Consciousness: Creeping up on the Hard Problem*. Oxford University Press.

Grey, Anthony (1970) *Hostage in Peking*. London: Michael Joseph.
  ([1970] 1988) *Hostage in Peking*. London: Weidenfeld and Nicolson.
  ([1971] 1990) *A Man Alone*. London: Pan Books.

Harré, Rom (1992) What is real in psychology: a plea for persons. *Theory and Psychology*, 2(2), 153–8.
  (1993) *Social Being*, 2nd edition. Oxford: Blackwell.
  (1998) *A Singular Self*. London: Sage.

(2000) Social construction and consciousness. In M. Velmans (ed.),
    Investigating Phenomenal Consciousness. Philadelphia, PA: John Benjamins.

Harré, Rom and Gillett, Grant (1994) *The Discursive Mind*. London: Sage.

Headlam Wells, Robin and McFadden, Johnjoe (eds.) (2006) *Human Nature: Fact and Fiction*. London: Continuum.

Hergenhahn, B. R. (2008) *An Introduction to the History of Psychology*, International edition. London: Wadsworth.

Hoare, Quintin and Nowell-Smith, Geoffrey (eds. and trans.) (1971) *Selections from the Prison Notebooks of Antonio Gramsci*. London: Lawrence and Wishart.

Hobsbawm, Eric (1997) *On History*. London: Abacus.

Hogg, Michael and Abrams, Dominic (1988) *Social Identifications: A Social Psychology of Intergroup Relations and Group Processes*. London: Routledge.

Honderich, Ted (ed.) (1995) *The Oxford Companion to Philosophy*. Oxford University Press.

Hoy, David Couzens and McCarthy, Thomas (1994) *Critical Theory*. Oxford: Blackwell.

Hume, David ([1739] 1969) *A Treatise on Human Nature*. Harmondsworth: Penguin.

Hunt, Peter (ed.) (1964) *The Shell Gardens Book*. London: Phoenix House.

Husserl, Edmund (1977) *Phenomenological Psychology*. The Hague: Martinus Nijhoff.

Hustvedt, Siri (2010) *The Shaking Woman*. London: Sceptre.

Hutchinson, John, Gombrich, Ernst and Njatin, Lela (1995) *Antony Gormley*. London: Phaidon Press.

Itard, Jean-Marc-Gaspard (1962) *The Wild Boy of Aveyron*, trans. from the French by George and Muriel Humphrey. Upper Saddle River, NJ: Prentice Hall.

Jackson, Frank (1982) Epiphenomenal Qualia. *The Philosophical Quarterly* 32(127), 127–36.

James, William ([1890] 2007). *The Principles of Psychology*, vol. 1. New York: Cosimo.

([1890] 1950). *The Principles of Psychology*, vol. 2. New York: Dover.

Jaynes, Julian ([1976] 1990) *The Origin of Consciousness in the Breakdown of the Bicameral Mind*. Boston: Houghton Mifflin.

Johnston, Alan (2007) *Kidnapped and Other Stories*. London: Profile Books / BBC.

Jones, Jonathan (2012) The story of British art: my 5,000 year hunt for treasure. *The Guardian*. 10 July, available from www.guardian.co.uk.

Josselson, Ruthellen and Lieblich, Amia (eds.) (1993) *The Narrative Study of Lives*, vol. 1. London: Sage.

Joyce, James ([1922] 1993) *Ulysses*. Oxford University Press.

Kearney, Richard (1988) *The Wake of Imagination: Ideas of Creativity in Western Culture*. London: Hutchinson Education.

(1991) *Poetics of Imagining: From Husserl to Lyotard*. London: HarperCollins.

Keenan, Brian (1992) *An Evil Cradling*. London: Vintage.

Koestler, Arthur (1981) *Kaleidoscope* (The Danube Edition). London: Hutchinson.

Lakoff, George and Johnson, Mark (1981) *Metaphors We Live By*. Chicago University Press.

Lancaster, Brian (Les) (2004) *Approaches to Consciousness. The Marriage of Science and Mysticism*. London: Palgrave Macmillan.

Lawson, Mark (2012) Big it up (an interview with Rachel Whiteread). *The Guardian*, g2, 13 June, 16–17.

Levi, Primo ([1958] 1996) *If This Is a Man*. London: Vintage.

Lodge, David (2002a) *Consciousness and the Novel*. London: Secker and Warburg.

(2002b) *Thinks. . ..* London: Penguin.

Ludlow, Peter, Nagasawa, Yujin and Stoljar, Daniel (eds.) (2004). *There's Something about Mary: Essays on Phenomenal Consciousness and Frank Jackson's Knowledge Argument*. Cambridge, MA: MIT Press.

Macfarlane, Robert (2004) *Mountains of the Mind*. London: Granta.

Maiers, Wolfgang, Bayer, Betty, Esgalhardo, Barbara Duarte, Jorna, René and Schraube, Ernst (eds.) (1999). *Challenges to Theoretical Psychology*. Concord, ON: Captus Press.

Maitland, Sara (2008) *A Book of Silence*. London: Granta.

Márquez, Gabriel García (1989) *Love in the Time of Cholera*. London: Penguin.

McEwan, Ian (2001) Only love and then oblivion. Love was all they had to set against their murderers. *The Guardian*, p. 1, 15 September.

McGinn, Colin (1993) *Problems in Philosophy*. Oxford: Blackwell.

Mead, George Herbert (1934) *Mind, Self and Society*. London and Chicago: University of Chicago Press.

([1938] 1972) *The Philosophy of the Act*, ed. Charles Morris. University of Chicago Press.

Meins, Elizabeth and Fernyhough, Charles (2006) Mind-mindedness coding manual. Unpublished manuscript, Durham University, UK.

Merleau-Ponty, Maurice ([1964a] 1968) *The Visible and the Invisible*, trans. from the French by Alphonso Lingis. Evanston: Northwestern University Press.

(1964b) *The Primacy of Perception*, trans. from the French by Alphonso Lingis. Evanston: Northwestern University Press.

Miłosz, Czesław ([1953] 1981) *The Captive Mind*. London: Penguin.

Morgan, John and Welton, Peter (1992) *See What I Mean? An Introduction to Visual Communication*. London: Edward Arnold.

Nagel, Thomas (1974). What is it like to be a bat? *Philosophical Review*, 83 (4), 435–50. (Reprinted in Nagel 1979)

(1979) *Mortal Questions*. Cambridge University Press.

Neisser, Ulric (1981) John Dean's memory: a case study. *Cognition*, 9, 1–22.

Newton, Michael (2002) *Savage Girls and Wild Boys*. London: Faber and Faber.

Nowell-Smith, Geoffrey (1990) On history and the cinema. *Screen*, 31(2), 160–71.

OED [online] *Oxford English Dictionary*.

Okri, Ben (1997) *A Way of Being Free*. London: Phoenix House.

Ost, James and Costall, Alan (2002) Misremembering Bartlett: a study in serial reproduction. *British Journal of Psychology*, 93(2), 245–55.

Paquet, Marcel (2006) *Magritte*. Cologne: Taschen.

Parfit, Derek (1984) *Reasons and Persons*. Oxford University Press.

(1987) Divided minds and the nature of persons. In C. Blakemore and S. Greenfield (eds.), *Mindwaves*. Oxford: Blackwell, 18–26.

(1995) The unimportance of identity. In Henry Harris (ed.), *Identity*. Oxford University Press, 13–45.

Parks, Rosa ([1992] 1999) *Rosa Parks: My Story*, written with Jim Haskins. Harmondsworth: Penguin.

Perry, Bruce (2002) Childhood experience and the expression of genetic potential: what childhood neglect tells us about nature and nurture. *Brain and Mind*, 3, 79–100.

Pickering, John and Skinner, Martin (1990) *From Sentience to Symbols: Readings on Consciousness*. Hemel Hempstead: Harvester Wheatsheaf.

Pogrund, Benjamin ([1990] 1997) *How Can Man Die Better: The Life of Robert Sobukwe*. Cape Town: Jonathan Ball.

Powers, Richard (1995) *Galatea 2.2*. London: Atlantic.

Premack, David and Woodruff, G. (1978) Does the chimpanzee have a theory of mind? *The Behavioural and Brain Sciences*, 1, 515–26.

Proust, Marcel ([1913] 1922) *Remembrance of Things Past*, trans. Charles Scott-Moncrieff. London: Vintage.

Pullman, Philip (2006) The cat, the chisel, and the grave. In Robin Headlam Wells and Johnjoe McFadden (eds.), *Human Nature: Fact and Fiction*. London: Continuum, 184–93.

Rayner, Alan (1997) *Degrees of Freedom: Living in Dynamic Boundaries*. London: Imperial College Press.

Reddy, Vasudevi (2010) *How Infants Know Minds*. Cambridge, MA: Harvard University Press.

Reicher, Steve (2011) Psychology, domination and resistance. *Europe's Journal of Psychology*, 7(2), 204–17.

Revonsuo, Antti (2010) *Consciousness: The Science of Subjectivity*. Hove: Psychology Press.

Richards, Graham (2002) *Putting Psychology in its Place*, 2nd edition. London: Routledge.

Richards, Martin (1974) *The Integration of a Child into a Social World*. Cambridge University Press.

Richardson, John (1996) *A Life of Picasso 1907–1917: The Painter of Modern Life*. London: Jonathan Cape.

Robinson, Marilynne (2010) *Absence of Mind*. New Haven, CT: Yale University Press.

Robinson, Peter (ed.) (1996) *Social Groups and Identities: Developing the Legacy of Henri Tajfel*. London: Butterworth-Heinemann.

Rose, David (2006) *Consciousness: Philosophical, Psychological and Neural Theories*. Oxford University Press.

Rowlands, Mark (2005) *The Philosopher at the End of the Universe: Philosophy Explained through Science Fiction Films*. London: Ebury Press.

Russon, Anne and Andrews, Kristin (2011) Pantomime in great apes. *Communicative and Integrative Biology*, 4(3), 315–17.

Ryle, Gilbert ([1949] 1975) *The Concept of Mind*. London: Hutchinson.

Sachs, Albie (1966) *The Jail Diary of Albie Sachs*. London: Harvill Press.

Sacks, Oliver (2008) *Musicophilia: Tales of Music and the Brain*. London: Vintage.

Sarbin, Theodore (ed.) (1986) *Narrative Psychology: The Storied Nature of Human Conduct*. New York: Praeger.

Saunders, Guy (1997) Captive flight: the storying of imagination constructed from accounts of confinement. In Man Cheung Chung (ed.), *Psychological Concepts from Philosophical and Historical Perspectives*. Leicester: The British Psychological Society.

(1998) Captive flight: the movement of imagination apprehended in accounts of confinement. Unpublished PhD thesis, University of Bath.

(2005) Existence and characterisation. In A. Gulerce, A. Hofmeister, I. Staeuble, G. Saunders and J. Kaye (eds.), *Contemporary Theorizing in Psychology: Global Perspectives*. Concord, ON: Captus Press.

(2007) Imagination. In M. Kiziewicz and I. Biggs (eds.), *Cascade: Creativity across Science, Art, Dyslexia, Education*. University of Bath, 79–83.

(2009) Consciousness and beliefs held about persons. Paper presented at Consciousness and Experiential Psychology section annual conference, St Anne's College, Oxford, September.

(2010) Conceptual issues in psychology from an arts' standpoint. Paper presented as part of symposium: 'Psychology and the Arts'. BPS annual conference. Stratford-upon-Avon. April.

Sennett, Richard (2012) *Together: The Rituals, Pleasures and Politics of Cooperation*. London: Allen Lane.

Shapin, Steven (1991) 'The mind is its own place': science and solitude in seventeenth-century England. *Science in Context*, 4(1), 191–218.

Shettleworth, Sara J. (2010) Clever animals and killjoy explanations in comparative psychology. *Trends in Cognitive Sciences*, 14(11), 477–81.

Shotter, John and Gergen, Kenneth J. (eds.) (1989) *Texts of Identity*. London: Sage.

Smolucha, Francine (1992) A reconstruction of Vygotsky's theory of creativity. *Creativity Research Journal*. Special Issue: Play, Vygotsky and Imagination, 5(1), 49–67. New Jersey: Ablex.

Storr, Anthony ([1988] 1994) *Solitude*. London: HarperCollins.

Strawson, Galen (1997) The Self. *Journal of Consciousness Studies*, 4, 405–28.

Sutton, Jon (2005) A higher consciousness: Jon Sutton interviews Susan Greenfield. *The Psychologist*, 18(10), 604–5.

Suu Kyi, Aung San ([1991] 2010) *Freedom from Fear (and other writings)*, 2nd edition ed. Michael Aris. Harmondsworth: Penguin.

Tajfel, Henri (1981) *Human Groups and Social Categories: Studies in Social Psychology*. London: Cambridge University Press.

Tallis, Raymond (2008) *The Kingdom of Infinite Space*. London: Atlantic Books.

(2010) *Michelangelo's Finger*. London: Atlantic Books.

Taylor, Charles (1985) Philosophy and the human sciences. *Philosophical Papers 2*. Cambridge University Press.

Turner, Graeme (1988) *Film as Social Practice*. London: Routledge.

Universal Declaration of Human Rights (1948) Available from www.un.org/en/documents/udhr/

Ursin, Rupert *et al.* (2007) Entanglement-based quantum communication over 144km. *Nature Physics*, 3, July, 481–6.

Valentine, Elizabeth (1982) *Conceptual Issues in Psychology*. London: George Allen & Unwin.

Velmans, Max (2000) *Understanding Consciousness*. London: Routledge.

Vernon, Jack ([1963] 1966) *Inside the Black Room*. Harmondsworth: Pelican.

Vidal, Gore (1996) *Palimpsest: A Memoir*. Little, Brown Book Group.

Vygotsky, Lev ([1933] 1966) Play and the mental development of the child. *Soviet Psychology*, 12(6), trans. Catherine Mulholland. Available from www.marxists.org/archive/vygotsky/index.htm

(1971) *The Psychology of Art*. Cambridge, MA: MIT Press.

(1987) *Collected Works*, vol. 1, *Problems of General Psychology, including Thinking and Speech*. New York and London: Plenum Press.

(1990) Imagination and creativity in childhood. *Soviet Psychology*, 28(1), 84–96.

(1991) Imagination and creativity in the adolescent. *Soviet Psychology*, 29(1), 73–8.

Waite, Terry (1993) *Taken on Trust*. London: Hodder and Stoughton.

Wallas, Graham ([1926] 1945) *The Art of Thought*. London: C. A. Watts and Co.

Wearing, Deborah (2005) *Forever Today*. London: Corgi.

Wegner, Daniel (2002) *The Illusion of Conscious Will*. A Bradford Book. Cambridge, MA: MIT Press.

Wertsch, James V. (1985) *Vygotsky and the Social Formation of Mind*. Cambridge, MA, and London: Harvard University Press.

White, Alison, and Hardy, Lew (1995) Use of different imagery perspectives on the learning and performance of different motor skills. *British Journal of Psychology*, 86, 169–80.

Whitehead, Charles (2008) *The Origins of Consciousness in the Social World*. Exeter: Imprint Academic.

Whitehead, John W. (c.2002) What it is to be humans in the Cybernetic State. At Gadfly online. Available from www.gadflyonline.com/ 02–18–02/film-blade_runner.html

Wittgenstein, Ludwig ([1953] 1992) *Philosophical Investigations*. Oxford: Blackwell.

Woods, Donald (1978) *Biko*. New York and London: Paddington Press.

Zelazo, Philip David; Moscovitch, Morris and Thompson, Evan (eds.) (2007) *The Cambridge Handbook of Consciousness*. Cambridge University Press.

Index

Index

Index

Lightning Source UK Ltd.
Milton Keynes UK
UKOW05f1435110514

231456UK00001B/12/P